Programming Hive

Edward Capriolo, Dean Wampler, and Jason Rutherglen

O'REILLY®

Beijing · Cambridge · Farnham · Köln · Sebastopol · Tokyo

Programming Hive
by Edward Capriolo, Dean Wampler, and Jason Rutherglen

Published by O'Reilly Media, Inc., 1005 Gravenstein Highway North, Sebastopol, CA 95472.

O'Reilly books may be purchased for educational, business, or sales promotional use. Online editions are also available for most titles (*http://my.safaribooksonline.com*). For more information, contact our corporate/institutional sales department: 800-998-9938 or *corporate@oreilly.com*.

Editors: Mike Loukides and Courtney Nash	**Indexer:** Bob Pfahler
Production Editors: Iris Febres and Rachel Steely	**Cover Designer:** Karen Montgomery
Proofreaders: Stacie Arellano and Kiel Van Horn	**Interior Designer:** David Futato
	Illustrator: Rebecca Demarest

October 2012:   First Edition.

Revision History for the First Edition:
     2012-09-17   First release
See *http://oreilly.com/catalog/errata.csp?isbn=9781449319335* for release details.

ISBN: 978-1-449-31933-5

[LSI]

1347905464

Table of Contents

Preface

Programming Hive introduces *Hive*, an essential tool in the *Hadoop* ecosystem that provides an *SQL* (Structured Query Language) dialect for querying data stored in the *Hadoop Distributed Filesystem* (HDFS), other filesystems that integrate with Hadoop, such as *MapR-FS* and Amazon's *S3* and databases like *HBase* (the Hadoop database) and *Cassandra*.

Most data warehouse applications are implemented using relational databases that use SQL as the query language. Hive lowers the barrier for moving these applications to Hadoop. People who know SQL can learn Hive easily. Without Hive, these users must learn new languages and tools to become productive again. Similarly, Hive makes it easier for developers to port SQL-based applications to Hadoop, compared to other tool options. Without Hive, developers would face a daunting challenge when porting their SQL applications to Hadoop.

Still, there are aspects of Hive that are different from other SQL-based environments. Documentation for Hive users and Hadoop developers has been sparse. We decided to write this book to fill that gap. We provide a pragmatic, comprehensive introduction to Hive that is suitable for SQL experts, such as database designers and business analysts. We also cover the in-depth technical details that Hadoop developers require for tuning and customizing Hive.

You can learn more at the book's catalog page (*http://oreil.ly/Programming_Hive*).

Conventions Used in This Book

The following typographical conventions are used in this book:

Italic
> Indicates new terms, URLs, email addresses, filenames, and file extensions. Definitions of most terms can be found in the Glossary.

`Constant width`
> Used for program listings, as well as within paragraphs to refer to program elements such as variable or function names, databases, data types, environment variables, statements, and keywords.

Constant width bold

Shows commands or other text that should be typed literally by the user.

Constant width italic

Shows text that should be replaced with user-supplied values or by values determined by context.

 This icon signifies a tip, suggestion, or general note.

 This icon indicates a warning or caution.

Using Code Examples

This book is here to help you get your job done. In general, you may use the code in this book in your programs and documentation. You do not need to contact us for permission unless you're reproducing a significant portion of the code. For example, writing a program that uses several chunks of code from this book does not require permission. Selling or distributing a CD-ROM of examples from O'Reilly books does require permission. Answering a question by citing this book and quoting example code does not require permission. Incorporating a significant amount of example code from this book into your product's documentation does require permission.

We appreciate, but do not require, attribution. An attribution usually includes the title, author, publisher, and ISBN. For example: "*Programming Hive* by Edward Capriolo, Dean Wampler, and Jason Rutherglen (O'Reilly). Copyright 2012 Edward Capriolo, Aspect Research Associates, and Jason Rutherglen, 978-1-449-31933-5."

If you feel your use of code examples falls outside fair use or the permission given above, feel free to contact us at *permissions@oreilly.com*.

Safari® Books Online

Safari Safari Books Online (*www.safaribooksonline.com*) is an on-demand digital library that delivers expert content in both book and video form from the world's leading authors in technology and business.

Technology professionals, software developers, web designers, and business and creative professionals use Safari Books Online as their primary resource for research, problem solving, learning, and certification training.

Safari Books Online offers a range of product mixes and pricing programs for organizations, government agencies, and individuals. Subscribers have access to thousands of books, training videos, and prepublication manuscripts in one fully searchable database from publishers like O'Reilly Media, Prentice Hall Professional, Addison-Wesley Professional, Microsoft Press, Sams, Que, Peachpit Press, Focal Press, Cisco Press, John Wiley & Sons, Syngress, Morgan Kaufmann, IBM Redbooks, Packt, Adobe Press, FT Press, Apress, Manning, New Riders, McGraw-Hill, Jones & Bartlett, Course Technology, and dozens more. For more information about Safari Books Online, please visit us online.

How to Contact Us

Please address comments and questions concerning this book to the publisher:

O'Reilly Media, Inc.
1005 Gravenstein Highway North
Sebastopol, CA 95472
800-998-9938 (in the United States or Canada)
707-829-0515 (international or local)
707-829-0104 (fax)

We have a web page for this book, where we list errata, examples, and any additional information. You can access this page at *http://oreil.ly/Programming_Hive*.

To comment or ask technical questions about this book, send email to *bookquestions@oreilly.com*.

For more information about our books, courses, conferences, and news, see our website at *http://www.oreilly.com*.

Find us on Facebook: *http://facebook.com/oreilly*

Follow us on Twitter: *http://twitter.com/oreillymedia*

Watch us on YouTube: *http://www.youtube.com/oreillymedia*

What Brought Us to Hive?

The three of us arrived here from different directions.

Edward Capriolo

When I first became involved with Hadoop, I saw the distributed filesystem and MapReduce as a great way to tackle computer-intensive problems. However, programming in the MapReduce model was a paradigm shift for me. Hive offered a fast and simple way to take advantage of MapReduce in an SQL-like world I was comfortable in. This approach also made it easy to prototype proof-of-concept applications and also to champion Hadoop as a solution internally. Even though I am now very familiar with Hadoop internals, Hive is still my primary method of working with Hadoop.

It is an honor to write a Hive book. Being a Hive Committer and a member of the Apache Software Foundation is my most valued accolade.

Dean Wampler

As a "big data" consultant at *Think Big Analytics*, I work with experienced "data people" who eat and breathe SQL. For them, Hive is a *necessary and sufficient condition* for Hadoop to be a viable tool to leverage their investment in SQL and open up new opportunities for data analytics.

Hive has lacked good documentation. I suggested to my previous editor at O'Reilly, Mike Loukides, that a Hive book was needed by the community. So, here we are...

Jason Rutherglen

I work at *Think Big Analytics* as a software architect. My career has involved an array of technologies including search, Hadoop, mobile, cryptography, and natural language processing. Hive is the ultimate way to build a data warehouse using open technologies on any amount of data. I use Hive regularly on a variety of projects.

Acknowledgments

Everyone involved with Hive. This includes committers, contributors, as well as end users.

Mark Grover wrote the chapter on Hive and Amazon Web Services. He is a contributor to the Apache Hive project and is active helping others on the Hive IRC channel.

David Ha and Rumit Patel, at M6D, contributed the case study and code on the Rank function. The ability to do Rank in Hive is a significant feature.

Ori Stitelman, at M6D, contributed the case study, Data Science using Hive and R, which demonstrates how Hive can be used to make first pass on large data sets and produce results to be used by a second R process.

David Funk contributed three use cases on in-site referrer identification, sessionization, and counting unique visitors. David's techniques show how rewriting and optimizing Hive queries can make large scale map reduce data analysis more efficient.

Ian Robertson read the entire first draft of the book and provided very helpful feedback on it. We're grateful to him for providing that feedback on short notice and a tight schedule.

John Sichi provided technical review for the book. John was also instrumental in driving through some of the newer features in Hive like StorageHandlers and Indexing Support. He has been actively growing and supporting the Hive community.

Alan Gates, author of *Programming Pig* (*http://shop.oreilly.com/product/0636920018087.do*), contributed the HCatalog chapter. Nanda Vijaydev contributed the chapter on how Karmasphere offers productized enhancements for Hive. Eric Lubow contributed the SimpleReach case study. Chris A. Mattmann, Paul Zimdars, Cameron Goodale, Andrew F. Hart, Jinwon Kim, Duane Waliser, and Peter Lean contributed the NASA JPL case study.

CHAPTER 1

Introduction

From the early days of the Internet's mainstream breakout, the major search engines and ecommerce companies wrestled with ever-growing quantities of data. More recently, social networking sites experienced the same problem. Today, many organizations realize that the data they gather is a valuable resource for understanding their customers, the performance of their business in the marketplace, and the effectiveness of their infrastructure.

The *Hadoop* ecosystem emerged as a cost-effective way of working with such large data sets. It imposes a particular programming model, called *MapReduce*, for breaking up computation tasks into units that can be distributed around a cluster of commodity, server class hardware, thereby providing cost-effective, horizontal scalability. Underneath this computation model is a distributed file system called the *Hadoop Distributed Filesystem* (HDFS). Although the filesystem is "pluggable," there are now several commercial and open source alternatives.

However, a challenge remains; how do you move an existing data infrastructure to Hadoop, when that infrastructure is based on traditional relational databases and the *Structured Query Language* (SQL)? What about the large base of SQL users, both expert database designers and administrators, as well as casual users who use SQL to extract information from their data warehouses?

This is where *Hive* comes in. Hive provides an *SQL* dialect, called *Hive Query Language* (abbreviated *HiveQL* or just *HQL*) for querying data stored in a Hadoop cluster.

SQL knowledge is widespread for a reason; it's an effective, reasonably intuitive model for organizing and using data. Mapping these familiar data operations to the low-level MapReduce Java API can be daunting, even for experienced Java developers. Hive does this dirty work for you, so you can focus on the query itself. Hive translates most queries to MapReduce jobs, thereby exploiting the scalability of Hadoop, while presenting a familiar SQL abstraction. If you don't believe us, see "Java Versus Hive: The Word Count Algorithm" on page 11 later in this chapter.

Hive is most suited for *data warehouse* applications, where relatively static data is analyzed, fast response times are not required, and when the data is not changing rapidly.

Hive is not a full database. The design constraints and limitations of Hadoop and HDFS impose limits on what Hive can do. The biggest limitation is that Hive does not provide record-level update, insert, nor delete. You can generate new tables from queries or output query results to files. Also, because Hadoop is a batch-oriented system, Hive queries have higher latency, due to the start-up overhead for MapReduce jobs. Queries that would finish in seconds for a traditional database take longer for Hive, even for relatively small data sets.[1] Finally, Hive does not provide transactions.

So, Hive doesn't provide crucial features required for OLTP, *Online Transaction Processing*. It's closer to being an OLAP tool, *Online Analytic Processing*, but as we'll see, Hive isn't ideal for satisfying the "online" part of OLAP, at least today, since there can be significant latency between issuing a query and receiving a reply, both due to the overhead of Hadoop and due to the size of the data sets Hadoop was designed to serve.

If you need OLTP features for large-scale data, you should consider using a *NoSQL* database. Examples include *HBase*, a *NoSQL* database integrated with Hadoop,[2] *Cassandra*,[3] and *DynamoDB*, if you are using Amazon's Elastic MapReduce (EMR) or Elastic Compute Cloud (EC2).[4] You can even integrate Hive with these databases (among others), as we'll discuss in Chapter 17.

So, Hive is best suited for data warehouse applications, where a large data set is maintained and mined for insights, reports, etc.

Because most data warehouse applications are implemented using SQL-based relational databases, Hive lowers the barrier for moving these applications to Hadoop. People who know SQL can learn Hive easily. Without Hive, these users would need to learn new languages and tools to be productive again.

Similarly, Hive makes it easier for developers to port SQL-based applications to Hadoop, compared with other Hadoop languages and tools.

However, like most SQL dialects, HiveQL does not conform to the ANSI SQL standard and it differs in various ways from the familiar SQL dialects provided by Oracle, MySQL, and SQL Server. (However, it is closest to MySQL's dialect of SQL.)

---

1. However, for the big data sets Hive is designed for, this start-up overhead is trivial compared to the actual processing time.

2. See the Apache HBase website, *http://hbase.apache.org*, and *HBase: The Definitive Guide* by Lars George (O'Reilly).

3. See the Cassandra website, *http://cassandra.apache.org/*, and *High Performance Cassandra Cookbook* by Edward Capriolo (Packt).

4. See the DynamoDB website, *http://aws.amazon.com/dynamodb/*.

So, this book has a dual purpose. First, it provides a comprehensive, example-driven introduction to HiveQL for all users, from developers, database administrators and architects, to less technical users, such as business analysts.

Second, the book provides the in-depth technical details required by developers and Hadoop administrators to tune Hive query performance and to customize Hive with *user-defined functions*, custom data formats, etc.

We wrote this book out of frustration that Hive lacked good documentation, especially for new users who aren't developers and aren't accustomed to browsing project artifacts like bug and feature databases, source code, etc., to get the information they need. The Hive Wiki[5] is an invaluable source of information, but its explanations are sometimes sparse and not always up to date. We hope this book remedies those issues, providing a single, comprehensive guide to all the essential features of Hive and how to use them effectively.[6]

An Overview of Hadoop and MapReduce

If you're already familiar with Hadoop and the *MapReduce* computing model, you can skip this section. While you don't need an intimate knowledge of MapReduce to use Hive, understanding the basic principles of MapReduce will help you understand what Hive is doing behind the scenes and how you can use Hive more effectively.

We provide a brief overview of Hadoop and MapReduce here. For more details, see *Hadoop: The Definitive Guide* (*http://shop.oreilly.com/product/0636920021773.do*) by Tom White (O'Reilly).

MapReduce

MapReduce is a computing model that decomposes large data manipulation *jobs* into individual *tasks* that can be executed in parallel across a cluster of servers. The results of the tasks can be joined together to compute the final results.

The *MapReduce* programming model was developed at Google and described in an influential paper called *MapReduce: simplified data processing on large clusters* (see the Appendix) on page 309. The *Google Filesystem* was described a year earlier in a paper called The Google filesystem on page 310. Both papers inspired the creation of Hadoop by Doug Cutting.

The term *MapReduce* comes from the two fundamental data-transformation operations used, *map* and *reduce*. A *map* operation converts the elements of a collection from one form to another. In this case, input key-value pairs are converted to zero-to-many

---

5. See *https://cwiki.apache.org/Hive/*.

6. It's worth bookmarking the wiki link, however, because the wiki contains some more obscure information we won't cover here.

output key-value pairs, where the input and output keys might be completely different and the input and output values might be completely different.

In *MapReduce*, all the key-pairs for a given key are sent to the same *reduce* operation. Specifically, the key and a collection of the values are passed to the reducer. The goal of "reduction" is to convert the collection to a value, such as summing or averaging a collection of numbers, or to another collection. A final key-value pair is emitted by the reducer. Again, the input versus output keys and values may be different. Note that if the job requires no reduction step, then it can be skipped.

An implementation infrastructure like the one provided by *Hadoop* handles most of the chores required to make jobs run successfully. For example, Hadoop determines how to decompose the submitted *job* into individual map and reduce *tasks* to run, it schedules those tasks given the available resources, it decides where to send a particular task in the cluster (usually where the corresponding data is located, when possible, to minimize network overhead), it monitors each task to ensure successful completion, and it restarts tasks that fail.

The *Hadoop Distributed Filesystem*, HDFS, or a similar distributed filesystem, manages data across the cluster. Each block is replicated several times (three copies is the usual default), so that no single hard drive or server failure results in data loss. Also, because the goal is to optimize the processing of very large data sets, HDFS and similar filesystems use very large block sizes, typically 64 MB or multiples thereof. Such large blocks can be stored contiguously on hard drives so they can be written and read with minimal seeking of the drive heads, thereby maximizing write and read performance.

To make MapReduce more clear, let's walk through a simple example, the *Word Count* algorithm that has become the "Hello World" of MapReduce.[7] Word Count returns a list of all the words that appear in a corpus (one or more documents) and the count of how many times each word appears. The output shows each word found and its count, one per line. By common convention, the word (output key) and count (output value) are usually separated by a tab separator.

Figure 1-1 shows how Word Count works in MapReduce.

There is a lot going on here, so let's walk through it from left to right.

Each *Input* box on the left-hand side of Figure 1-1 is a separate document. Here are four documents, the third of which is empty and the others contain just a few words, to keep things simple.

By default, a separate *Mapper* process is invoked to process each document. In real scenarios, large documents might be split and each split would be sent to a separate Mapper. Also, there are techniques for combining many small documents into a single *split* for a Mapper. We won't worry about those details now.

---

7. If you're not a developer, a "Hello World" program is the traditional first program you write when learning a new language or tool set.

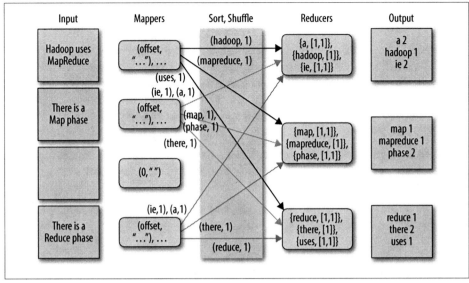

Figure 1-1. Word Count algorithm using MapReduce

The fundamental data structure for input and output in MapReduce is the key-value pair. After each Mapper is started, it is called repeatedly for each line of text from the document. For each call, the key passed to the mapper is the character offset into the document at the start of the line. The corresponding value is the text of the line.

In Word Count, the character offset (key) is discarded. The value, the line of text, is tokenized into words, using one of several possible techniques (e.g., splitting on white-space is the simplest, but it can leave in undesirable punctuation). We'll also assume that the Mapper converts each word to lowercase, so for example, "FUN" and "fun" will be counted as the same word.

Finally, for each word in the line, the mapper outputs a key-value pair, with the word as the key and the number 1 as the value (i.e., the count of "one occurrence"). Note that the output *types* of the keys and values are different from the input types.

Part of Hadoop's magic is the *Sort and Shuffle* phase that comes next. Hadoop sorts the key-value pairs by key and it "shuffles" all pairs with the same key to the same *Reducer*. There are several possible techniques that can be used to decide which reducer gets which range of keys. We won't worry about that here, but for illustrative purposes, we have assumed in the figure that a particular alphanumeric partitioning was used. In a real implementation, it would be different.

For the mapper to simply output a count of 1 every time a word is seen is a bit wasteful of network and disk I/O used in the sort and shuffle. (It does minimize the memory used in the Mappers, however.) One optimization is to keep track of the count for each word and then output only one count for each word when the Mapper finishes. There are several ways to do this optimization, but the simple approach is logically correct and sufficient for this discussion.

The inputs to each *Reducer* are again key-value pairs, but this time, each key will be one of the words found by the mappers and the value will be a *collection* of all the counts emitted by all the mappers for that word. Note that the type of the key and the type of the value collection elements are the same as the types used in the Mapper's output. That is, the key type is a character string and the value collection element type is an integer.

To finish the algorithm, all the reducer has to do is add up all the counts in the value collection and write a final key-value pair consisting of each word and the count for that word.

Word Count isn't a toy example. The data it produces is used in spell checkers, language detection and translation systems, and other applications.

Hive in the Hadoop Ecosystem

The Word Count algorithm, like most that you might implement with Hadoop, is a little involved. When you actually implement such algorithms using the Hadoop Java API, there are even more low-level details you have to manage yourself. It's a job that's only suitable for an experienced Java developer, potentially putting Hadoop out of reach of users who aren't programmers, even when they understand the algorithm they want to use.

In fact, many of those low-level details are actually quite repetitive from one job to the next, from low-level chores like wiring together Mappers and Reducers to certain data manipulation constructs, like filtering for just the data you want and performing SQL-like joins on data sets. There's a real opportunity to eliminate reinventing these idioms by letting "higher-level" tools handle them automatically.

That's where Hive comes in. It not only provides a familiar programming model for people who know SQL, it also eliminates lots of boilerplate and sometimes-tricky coding you would have to do in Java.

This is why Hive is so important to Hadoop, whether you are a DBA or a Java developer. Hive lets you complete a lot of work with relatively little effort.

Figure 1-2 shows the major "modules" of Hive and how they work with Hadoop.

There are several ways to interact with Hive. In this book, we will mostly focus on the CLI, *command-line interface*. For people who prefer graphical user interfaces, commercial and open source options are starting to appear, including a commercial product from Karmasphere (*http://karmasphere.com*), Cloudera's open source *Hue* (*https://git hub.com/cloudera/hue*), a new "Hive-as-a-service" offering from Qubole (*http://qubole .com*), and others.

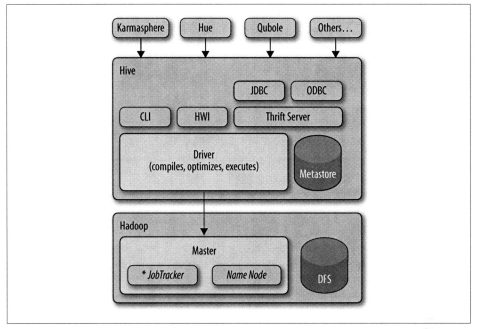

Figure 1-2. Hive modules

Bundled with the Hive distribution is the CLI, a simple web interface called *Hive web interface* (HWI), and programmatic access through JDBC, ODBC, and a Thrift server (see Chapter 16).

All commands and queries go to the Driver, which compiles the input, optimizes the computation required, and executes the required steps, usually with MapReduce jobs.

When MapReduce jobs are required, Hive doesn't generate Java MapReduce programs. Instead, it uses built-in, generic Mapper and Reducer modules that are driven by an XML file representing the "job plan." In other words, these generic modules function like mini language interpreters and the "language" to drive the computation is encoded in XML.

Hive communicates with the *JobTracker* to initiate the MapReduce job. Hive does not have to be running on the same master node with the JobTracker. In larger clusters, it's common to have edge nodes where tools like Hive run. They communicate remotely with the JobTracker on the master node to execute jobs. Usually, the data files to be processed are in HDFS, which is managed by the *NameNode*.

The Metastore is a separate relational database (usually a MySQL instance) where Hive persists table schemas and other system metadata. We'll discuss it in detail in Chapter 2.

While this is a book about Hive, it's worth mentioning other higher-level tools that you should consider for your needs. Hive is best suited for data warehouse applications, where real-time responsiveness to queries and record-level inserts, updates, and deletes are not required. Of course, Hive is also very nice for people who know SQL already. However, some of your work may be easier to accomplish with alternative tools.

Pig

The best known alternative to Hive is Pig (see *http://pig.apache.org*), which was developed at Yahoo! about the same time Facebook was developing Hive. Pig is also now a top-level Apache project that is closely associated with Hadoop.

Suppose you have one or more sources of input data and you need to perform a complex set of transformations to generate one or more collections of output data. Using Hive, you might be able to do this with nested queries (as we'll see), but at some point it will be necessary to resort to temporary tables (which you have to manage yourself) to manage the complexity.

Pig is described as a *data flow* language, rather than a query language. In Pig, you write a series of declarative statements that define *relations* from other relations, where each new relation performs some new data transformation. Pig looks at these declarations and then builds up a sequence of MapReduce jobs to perform the transformations until the final results are computed the way that you want.

This step-by-step "flow" of data can be more intuitive than a complex set of queries. For this reason, Pig is often used as part of ETL (Extract, Transform, and Load) processes used to ingest external data into a Hadoop cluster and transform it into a more desirable form.

A drawback of Pig is that it uses a custom language not based on SQL. This is appropriate, since it is not designed as a query language, but it also means that Pig is less suitable for porting over SQL applications and experienced SQL users will have a larger learning curve with Pig.

Nevertheless, it's common for Hadoop teams to use a combination of Hive and Pig, selecting the appropriate tool for particular jobs.

Programming Pig (http://shop.oreilly.com/product/0636920018087.do) by Alan Gates (O'Reilly) provides a comprehensive introduction to Pig.

HBase

What if you need the database features that Hive doesn't provide, like row-level updates, rapid query response times, and transactions?

HBase (*http://hbase.apache.org/*) is a distributed and scalable data store that supports row-level updates, rapid queries, and row-level transactions (but not multirow transactions).

HBase is inspired by Google's *Big Table*, although it doesn't implement all Big Table features. One of the important features HBase supports is column-oriented storage, where columns can be organized into *column families*. Column families are physically stored together in a distributed cluster, which makes reads and writes faster when the typical query scenarios involve a small subset of the columns. Rather than reading entire rows and discarding most of the columns, you read only the columns you need.

HBase can be used like a key-value store, where a single key is used for each row to provide very fast reads and writes of the row's columns or column families. HBase also keeps a configurable number of versions of each column's values (marked by timestamps), so it's possible to go "back in time" to previous values, when needed.

Finally, what is the relationship between HBase and Hadoop? HBase uses HDFS (or one of the other distributed filesystems) for durable file storage of data. To provide row-level updates and fast queries, HBase also uses in-memory caching of data and local files for the append log of updates. Periodically, the durable files are updated with all the append log updates, etc.

HBase doesn't provide a query language like SQL, but Hive is now integrated with HBase. We'll discuss this integration in "HBase" on page 222.

For more on HBase, see the HBase website (*http://hbase.apache.org/*), and *HBase: The Definitive Guide* (*http://shop.oreilly.com/product/0636920014348.do*) by Lars George.

Cascading, Crunch, and Others

There are several other "high-level" languages that have emerged outside of the Apache Hadoop umbrella, which also provide nice abstractions on top of Hadoop to reduce the amount of low-level boilerplate code required for typical jobs. For completeness, we list several of them here. All are JVM (Java Virtual Machine) libraries that can be used from programming languages like Java, Clojure, Scala, JRuby, Groovy, and Jython, as opposed to tools with their own languages, like Hive and Pig.

Using one of these programming languages has advantages and disadvantages. It makes these tools less attractive to nonprogrammers who already know SQL. However, for developers, these tools provide the full power of a *Turing complete* programming language. Neither Hive nor Pig are Turing complete. We'll learn how to extend Hive with Java code when we need additional functionality that Hive doesn't provide (Table 1-1).

Table 1-1. Alternative higher-level libraries for Hadoop

Name	URL	Description
Cascading	*http://cascading.org*	Java API with Data Processing abstractions. There are now many Domain Specific Languages (DSLs) for Cascading in other languages, e.g., Scala (*https://github.com/twitter/scalding*), Groovy (*http://www.cascading.org/documentation/groovy.html*), JRuby (*http://github.com/etsy/cascading.jruby/*), and Jython (*https://github.com/twitter/pycascading/*).

Name	URL	Description
Cascalog	https://github.com/nathanmarz/cascalog	A Clojure DSL for Cascading that provides additional functionality inspired by Datalog for data processing and query abstractions.
Crunch	https://github.com/cloudera/crunch	A Java and Scala API for defining data flow pipelines.

Because Hadoop is a batch-oriented system, there are tools with different distributed computing models that are better suited for *event stream* processing, where closer to "real-time" responsiveness is required. Here we list several of the many alternatives (Table 1-2).

Table 1-2. Distributed data processing tools that don't use MapReduce

Name	URL	Description
Spark	http://www.spark-project.org/	A distributed computing framework based on the idea of distributed data sets with a Scala API. It can work with HDFS files and it offers notable performance improvements over Hadoop MapReduce for many computations. There is also a project to port Hive to Spark, called Shark (http://shark.cs.berkeley.edu/).
Storm	https://github.com/nathanmarz/storm	A real-time event stream processing system.
Kafka	http://incubator.apache.org/kafka/index.html	A distributed publish-subscribe messaging system.

Finally, it's important to consider when you *don't* need a full cluster (e.g., for smaller data sets or when the time to perform a computation is less critical). Also, many alternative tools are easier to use when prototyping algorithms or doing exploration with a subset of data. Some of the more popular options are listed in Table 1-3.

Table 1-3. Other data processing languages and tools

Name	URL	Description
R	http://r-project.org/	An open source language for statistical analysis and graphing of data that is popular with statisticians, economists, etc. It's not a distributed system, so the data sizes it can handle are limited. There are efforts to integrate R with Hadoop.
Matlab	http://www.mathworks.com/products/matlab/index.html	A commercial system for data analysis and numerical methods that is popular with engineers and scientists.
Octave	http://www.gnu.org/software/octave/	An open source clone of MatLab.
Mathematica	http://www.wolfram.com/mathematica/	A commercial data analysis, symbolic manipulation, and numerical methods system that is also popular with scientists and engineers.
SciPy, NumPy	http://scipy.org	Extensive software package for scientific programming in Python, which is widely used by data scientists.

Java Versus Hive: The Word Count Algorithm

If you are not a Java programmer, you can skip to the next section.

If you are a Java programmer, you might be reading this book because you'll need to support the Hive users in your organization. You might be skeptical about using Hive for your own work. If so, consider the following example that implements the Word Count algorithm we discussed above, first using the Java MapReduce API and then using Hive.

It's very common to use Word Count as the first Java MapReduce program that people write, because the algorithm is simple to understand, so you can focus on the API. Hence, it has become the "Hello World" of the Hadoop world.

The following Java implementation is included in the Apache Hadoop distribution.[8] If you don't know Java (and you're still reading this section), don't worry, we're only showing you the code for the size comparison:

```java
package org.myorg;

import java.io.IOException;
import java.util.*;

import org.apache.hadoop.fs.Path;
import org.apache.hadoop.conf.*;
import org.apache.hadoop.io.*;
import org.apache.hadoop.mapreduce.*;
import org.apache.hadoop.mapreduce.lib.input.FileInputFormat;
import org.apache.hadoop.mapreduce.lib.input.TextInputFormat;
import org.apache.hadoop.mapreduce.lib.output.FileOutputFormat;
import org.apache.hadoop.mapreduce.lib.output.TextOutputFormat;

public class WordCount {

  public static class Map extends Mapper<LongWritable, Text, Text, IntWritable> {
    private final static IntWritable one = new IntWritable(1);
    private Text word = new Text();

    public void map(LongWritable key, Text value, Context context)
      throws IOException, InterruptedException {
      String line = value.toString();
      StringTokenizer tokenizer = new StringTokenizer(line);
      while (tokenizer.hasMoreTokens()) {
        word.set(tokenizer.nextToken());
        context.write(word, one);
      }
    }
  }

  public static class Reduce extends Reducer<Text, IntWritable, Text, IntWritable> {
```

---

8. Apache Hadoop word count: *http://wiki.apache.org/hadoop/WordCount*.

```
    public void reduce(Text key, Iterable<IntWritable> values, Context context)
      throws IOException, InterruptedException {
        int sum = 0;
        for (IntWritable val : values) {
            sum += val.get();
        }
        context.write(key, new IntWritable(sum));
    }
}

public static void main(String[] args) throws Exception {
    Configuration conf = new Configuration();

    Job job = new Job(conf, "wordcount");

    job.setOutputKeyClass(Text.class);
    job.setOutputValueClass(IntWritable.class);

    job.setMapperClass(Map.class);
    job.setReducerClass(Reduce.class);

    job.setInputFormatClass(TextInputFormat.class);
    job.setOutputFormatClass(TextOutputFormat.class);

    FileInputFormat.addInputPath(job, new Path(args[0]));
    FileOutputFormat.setOutputPath(job, new Path(args[1]));

    job.waitForCompletion(true);
}

}
```

That was 63 lines of Java code. We won't explain the API details.[9] Here is the *same* calculation written in HiveQL, which is just 8 lines of code, and does not require compilation nor the creation of a "JAR" (Java ARchive) file:

```
CREATE TABLE docs (line STRING);

LOAD DATA INPATH 'docs' OVERWRITE INTO TABLE docs;

CREATE TABLE word_counts AS
SELECT word, count(1) AS count FROM
  (SELECT explode(split(line, '\s')) AS word FROM docs) w
GROUP BY word
ORDER BY word;
```

We'll explain all this HiveQL syntax later on.

---

9. See *Hadoop: The Definitive Guide* by Tom White for the details.

In both examples, the files were tokenized into words using the simplest possible approach; splitting on whitespace boundaries. This approach doesn't properly handle punctuation, it doesn't recognize that singular and plural forms of words are the same word, etc. However, it's good enough for our purposes here.[10]

The virtue of the Java API is the ability to customize and fine-tune every detail of an algorithm implementation. However, most of the time, you just don't need that level of control and it slows you down considerably when you have to manage all those details.

If you're not a programmer, then writing Java MapReduce code is out of reach. However, if you already know SQL, learning Hive is relatively straightforward and many applications are quick and easy to implement.

What's Next

We described the important role that Hive plays in the Hadoop ecosystem. Now let's get started!

---

10. There is one other minor difference. The Hive query hardcodes a path to the data, while the Java code takes the path as an argument. In Chapter 2, we'll learn how to use Hive *variables* in scripts to avoid hardcoding such details.

Getting Started

Let's install Hadoop and Hive on our personal workstation. This is a convenient way to learn and experiment with Hadoop. Then we'll discuss how to configure Hive for use on Hadoop clusters.

If you already use Amazon Web Services, the fastest path to setting up Hive for learning is to run a Hive-configured *job flow* on *Amazon Elastic MapReduce (EMR)*. We discuss this option in Chapter 21.

If you have access to a Hadoop cluster with Hive already installed, we encourage you to skim the first part of this chapter and pick up again at "What Is Inside Hive?" on page 22.

Installing a Preconfigured Virtual Machine

There are several ways you can install Hadoop and Hive. An easy way to install a complete Hadoop system, including Hive, is to download a preconfigured *virtual machine* (VM) that runs in *VMWare*[1] or *VirtualBox*[2]. For VMWare, either *VMWare Player* for Windows and Linux (free) or *VMWare Fusion* for Mac OS X (inexpensive) can be used. VirtualBox is free for all these platforms, and also Solaris.

The virtual machines use Linux as the operating system, which is currently the only recommended operating system for running Hadoop in production.[3]

 Using a virtual machine is currently the only way to run Hadoop on Windows systems, even when *Cygwin* or similar Unix-like software is installed.

---

1. *http://vmware.com.*

2. *https://www.virtualbox.org/.*

3. However, some vendors are starting to support Hadoop on other systems. Hadoop has been used in production on various Unix systems and it works fine on Mac OS X for development use.

Most of the preconfigured virtual machines (VMs) available are only designed for VMWare, but if you prefer VirtualBox you may find instructions on the Web that explain how to import a particular VM into VirtualBox.

You can download preconfigured virtual machines from one of the websites given in Table 2-1.[4] Follow the instructions on these web sites for loading the VM into VMWare.

Table 2-1. Preconfigured Hadoop virtual machines for VMWare

Provider	URL	Notes
Cloudera, Inc.	*https://ccp.cloudera.com/display/SUPPORT/Clou dera's+Hadoop+Demo+VM*	Uses Cloudera's own distribution of Hadoop, CDH3 or CDH4.
MapR, Inc.	*http://www.mapr.com/doc/display/MapR/Quick +Start+-+Test+Drive+MapR+on+a+Virtual +Machine*	MapR's Hadoop distribution, which replaces *HDFS* with the MapR Filesystem (*MapR-FS*).
Hortonworks, Inc.	*http://docs.hortonworks.com/HDP-1.0.4-PREVIEW -6/Using_HDP_Single_Box_VM/HDP_Single_Box _VM.htm*	Based on the latest, stable Apache releases.
Think Big An-alytics, Inc.	*http://thinkbigacademy.s3-website-us-east-1.ama zonaws.com/vm/README.html*	Based on the latest, stable Apache releases.

Next, go to "What Is Inside Hive?" on page 22.

Detailed Installation

While using a preconfigured virtual machine may be an easy way to run Hive, installing Hadoop and Hive yourself will give you valuable insights into how these tools work, especially if you are a developer.

The instructions that follow describe the minimum necessary Hadoop and Hive installation steps for your personal Linux or Mac OS X workstation. For production installations, consult the recommended installation procedures for your Hadoop distributor.

Installing Java

Hive requires Hadoop and Hadoop requires Java. Ensure your system has a recent v1.6.X or v1.7.X JVM (Java Virtual Machine). Although the JRE (Java Runtime Environment) is all you need to run Hive, you will need the full JDK (Java Development Kit) to build examples in this book that demonstrate how to extend Hive with Java code. However, if you are not a programmer, the companion source code distribution for this book (see the Preface) contains prebuilt examples.

---

4. These are the current URLs at the time of this writing.

After the installation is complete, you'll need to ensure that Java is in your path and the JAVA_HOME environment variable is set.

Linux-specific Java steps

On Linux systems, the following instructions set up a *bash* file in the */etc/profile.d/* directory that defines *JAVA_HOME* for all users. Changing environmental settings in this folder requires root access and affects all users of the system. (We're using **$** as the *bash* shell prompt.) The Oracle JVM installer typically installs the software in */usr/java/ jdk-1.6.X* (for v1.6) and it creates sym-links from */usr/java/default* and */usr/java/latest* to the installation:

```
$ /usr/java/latest/bin/java -version
java version "1.6.0_23"
Java(TM) SE Runtime Environment (build 1.6.0_23-b05)
Java HotSpot(TM) 64-Bit Server VM (build 19.0-b09, mixed mode)
$ sudo echo "export JAVA_HOME=/usr/java/latest" > /etc/profile.d/java.sh
$ sudo echo "PATH=$PATH:$JAVA_HOME/bin" >> /etc/profile.d/java.sh
$ . /etc/profile
$ echo $JAVA_HOME
/usr/java/latest
```

 If you've never used sudo ("super user do *something*") before to run a command as a "privileged" user, as in two of the commands, just type your normal password when you're asked for it. If you're on a personal machine, your user account probably has "sudo rights." If not, ask your administrator to run those commands.

However, if you don't want to make permanent changes that affect all users of the system, an alternative is to put the definitions shown for *PATH* and *JAVA_HOME* in your *$HOME/.bashrc* file:

```
export JAVA_HOME=/usr/java/latest
export PATH=$PATH:$JAVA_HOME/bin
```

Mac OS X–specific Java steps

Mac OS X systems don't have the */etc/profile.d* directory and they are typically single-user systems, so it's best to put the environment variable definitions in your *$HOME/.bashrc*. The Java paths are different, too, and they may be in one of several places.[5]

Here are a few examples. You'll need to determine where Java is installed on your Mac and adjust the definitions accordingly. Here is a Java 1.6 example for Mac OS X:

```
$ export JAVA_HOME=/System/Library/Frameworks/JavaVM.framework/Versions/1.6/Home
$ export PATH=$PATH:$JAVA_HOME/bin
```

---

5. At least that's the current situation on Dean's Mac. This discrepancy may actually reflect the fact that stewardship of the Mac OS X Java port is transitioning from Apple to Oracle as of Java 1.7.

Here is a Java 1.7 example for Mac OS X:

```
$ export JAVA_HOME=/Library/Java/JavaVirtualMachines/1.7.0.jdk/Contents/Home
$ export PATH=$PATH:$JAVA_HOME/bin
```

OpenJDK 1.7 releases also install under */Library/Java/JavaVirtualMachines*.

Installing Hadoop

Hive runs on top of Hadoop. Hadoop is an active open source project with many releases and branches. Also, many commercial software companies are now producing
their own distributions of Hadoop, sometimes with custom enhancements or replace-
ments for some components. This situation promotes innovation, but also potential
confusion and compatibility issues.

Keeping software up to date lets you exploit the latest performance enhancements and
bug fixes. However, sometimes you introduce *new* bugs and compatibility issues. So,
for this book, we'll show you how to install the Apache Hadoop release v0.20.2. This
edition is not the most recent stable release, but it has been the reliable gold standard
for some time for performance and compatibility.

However, you should be able to choose a different version, distribution, or release
without problems for learning and using Hive, such as the Apache Hadoop v0.20.205
or 1.0.X releases, Cloudera CDH3 or CDH4, MapR M3 or M5, and the forthcoming
Hortonworks distribution. Note that the bundled Cloudera, MapR, and planned
Hortonworks distributions all include a Hive release.

However, we don't recommend installing the new, alpha-quality, "Next Generation"
Hadoop v2.0 (also known as v0.23), at least for the purposes of this book. While this
release will bring significant enhancements to the Hadoop ecosystem, it is too new for
our purposes.

To install Hadoop on a Linux system, run the following commands. Note that we
wrapped the long line for the wget command:

```
$ cd ~                    # or use another directory of your choice.
$ wget \
 http://www.us.apache.org/dist/hadoop/common/hadoop-0.20.2/hadoop-0.20.2.tar.gz
$ tar -xzf hadoop-0.20.2.tar.gz
$ sudo echo "export HADOOP_HOME=$PWD/hadoop-0.20.2" > /etc/profile.d/hadoop.sh
$ sudo echo "PATH=$PATH:$HADOOP_HOME/bin" >> /etc/profile.d/hadoop.sh
$ . /etc/profile
```

To install Hadoop on a Mac OS X system, run the following commands. Note that we
wrapped the long line for the curl command:

```
$ cd ~                    # or use another directory of your choice.
$ curl -o \
 http://www.us.apache.org/dist/hadoop/common/hadoop-0.20.2/hadoop-0.20.2.tar.gz
$ tar -xzf hadoop-0.20.2.tar.gz
$ echo "export HADOOP_HOME=$PWD/hadoop-0.20.2" >> $HOME/.bashrc
```

```
$ echo "PATH=$PATH:$HADOOP_HOME/bin" >> $HOME/.bashrc
$ . $HOME/.bashrc
```

In what follows, we will assume that you added $HADOOP_HOME/bin to your path, as in the previous commands. This will allow you to simply type the hadoop command without the path prefix.

Local Mode, Pseudodistributed Mode, and Distributed Mode

Before we proceed, let's clarify the different runtime modes for Hadoop. We mentioned above that the default mode is *local mode*, where filesystem references use the local filesystem. Also in local mode, when Hadoop jobs are executed (including most Hive queries), the Map and Reduce tasks are run as part of the same process.

Actual clusters are configured in *distributed mode*, where all filesystem references that aren't full URIs default to the distributed filesystem (usually HDFS) and jobs are managed by the *JobTracker* service, with individual tasks executed in separate processes.

A dilemma for developers working on personal machines is the fact that local mode doesn't closely resemble the behavior of a real cluster, which is important to remember when testing applications. To address this need, a single machine can be configured to run in *pseudodistributed mode*, where the behavior is identical to distributed mode, namely filesystem references default to the distributed filesystem and jobs are managed by the *JobTracker* service, but there is just a single machine. Hence, for example, HDFS file block replication is limited to one copy. In other words, the behavior is like a single-node "cluster." We'll discuss these configuration options in "Configuring Your Hadoop Environment" on page 24.

Because Hive uses Hadoop jobs for most of its work, its behavior reflects the Hadoop mode you're using. However, even when running in distributed mode, Hive can decide on a per-query basis whether or not it can perform the query using just local mode, where it reads the data files and manages the MapReduce tasks itself, providing faster turnaround. Hence, the distinction between the different modes is more of an *execution* style for Hive than a *deployment* style, as it is for Hadoop.

For most of the book, it won't matter which mode you're using. We'll assume you're working on a personal machine in local mode and we'll discuss the cases where the mode matters.

 When working with small data sets, using local mode execution will make Hive queries much faster. Setting the property set hive.exec.mode.local.auto=true; will cause Hive to use this mode more aggressively, even when you are running Hadoop in distributed or pseudodistributed mode. To always use this setting, add the command to your *$HOME/.hiverc* file (see "The .hiverc File" on page 36).

Testing Hadoop

Assuming you're using local mode, let's look at the local filesystem two different ways. The following output of the Linux ls command shows the typical contents of the "root" directory of a Linux system:

```
$ ls /
bin   cgroup  etc   lib    lost+found  mnt   opt   root  selinux  sys  user  var
boot  dev     home  lib64  media       null  proc  sbin  srv      tmp  usr
```

Hadoop provides a dfs tool that offers basic filesystem functionality like ls for the *default* filesystem. Since we're using local mode, the default filesystem is the local file-system:[6]

```
$ hadoop dfs -ls /
Found 26 items
drwxrwxrwx   - root root     24576 2012-06-03 14:28 /tmp
drwxr-xr-x   - root root      4096 2012-01-25 22:43 /opt
drwx------   - root root     16384 2010-12-30 14:56 /lost+found
drwxr-xr-x   - root root         0 2012-05-11 16:44 /selinux
dr-xr-x---   - root root      4096 2012-05-23 22:32 /root
...
```

If instead you get an error message that hadoop isn't found, either invoke the command with the full path (e.g., $HOME/hadoop-0.20.2/bin/hadoop) or add the bin directory to your PATH variable, as discussed in "Installing Hadoop" on page 18 above.

 If you find yourself using the hadoop dfs command frequently, it's convenient to define an alias for it (e.g., alias hdfs="hadoop dfs").

Hadoop offers a framework for *MapReduce*. The Hadoop distribution contains an implementation of the *Word Count* algorithm we discussed in Chapter 1. Let's run it!

Start by creating an input directory (inside your current working directory) with files to be processed by Hadoop:

```
$ mkdir wc-in
$ echo "bla bla" > wc-in/a.txt
$ echo "bla wa wa " > wc-in/b.txt
```

Use the hadoop command to launch the Word Count application on the input directory we just created. Note that it's conventional to always specify *directories* for input and output, not individual *files*, since there will often be multiple input and/or output files per directory, a consequence of the parallelism of the system.

---

6. Unfortunately, the dfs -ls command only provides a "long listing" format. There is no short format, like the default for the Linux ls command.

If you are running these commands on your local installation that was configured to use *local mode*, the hadoop command will launch the MapReduce components in the same process. If you are running on a cluster or on a single machine using *pseudodistributed* mode, the hadoop command will launch one or more separate processes using the *JobTracker* service (and the output below will be slightly different). Also, if you are running with a different version of Hadoop, change the name of the *examples.jar* as needed:

```
$ hadoop jar $HADOOP_HOME/hadoop-0.20.2-examples.jar wordcount wc-in wc-out
12/06/03 15:40:26 INFO input.FileInputFormat: Total input paths to process : 2
...
12/06/03 15:40:27 INFO mapred.JobClient: Running job: job_local_0001
12/06/03 15:40:30 INFO mapred.JobClient:  map 100% reduce 0%
12/06/03 15:40:41 INFO mapred.JobClient:  map 100% reduce 100%
12/06/03 15:40:41 INFO mapred.JobClient: Job complete: job_local_0001
```

The results of the Word count application can be viewed through local filesystem commands:

```
$ ls wc-out/*
part-r-00000
$ cat wc-out/*
bla    3
wa     2
```

They can also be viewed by the equivalent dfs command (again, because we assume you are running in *local mode*):

```
$ hadoop dfs -cat wc-out/*
bla    3
wa     2
```

 For very big files, if you want to view just the first or last parts, there is no -more, -head, nor -tail subcommand. Instead, just pipe the output of the -cat command through the shell's more, head, or tail. For example: hadoop dfs -cat wc-out/* | more.

Now that we have installed and tested an installation of Hadoop, we can install Hive.

Installing Hive

Installing Hive is similar to installing Hadoop. We will download and extract a tarball for Hive, which does not include an embedded version of Hadoop. A single Hive binary is designed to work with multiple versions of Hadoop. This means it's often easier and less risky to upgrade to newer Hive releases than it is to upgrade to newer Hadoop releases.

Hive uses the environment variable HADOOP_HOME to locate the Hadoop JARs and configuration files. So, make sure you set that variable as discussed above before proceeding. The following commands work for both Linux and Mac OS X:

```
$ cd ~                    # or use another directory of your choice.
$ curl -o http://archive.apache.org/dist/hive/hive-0.9.0/hive-0.9.0-bin.tar.gz
$ tar -xzf hive-0.9.0.tar.gz
$ sudo mkdir -p /user/hive/warehouse
$ sudo chmod a+rwx /user/hive/warehouse
```

As you can infer from these commands, we are using the latest stable release of Hive at the time of this writing, v0.9.0. However, most of the material in this book works with Hive v0.7.X and v0.8.X. We'll call out the differences as we come to them.

You'll want to add the hive command to your path, like we did for the hadoop command. We'll follow the same approach, by first defining a HIVE_HOME variable, but unlike HADOOP_HOME, this variable isn't really essential. We'll assume it's defined for some examples later in the book.

For Linux, run these commands:

```
$ sudo echo "export HIVE_HOME=$PWD/hive-0.9.0" > /etc/profile.d/hive.sh
$ sudo echo "PATH=$PATH:$HIVE_HOME/bin >> /etc/profile.d/hive.sh
$ . /etc/profile
```

For Mac OS X, run these commands:

```
$ echo "export HIVE_HOME=$PWD/hive-0.9.0" >> $HOME/.bashrc
$ echo "PATH=$PATH:$HIVE_HOME/bin" >> $HOME/.bashrc
$ . $HOME/.bashrc
```

What Is Inside Hive?

The core of a Hive binary distribution contains three parts. The main part is the Java code itself. Multiple JAR (Java archive) files such as hive-exec*.jar and hive-meta store*.jar are found under the *$HIVE_HOME/lib* directory. Each JAR file implements a particular subset of Hive's functionality, but the details don't concern us now.

The *$HIVE_HOME/bin* directory contains executable scripts that launch various Hive services, including the hive *command-line interface* (CLI). The CLI is the most popular way to use Hive. We will use hive (in lowercase, with a fixed-width font) to refer to the CLI, except where noted. The CLI can be used interactively to type in statements one at a time or it can be used to run "scripts" of Hive statements, as we'll see.

Hive also has other components. A *Thrift* service provides remote access from other processes. Access using *JDBC* and *ODBC* are provided, too. They are implemented on top of the Thrift service. We'll describe these features in later chapters.

All Hive installations require a *metastore* service, which Hive uses to store table schemas and other *metadata*. It is typically implemented using tables in a relational database. By default, Hive uses a built-in *Derby SQL* server, which provides limited, single-process storage. For example, when using Derby, you can't run two simultaneous instances of the Hive CLI. However, this is fine for learning Hive on a personal machine and some developer tasks. For clusters, MySQL or a similar relational database is required. We will discuss the details in "Metastore Using JDBC" on page 28.

Finally, a simple web interface, called *Hive Web Interface* (HWI), provides remote access to Hive.

The conf directory contains the files that configure Hive. Hive has a number of configuration properties that we will discuss as needed. These properties control features such as the *metastore* (where data is stored), various optimizations, and "safety controls," etc.

Starting Hive

Let's finally start the Hive command-line interface (CLI) and run a few commands! We'll briefly comment on what's happening, but save the details for discussion later.

In the following session, we'll use the $HIVE_HOME/bin/hive command, which is a bash shell script, to start the CLI. Substitute the directory where Hive is installed on your system whenever $HIVE_HOME is listed in the following script. Or, if you added $HIVE_HOME/bin to your PATH, you can just type hive to run the command. We'll make that assumption for the rest of the book.

As before, $ is the bash prompt. In the Hive CLI, the hive> string is the hive prompt, and the indented > is the *secondary* prompt. Here is a sample session, where we have added a blank line after the output of each command, for clarity:

```
$ cd $HIVE_HOME
$ bin/hive
Hive history file=/tmp/myname/hive_job_log_myname_201201271126_1992326118.txt
hive> CREATE TABLE x (a INT);
OK
Time taken: 3.543 seconds

hive> SELECT * FROM x;
OK
Time taken: 0.231 seconds

hive> SELECT *
    > FROM x;
OK
Time taken: 0.072 seconds

hive> DROP TABLE x;
OK
Time taken: 0.834 seconds

hive> exit;
$
```

The first line printed by the CLI is the local filesystem location where the CLI writes log data about the commands and queries you execute. If a command or query is successful, the first line of output will be `OK`, followed by the output, and finished by the line showing the amount of time taken to run the command or query.

 Throughout the book, we will follow the SQL convention of showing Hive keywords in uppercase (e.g., `CREATE`, `TABLE`, `SELECT` and `FROM`), even though case is ignored by Hive, following SQL conventions.

> Going forward, we'll usually add the blank line after the command output for all sessions. Also, when starting a session, we'll omit the line about the logfile. For individual commands and queries, we'll omit the `OK` and `Time taken:...` lines, too, except in special cases, such as when we want to emphasize that a command or query was successful, but it had no other output.

At the successive prompts, we create a simple table named x with a single `INT` (4-byte integer) column named a, then query it twice, the second time showing how queries and commands can spread across multiple lines. Finally, we drop the table.

If you are running with the default *Derby* database for the metastore, you'll notice that your current working directory now contains a new subdirectory called *metastore_db* that was created by *Derby* during the short `hive` session you just executed. If you are running one of the VMs, it's possible it has configured different behavior, as we'll discuss later.

Creating a *metastore_db* subdirectory under whatever working directory you happen to be in is not convenient, as *Derby* "forgets" about previous metastores when you change to a new working directory! In the next section, we'll see how to configure a permanent location for the metastore database, as well as make other changes.

Configuring Your Hadoop Environment

Let's dive a little deeper into the different Hadoop modes and discuss more configuration issues relevant to Hive.

You can skip this section if you're using Hadoop on an existing cluster or you are using a virtual machine instance. If you are a developer or you installed Hadoop and Hive yourself, you'll want to understand the rest of this section. However, we won't provide a complete discussion. See *Appendix A* of *Hadoop: The Definitive Guide (http://shop .oreilly.com/product/0636920021773.do)* by Tom White for the full details on configuring the different modes.

Local Mode Configuration

Recall that in *local mode*, all references to files go to your local filesystem, not the distributed filesystem. There are no services running. Instead, your jobs run all tasks in a single JVM instance.

Figure 2-1 illustrates a Hadoop job running in local mode.

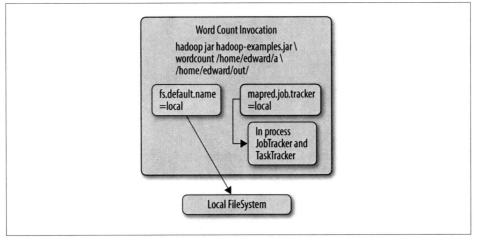

Figure 2-1. Hadoop in local mode

If you plan to use the local mode regularly, it's worth configuring a standard location for the *Derby metastore_db*, where Hive stores metadata about your tables, etc.

You can also configure a different directory for Hive to store table data, if you don't want to use the default location, which is *file:///user/hive/warehouse*, for local mode, and *hdfs://namenode_server/user/hive/warehouse* for the other modes discussed next.

First, go to the *$HIVE_HOME/conf* directory. The curious may want to peek at the large *hive-default.xml.template* file, which shows the different configuration properties supported by Hive and their default values. Most of these properties you can safely ignore. Changes to your configuration are done by editing the *hive-site.xml* file. Create one if it doesn't already exist.

Here is an example configuration file where we set several properties for local mode execution (Example 2-1).

Example 2-1. Local-mode hive-site.xml

```
<?xml version="1.0"?>
<?xml-stylesheet type="text/xsl" href="configuration.xsl"?>
<configuration>
  <property>
    <name>hive.metastore.warehouse.dir</name>
    <value>/home/me/hive/warehouse</value>
    <description>
      Local or HDFS directory where Hive keeps table contents.
    </description>
  </property>
  <property>
    <name>hive.metastore.local</name>
```

```
    <value>true</value>
    <description>
      Use false if a production metastore server is used.
    </description>
  </property>
  <property>
    <name>javax.jdo.option.ConnectionURL</name>
    <value>jdbc:derby:;databaseName=/home/me/hive/metastore_db;create=true</value>
    <description>
      The JDBC connection URL.
    </description>
  </property>
</configuration>
```

You can remove any of these `<property>...</property>` tags you don't want to change.

As the `<description>` tags indicate, the `hive.metastore.warehouse.dir` tells Hive where in your local filesystem to keep the data contents for Hive's tables. (This value is appended to the value of `fs.default.name` defined in the Hadoop configuration and defaults to *file:///*.) You can use any directory path you want for the value. Note that this directory will not be used to store the table metadata, which goes in the separate *metastore*.

The `hive.metastore.local` property defaults to `true`, so we don't really need to show it in Example 2-1. It's there more for documentation purposes. This property controls whether to connect to a remote metastore server or open a new metastore server as part of the Hive Client JVM. This setting is almost always set to `true` and JDBC is used to communicate directly to a relational database. When it is set to `false`, Hive will communicate through a metastore server, which we'll discuss in "Metastore Methods" on page 216.

The value for the `javax.jdo.option.ConnectionURL` property makes one small but convenient change to the default value for this property. This property tells Hive how to connect to the *metastore* server. By default, it uses the current working directory for the `databaseName` part of the value string. As shown in Example 2-1, we use `database Name=/home/me/hive/metastore_db` as the absolute path instead, which is the location where the *metastore_db* directory will always be located. This change eliminates the problem of Hive dropping the *metastore_db* directory in the current working directory every time we start a new Hive session. Now, we'll always have access to all our metadata, no matter what directory we are working in.

Distributed and Pseudodistributed Mode Configuration

In *distributed* mode, several services run in the cluster. The *JobTracker* manages jobs and the *NameNode* is the HDFS master. Worker nodes run individual job tasks, managed by a *TaskTracker* service on each node, and then hold blocks for files in the distributed filesystem, managed by *DataNode* services.

Figure 2-2 shows a typical distributed mode configuration for a Hadoop cluster.

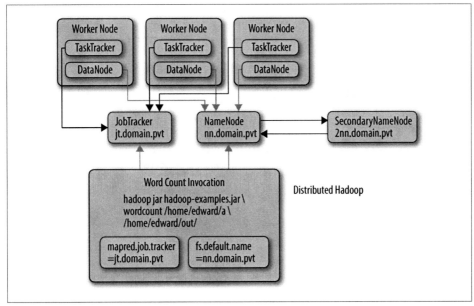

Figure 2-2. Hadoop in distributed mode

We're using the convention that `*.domain.pvt` is our DNS naming convention for the cluster's private, internal network.

Pseudodistributed mode is nearly identical; it's effectively a one-node cluster.

We'll assume that your administrator has already configured Hadoop, including your distributed filesystem (e.g., HDFS, or see *Appendix A* of *Hadoop: The Definitive Guide* by Tom White). Here, we'll focus on the unique configuration steps required by Hive.

One Hive property you might want to configure is the top-level directory for table storage, which is specified by the property `hive.metastore.warehouse.dir`, which we also discussed in "Local Mode Configuration" on page 24.

The default value for this property is `/user/hive/warehouse` in the Apache Hadoop and MapR distributions, which will be interpreted as a distributed filesystem path when Hadoop is configured for distributed or pseudodistributed mode. For Amazon Elastic MapReduce (EMR), the default value is `/mnt/hive_0M_N/warehouse` when using Hive v0.M.N (e.g., `/mnt/hive_08_1/warehouse`).

Specifying a different value here allows each user to define their own warehouse directory, so they don't affect other system users. Hence, each user might use the following statement to define their own warehouse directory:

```
set hive.metastore.warehouse.dir=/user/myname/hive/warehouse;
```

It's tedious to type this each time you start the Hive CLI or to remember to add it to every Hive script. Of course, it's also easy to forget to define this property. Instead, it's best to put commands like this in the *$HOME/.hiverc* file, which will be processed when Hive starts. See "The .hiverc File" on page 36 for more details.

We'll assume the value is /user/hive/warehouse from here on.

Metastore Using JDBC

Hive requires only one extra component that Hadoop does not already have; the *metastore* component. The metastore stores metadata such as table schema and partition information that you specify when you run commands such as `create table x...`, or `alter table y...`, etc. Because multiple users and systems are likely to need concurrent access to the metastore, the default embedded database is not suitable for production.

 If you are using a single node in *pseudodistributed* mode, you may not find it useful to set up a full relational database for the *metastore*. Rather, you may wish to continue using the default *Derby* store, but configure it to use a central location for its data, as described in "Local Mode Configuration" on page 24.

Any JDBC-compliant database can be used for the metastore. In practice, most installations of Hive use MySQL (*http://www.mysql.com*). We'll discuss how to use MySQL. It is straightforward to adapt this information to other JDBC-compliant databases.

 The information required for table schema, partition information, etc., is small, typically much smaller than the large quantity of data stored in Hive. As a result, you typically don't need a powerful dedicated database server for the metastore. However because it represents a Single Point of Failure (SPOF), it is strongly recommended that you replicate and back up this database using the standard techniques you would normally use with other relational database instances. We won't discuss those techniques here.

For our MySQL configuration, we need to know the host and port the service is running on. We will assume db1.mydomain.pvt and port 3306, which is the standard MySQL port. Finally, we will assume that hive_db is the name of our catalog. We define these properties in Example 2-2.

Example 2-2. Metastore database configuration in hive-site.xml

```
<?xml version="1.0"?>
<?xml-stylesheet type="text/xsl" href="configuration.xsl"?>
<configuration>
  <property>
    <name>javax.jdo.option.ConnectionURL</name>
    <value>jdbc:mysql://db1.mydomain.pvt/hive_db?createDatabaseIfNotExist=true</value>
  </property>
```

```
<property>
  <name>javax.jdo.option.ConnectionDriverName</name>
  <value>com.mysql.jdbc.Driver</value>
</property>
<property>
  <name>javax.jdo.option.ConnectionUserName</name>
  <value>database_user</value>
</property>
<property>
  <name>javax.jdo.option.ConnectionPassword</name>
  <value>database_pass</value>
</property>
</configuration>
```

You may have noticed the `ConnectionURL` property starts with a prefix of `jdbc:mysql`. For Hive to be able to connect to MySQL, we need to place the JDBC driver in our classpath. Download the MySQL JDBC driver (`Jconnector`) from *http://www.mysql .com/downloads/connector/j/*. The driver can be placed in the Hive library path, `$HIVE_HOME/lib`. Some teams put all such support libraries in their Hadoop `lib` directory.

With the driver and the configuration settings in place, Hive will store its metastore information in MySQL.

The Hive Command

The `$HIVE_HOME/bin/hive` shell command, which we'll simply refer to as `hive` from now on, is the gateway to Hive services, including the *command-line interface* or CLI.

We'll also assume that you have added `$HIVE_HOME/bin` to your environment's `PATH` so you can type `hive` at the shell prompt and your shell environment (e.g., bash) will find the command.

Command Options

If you run the following command, you'll see a brief list of the options for the `hive` command. Here is the output for Hive v0.8.X and v0.9.X:

```
$ bin/hive --help
Usage ./hive <parameters> --service serviceName <service parameters>
Service List: cli help hiveserver hwi jar lineage metastore rcfilecat
Parameters parsed:
  --auxpath : Auxiliary jars
  --config : Hive configuration directory
  --service : Starts specific service/component. cli is default
Parameters used:
  HADOOP_HOME : Hadoop install directory
  HIVE_OPT : Hive options
```

```
For help on a particular service:
  ./hive --service serviceName --help
Debug help:  ./hive --debug --help
```

Note the *Service List*. There are several services available, including the CLI that we will spend most of our time using. You can invoke a service using the `--service name` option, although there are shorthand invocations for some of the services, as well. Table 2-2 describes the most useful services.

Table 2-2. Hive services

Option	Name	Description
cli	Command-line interface	Used to define tables, run queries, etc. It is the default service if no other service is specified. See "The Command-Line Interface" on page 30.
hiveserver	Hive Server	A daemon that listens for Thrift connections from other processes. See Chapter 16 for more details.
hwi	Hive Web Interface	A simple web interface for running queries and other commands without logging into a cluster machine and using the CLI.
jar		An extension of the hadoop jar command for running an application that also requires the Hive environment.
metastore		Start an external Hive *metastore* service to support multiple clients (see also "Metastore Using JDBC" on page 28).
rcfilecat		A tool for printing the contents of an RCFile (see "RCFile" on page 202).

The `--auxpath` option lets you specify a colon-separated list of "auxiliary" Java archive (JAR) files that contain custom extensions, etc., that you might require.

The `--config` directory is mostly useful if you have to override the default configuration properties in $HIVE_HOME/conf in a new directory.

The Command-Line Interface

The *command-line interface* or CLI is the most common way to interact with Hive. Using the CLI, you can create tables, inspect schema and query tables, etc.

CLI Options

The following command shows a brief list of the options for the CLI. Here we show the output for Hive v0.8.X and v0.9.X:

```
$ hive --help --service cli
usage: hive
 -d,--define <key=value>          Variable substitution to apply to hive
                                  commands. e.g. -d A=B or --define A=B
 -e <quoted-query-string>         SQL from command line
 -f <filename>                    SQL from files
 -H,--help                        Print help information
 -h <hostname>                    connecting to Hive Server on remote host
    --hiveconf <property=value>   Use value for given property
    --hivevar <key=value>         Variable substitution to apply to hive
                                  commands. e.g. --hivevar A=B
 -i <filename>                    Initialization SQL file
 -p <port>                        connecting to Hive Server on port number
 -S,--silent                      Silent mode in interactive shell
 -v,--verbose                     Verbose mode (echo executed SQL to the
                                  console)
```

A shorter version of this command is `hive -h`. However, that's technically an unsupported option, but it produces the help output with an additional line that complains about `Missing argument for option: h`.

For Hive v0.7.X, the `-d`, `--hivevar`, and `-p` options are not supported.

Let's explore these options in more detail.

Variables and Properties

The `--define key=value` option is effectively equivalent to the `--hivevar key=value` option. Both let you define on the command line custom variables that you can reference in Hive scripts to customize execution. This feature is only supported in Hive v0.8.0 and later versions.

When you use this feature, Hive puts the key-value pair in the `hivevar` "namespace" to distinguish these definitions from three other built-in namespaces, `hiveconf`, `system`, and `env`.

> The terms *variable* or *property* are used in different contexts, but they function the same way in most cases.

The namespace options are described in Table 2-3.

Table 2-3. Hive namespaces for variables and properties

Namespace	Access	Description
hivevar	Read/Write	(v0.8.0 and later) User-defined custom variables.
hiveconf	Read/Write	Hive-specific configuration properties.
system	Read/Write	Configuration properties defined by Java.
env	Read only	Environment variables defined by the shell environment (e.g., bash).

Hive's variables are internally stored as Java Strings. You can reference variables in queries; Hive replaces the reference with the variable's value before sending the query to the query processor.

Inside the CLI, variables are displayed and changed using the SET command. For example, the following session shows the value for one variable, in the env namespace, and then all variable definitions! Here is a Hive session where some output has been omitted and we have added a blank line after the output of each command for clarity:

```
$ hive
hive> set env:HOME;
env:HOME=/home/thisuser

hive> set;
... lots of output including these variables:
hive.stats.retries.wait=3000
env:TERM=xterm
system:user.timezone=America/New_York
...

hive> set -v;
... even more output!...
```

Without the -v flag, set prints all the variables in the namespaces hivevar, hiveconf, system, and env. With the -v option, it also prints all the properties defined by Hadoop, such as properties controlling HDFS and MapReduce.

The set command is also used to set new values for variables. Let's look specifically at the hivevar namespace and a variable that is defined for it on the command line:

```
$ hive --define foo=bar
hive> set foo;
foo=bar;

hive> set hivevar:foo;
hivevar:foo=bar;

hive> set hivevar:foo=bar2;

hive> set foo;
foo=bar2
```

```
hive> set hivevar:foo;
hivevar:foo=bar2
```

As we can see, the `hivevar:` prefix is optional. The `--hivevar` flag is the same as the `--define` flag.

Variable references in queries are replaced in the CLI before the query is sent to the query processor. Consider the following `hive` CLI session (v0.8.X only):

```
hive> create table toss1(i int, ${hivevar:foo} string);

hive> describe toss1;
i       int
bar2    string

hive> create table toss2(i2 int, ${foo} string);

hive> describe toss2;
i2      int
bar2    string

hive> drop table toss1;
hive> drop table toss2;
```

Let's look at the `--hiveconf` option, which is supported in Hive v0.7.X. It is used for all properties that configure Hive behavior. We'll use it with a property `hive.cli.print.current.db` that was added in Hive v0.8.0. It turns on printing of the current working database name in the CLI prompt. (See "Databases in Hive" on page 49 for more on Hive databases.) The default database is named `default`. This property is `false` by default:

```
$ hive --hiveconf hive.cli.print.current.db=true
hive (default)> set hive.cli.print.current.db;
hive.cli.print.current.db=true

hive (default)> set hiveconf:hive.cli.print.current.db;
hiveconf:hive.cli.print.current.db=true

hive (default)> set hiveconf:hive.cli.print.current.db=false;

hive> set hiveconf:hive.cli.print.current.db=true;

hive (default)> ...
```

We can even add new `hiveconf` entries, which is the only supported option for Hive versions earlier than v0.8.0:

```
$ hive --hiveconf y=5
hive> set y;
y=5

hive> CREATE TABLE whatsit(i int);

hive> ... load data into whatsit ...
```

```
hive> SELECT * FROM whatsit WHERE i = ${hiveconf:y};
...
```

It's also useful to know about the **system** namespace, which provides read-write access to Java system properties, and the **env** namespace, which provides read-only access to environment variables:

```
hive> set system:user.name;
system:user.name=myusername

hive> set system:user.name=yourusername;

hive> set system:user.name;
system:user.name=yourusername

hive> set env:HOME;
env:HOME=/home/yourusername

hive> set env:HOME;
env:* variables can not be set.
```

Unlike **hivevar** variables, you have to use the **system:** or **env:** prefix with system properties and environment variables.

The **env** namespace is useful as an alternative way to pass variable definitions to Hive, especially for Hive v0.7.X. Consider the following example:

```
$ YEAR=2012 hive -e "SELECT * FROM mytable WHERE year = ${env:YEAR}";
```

The query processor will see the literal number **2012** in the **WHERE** clause.

If you are using Hive v0.7.X, some of the examples in this book that use parameters and variables may not work as written. If so, replace the variable reference with the corresponding value.

All of Hive's built-in properties are listed in $HIVE_HOME/conf/hive-default.xml.template, the "sample" configuration file. It also shows the default values for each property.

Hive "One Shot" Commands

The user may wish to run one or more queries (semicolon separated) and then have the hive CLI exit immediately after completion. The CLI accepts a -e command argument that enables this feature. If **mytable** has a string and integer column, we might see the following output:

```
$ hive -e "SELECT * FROM mytable LIMIT 3";
OK
name1 10
name2 20
name3 30
```

```
Time taken: 4.955 seconds
$
```

A quick and dirty technique is to use this feature to output the query results to a file. Adding the -S for silent mode removes the OK and Time taken … lines, as well as other inessential output, as in this example:

```
$ hive -S -e "select * FROM mytable LIMIT 3" > /tmp/myquery
$ cat /tmp/myquery
name1   10
name2   20
name3   30
```

Note that hive wrote the output to the *standard output* and the shell command redirected that output to the local filesystem, not to HDFS.

Finally, here is a useful trick for finding a property name that you can't quite remember, without having to scroll through the list of the set output. Suppose you can't remember the name of the property that specifies the "warehouse" location for managed tables:

```
$ hive -S -e "set" | grep warehouse
hive.metastore.warehouse.dir=/user/hive/warehouse
hive.warehouse.subdir.inherit.perms=false
```

It's the first one.

Executing Hive Queries from Files

Hive can execute one or more queries that were saved to a file using the -f file argument. By convention, saved Hive query files use the *.q* or *.hql* extension.

```
$ hive -f /path/to/file/withqueries.hql
```

If you are already inside the Hive shell you can use the SOURCE command to execute a script file. Here is an example:

```
$ cat /path/to/file/withqueries.hql
SELECT x.* FROM src x;
$ hive
hive> source /path/to/file/withqueries.hql;
...
```

By the way, we'll occasionally use the name src ("source") for tables in queries when the name of the table is irrelevant for the example. This convention is taken from the *unit tests* in Hive's source code; first create a src table before all tests.

For example, when experimenting with a built-in function, it's convenient to write a "query" that passes literal arguments to the function, as in the following example taken from later in the book, "XPath-Related Functions" on page 207:

```
hive> SELECT xpath(\'<a><b id="foo">b1</b><b id="bar">b2</b></a>\',\'//@id\')
    > FROM src LIMIT 1;
[foo","bar]
```

The details for xpath don't concern us here, but note that we pass string literals to the xpath function and use FROM src LIMIT 1 to specify the required FROM clause and to limit the output. Substitute src with the name of a table you have already created or create a dummy table named src:

```
CREATE TABLE src(s STRING);
```

Also the source table must have at least one row of content in it:

```
$ echo "one row" > /tmp/myfile
$ hive -e "LOAD DATA LOCAL INPATH '/tmp/myfile' INTO TABLE src;
```

The .hiverc File

The last CLI option we'll discuss is the -i file option, which lets you specify a file of commands for the CLI to run as it starts, before showing you the prompt. Hive automatically looks for a file named .hiverc in your HOME directory and runs the commands it contains, if any.

These files are convenient for commands that you run frequently, such as setting system properties (see "Variables and Properties" on page 31) or adding Java archives (JAR files) of custom Hive extensions to Hadoop's distributed cache (as discussed in Chapter 15).

The following shows an example of a typical $HOME/.hiverc file:

```
ADD JAR /path/to/custom_hive_extensions.jar;
set hive.cli.print.current.db=true;
set hive.exec.mode.local.auto=true;
```

The first line adds a JAR file to the Hadoop distributed cache. The second line modifies the CLI prompt to show the current working Hive database, as we described earlier in "Variables and Properties" on page 31. The last line "encourages" Hive to be more aggressive about using local-mode execution when possible, even when Hadoop is running in distributed or pseudo-distributed mode, which speeds up queries for small data sets.

 An easy mistake to make is to forget the semicolon at the end of lines like this. When you make this mistake, the definition of the property will include *all the text from all the subsequent lines in the file until the next semicolon.*

More on Using the Hive CLI

The CLI supports a number of other useful features.

Autocomplete

If you start typing and hit the Tab key, the CLI will autocomplete possible keywords and function names. For example, if you type SELE and then the Tab key, the CLI will complete the word SELECT.

If you type the Tab key at the prompt, you'll get this reply:

```
hive>
Display all 407 possibilities? (y or n)
```

If you enter y, you'll get a long list of all the keywords and built-in functions.

 A common source of error and confusion when pasting statements into the CLI occurs where some lines begin with a tab. You'll get the prompt about displaying all possibilities, and subsequent characters in the stream will get misinterpreted as answers to the prompt, causing the command to fail.

Command History

You can use the up and down arrow keys to scroll through previous commands. Actually, each previous line of input is shown separately; the CLI does not combine multiline commands and queries into a single history entry. Hive saves the last 100,00 lines into a file *$HOME/.hivehistory*.

If you want to repeat a previous command, scroll to it and hit Enter. If you want to edit the line before entering it, use the left and right arrow keys to navigate to the point where changes are required and edit the line. You can hit Return to submit it without returning to the end of the line.

 Most navigation keystrokes using the Control key work as they do for the bash shell (e.g., Control-A goes to the beginning of the line and Control-E goes to the end of the line). However, similar "meta," Option, or Escape keys don't work (e.g., Option-F to move forward a word at a time). Similarly, the Delete key will delete the character to the *left* of the cursor, but the Forward Delete key doesn't delete the character *under* the cursor.

Shell Execution

You don't need to leave the hive CLI to run simple bash shell commands. Simply type ! followed by the command and terminate the line with a semicolon (;):

```
hive> ! /bin/echo "what up dog";
"what up dog"
hive> ! pwd;
/home/me/hiveplay
```

Don't invoke interactive commands that require user input. Shell "pipes" don't work and neither do file "globs." For example, ! ls *.hql; will look for a file named *.hql;, rather than all files that end with the .hql extension.

Hadoop dfs Commands from Inside Hive

You can run the `hadoop dfs ...` commands from within the `hive` CLI; just drop the `hadoop` word from the command and add the semicolon at the end:

```
hive> dfs -ls / ;
Found 3 items
drwxr-xr-x   - root    supergroup          0 2011-08-17 16:27 /etl
drwxr-xr-x   - edward  supergroup          0 2012-01-18 15:51 /flag
drwxrwxr-x   - hadoop  supergroup          0 2010-02-03 17:50 /users
```

This method of accessing `hadoop` commands is actually more efficient than using the `hadoop dfs ...` equivalent at the bash shell, because the latter starts up a new JVM instance each time, whereas Hive just runs the same code in its current process.

You can see a full listing of help on the options supported by `dfs` using this command:

```
hive> dfs -help;
```

See also *http://hadoop.apache.org/common/docs/r0.20.205.0/file_system_shell.html* or similar documentation for your Hadoop distribution.

Comments in Hive Scripts

As of Hive v0.8.0, you can embed lines of comments that start with the string --, for example:

```
-- Copyright (c) 2012 Megacorp, LLC.
-- This is the best Hive script evar!!

SELECT * FROM massive_table;
...
```

 The CLI does not parse these comment lines. If you paste them into the CLI, you'll get errors. They only work when used in scripts executed with `hive -f script_name`.

Query Column Headers

As a final example that pulls together a few things we've learned, let's tell the CLI to print column headers, which is disabled by default. We can enable this feature by setting the `hiveconf` property `hive.cli.print.header` to `true`:

```
hive> set hive.cli.print.header=true;

hive> SELECT * FROM system_logs LIMIT 3;
tstamp          severity server message
1335667117.337715 ERROR server1 Hard drive hd1 is 90% full!
1335667117.338012 WARN  server1 Slow response from server2.
1335667117.339234 WARN  server2 Uh, Dude, I'm kinda busy right now...
```

If you always prefer seeing the headers, put the first line in your *$HOME/.hiverc* file.

CHAPTER 3

Data Types and File Formats

Hive supports many of the *primitive* data types you find in relational databases, as well as three *collection* data types that are rarely found in relational databases, for reasons we'll discuss shortly.

A related concern is how these types are represented in text files, as well as alternatives to text storage that address various performance and other concerns. A unique feature of Hive, compared to most databases, is that it provides great flexibility in how data is encoded in files. Most databases take total control of the data, both how it is persisted to disk and its life cycle. By letting you control all these aspects, Hive makes it easier to manage and process data with a variety of tools.

Primitive Data Types

Hive supports several sizes of integer and floating-point types, a Boolean type, and character strings of arbitrary length. Hive v0.8.0 added types for timestamps and binary fields.

Table 3-1 lists the *primitive* types supported by Hive.

Table 3-1. Primitive data types

Type	Size	Literal syntax examples
TINYINT	1 byte signed integer.	20
SMALLINT	2 byte signed integer.	20
INT	4 byte signed integer.	20
BIGINT	8 byte signed integer.	20
BOOLEAN	Boolean true or false.	TRUE
FLOAT	Single precision floating point.	3.14159
DOUBLE	Double precision floating point.	3.14159

Type	Size	Literal syntax examples
STRING	Sequence of characters. The character set can be specified. Single or double quotes can be used.	'Now is the time', "for all good men"
TIMESTAMP (v0.8.0+)	Integer, float, or string.	1327882394 (Unix epoch seconds), 1327882394.123456789 (Unix epoch seconds plus nanoseconds), and '2012-02-03 12:34:56.123456789' (JDBC-compliant java.sql.Timestamp format)
BINARY (v0.8.0+)	Array of bytes.	See discussion below

As for other SQL dialects, the case of these names is ignored.

It's useful to remember that each of these types is implemented in Java, so the particular behavior details will be exactly what you would expect from the corresponding Java types. For example, STRING is implemented by the Java String, FLOAT is implemented by Java float, etc.

Note that Hive does not support "character arrays" (strings) with maximum-allowed lengths, as is common in other SQL dialects. Relational databases offer this feature as a performance optimization; fixed-length records are easier to index, scan, etc. In the "looser" world in which Hive lives, where it may not own the data files and has to be flexible on file format, Hive relies on the presence of delimiters to separate fields. Also, Hadoop and Hive emphasize optimizing disk reading and writing performance, where fixing the lengths of column values is relatively unimportant.

Values of the new TIMESTAMP type can be integers, which are interpreted as seconds since the Unix epoch time (Midnight, January 1, 1970), floats, which are interpreted as seconds since the epoch time with nanosecond resolution (up to 9 decimal places), and strings, which are interpreted according to the JDBC date string format convention, YYYY-MM-DD hh:mm:ss.fffffffff.

TIMESTAMPS are interpreted as UTC times. Built-in functions for conversion to and from timezones are provided by Hive, to_utc_timestamp and from_utc_timestamp, respectively (see Chapter 13 for more details).

The BINARY type is similar to the VARBINARY type found in many relational databases. It's not like a BLOB type, since BINARY columns are stored within the record, not separately like BLOBs. BINARY can be used as a way of including arbitrary bytes in a record and preventing Hive from attempting to parse them as numbers, strings, etc.

Note that you don't need BINARY if your goal is to ignore the tail end of each record. If a table schema specifies three columns and the data files contain five values for each record, the last two will be ignored by Hive.

What if you run a query that wants to compare a float column to a double column or compare a value of one integer type with a value of a different integer type? Hive will implicitly *cast* any integer to the larger of the two integer types, cast FLOAT to DOUBLE, and cast any integer value to DOUBLE, as needed, so it is comparing identical types.

What if you run a query that wants to interpret a string column as a number? You can explicitly cast one type to another as in the following example, where s is a string column that holds a value representing an integer:

```
... cast(s AS INT) ...;
```

(To be clear, the AS INT are keywords, so lowercase would be fine.)

We'll discuss data conversions in more depth in "Casting" on page 109.

Collection Data Types

Hive supports columns that are structs, maps, and arrays. Note that the literal syntax examples in Table 3-2 are actually calls to built-in functions.

Table 3-2. Collection data types

Type	Description	Literal syntax examples
STRUCT	Analogous to a C struct or an "object." Fields can be accessed using the "dot" notation. For example, if a column name is of type STRUCT {first STRING; last STRING}, then the first name field can be referenced using name.first.	struct('John', 'Doe')
MAP	A collection of key-value tuples, where the fields are accessed using array notation (e.g., ['key']). For example, if a column name is of type MAP with key→value pairs 'first'→'John' and 'last'→'Doe', then the last name can be referenced using name['last'].	map('first', 'John', 'last', 'Doe')
ARRAY	Ordered sequences of the *same* type that are indexable using zero-based integers. For example, if a column name is of type ARRAY of strings with the value ['John', 'Doe'], then the second element can be referenced using name[1].	array('John', 'Doe')

As for simple types, the case of the type name is ignored.

Most relational databases don't support such collection types, because using them tends to break *normal form*. For example, in traditional data models, structs might be captured in separate tables, with foreign key relations between the tables, as appropriate.

A practical problem with breaking normal form is the greater risk of data duplication, leading to unnecessary disk space consumption and potential data inconsistencies, as duplicate copies can grow out of sync as changes are made.

However, in *Big Data* systems, a benefit of sacrificing normal form is higher processing throughput. Scanning data off hard disks with minimal "head seeks" is essential when processing terabytes to petabytes of data. Embedding collections in records makes retrieval faster with minimal seeks. Navigating each foreign key relationship requires seeking across the disk, with significant performance overhead.

 Hive doesn't have the concept of keys. However, you can index tables, as we'll see in Chapter 7.

Here is a table declaration that demonstrates how to use these types, an *employees* table in a fictitious Human Resources application:

```
CREATE TABLE employees (
    name          STRING,
    salary        FLOAT,
    subordinates  ARRAY<STRING>,
    deductions    MAP<STRING, FLOAT>,
    address       STRUCT<street:STRING, city:STRING, state:STRING, zip:INT>);
```

The name is a simple string and for most employees, a float is large enough for the salary. The list of subordinates is an array of string values, where we treat the name as a "primary key," so each element in subordinates would reference another record in the table. Employees without subordinates would have an empty array. In a traditional model, the relationship would go the other way, from an employee to his or her manager. We're not arguing that our model is better for Hive; it's just a contrived example to illustrate the use of arrays.

The deductions is a map that holds a key-value pair for every deduction that will be subtracted from the employee's salary when paychecks are produced. The key is the name of the deduction (e.g., "Federal Taxes"), and the key would either be a percentage value or an absolute number. In a traditional data model, there might be separate tables for deduction type (each key in our map), where the rows contain particular deduction values and a foreign key pointing back to the corresponding employee record.

Finally, the home address of each employee is represented as a struct, where each field is named and has a particular type.

Note that Java syntax conventions for *generics* are followed for the collection types. For example, MAP<STRING, FLOAT> means that every key in the map will be of type STRING and every value will be of type FLOAT. For an ARRAY<STRING>, every item in the array will be a STRING. STRUCTs can mix different types, but the locations are fixed to the declared position in the STRUCT.

Text File Encoding of Data Values

Let's begin our exploration of file formats by looking at the simplest example, text files.

You are no doubt familiar with text files delimited with commas or tabs, the so-called *comma-separated values* (CSVs) or *tab-separated values* (TSVs), respectively. Hive can use those formats if you want and we'll show you how shortly. However, there is a drawback to both formats; you have to be careful about commas or tabs embedded in text and not intended as field or column delimiters. For this reason, Hive uses various control characters by default, which are less likely to appear in value strings. Hive uses the term `field` when overriding the default delimiter, as we'll see shortly. They are listed in Table 3-3.

Table 3-3. Hive's default record and field delimiters

Delimiter	Description
\n	For text files, each line is a record, so the line feed character separates records.
^A ("control" A)	Separates all fields (columns). Written using the octal code \001 when explicitly specified in CREATE TABLE statements.
^B	Separate the elements in an ARRAY or STRUCT, or the key-value pairs in a MAP. Written using the octal code \002 when explicitly specified in CREATE TABLE statements.
^C	Separate the key from the corresponding value in MAP key-value pairs. Written using the octal code \003 when explicitly specified in CREATE TABLE statements.

Records for the `employees` table declared in the previous section would look like the following example, where we use ^A, etc., to represent the field delimiters. A text editor like Emacs will show the delimiters this way. Note that the lines have been wrapped in the example because they are too long for the printed page. To clearly indicate the division between records, we have added blank lines between them that would not appear in the file:

John Doe^A100000.0^AMary Smith^BTodd Jones^AFederal Taxes^C.2^BState Taxes^C.05^BInsurance^C.1^A1 Michigan Ave.^BChicago^BIL^B60600

Mary Smith^A80000.0^ABill King^AFederal Taxes^C.2^BState Taxes^C. 05^BInsurance^C.1^A100 Ontario St.^BChicago^BIL^B60601

Todd Jones^A70000.0^AFederal Taxes^C.15^BState Taxes^C.03^BInsurance^C. 1^A200 Chicago Ave.^BOak Park^BIL^B60700

Bill King^A60000.0^AFederal Taxes^C.15^BState Taxes^C.03^BInsurance^C. 1^A300 Obscure Dr.^BObscuria^BIL^B60100

This is a little hard to read, but you would normally let Hive do that for you, of course. Let's walk through the first line to understand the structure. First, here is what it would look like in JavaScript Object Notation (JSON), where we have also inserted the names from the table schema:

```
{
  "name":  "John Doe",
  "salary": 100000.0,
  "subordinates": ["Mary Smith", "Todd Jones"],
  "deductions": {
    "Federal Taxes": .2,
    "State Taxes":   .05,
    "Insurance":     .1
  },
  "address": {
    "street": "1 Michigan Ave.",
    "city":   "Chicago",
    "state":  "IL",
    "zip":    60600
  }
}
```

You'll note that maps and structs are effectively the same thing in JSON.

Now, here's how the first line of the text file breaks down:

- John Doe is the name.
- 100000.0 is the salary.
- Mary Smith^BTodd Jones are the subordinates "Mary Smith" and "Todd Jones."
- Federal Taxes^C.2^BState Taxes^C.05^BInsurance^C.1 are the deductions, where 20% is deducted for "Federal Taxes," 5% is deducted for "State Taxes," and 10% is deducted for "Insurance."
- 1 Michigan Ave.^BChicago^BIL^B60600 is the address, "1 Michigan Ave., Chicago, 60600."

You can override these default delimiters. This might be necessary if another application writes the data using a different convention. Here is the same table declaration again, this time with all the format defaults explicitly specified:

```
CREATE TABLE employees (
    name          STRING,
    salary        FLOAT,
    subordinates  ARRAY<STRING>,
    deductions    MAP<STRING, FLOAT>,
    address       STRUCT<street:STRING, city:STRING, state:STRING, zip:INT>
)
ROW FORMAT DELIMITED
FIELDS TERMINATED BY '\001'
COLLECTION ITEMS TERMINATED BY '\002'
MAP KEYS TERMINATED BY '\003'
LINES TERMINATED BY '\n'
STORED AS TEXTFILE;
```

The ROW FORMAT DELIMITED sequence of keywords must appear before any of the other clauses, with the exception of the STORED AS … clause.

The character \001 is the octal code for ^A. The clause ROW FORMAT DELIMITED FIELDS TERMINATED BY '\001' means that Hive will use the ^A character to separate *fields*.

Similarly, the character \002 is the octal code for ^B. The clause ROW FORMAT DELIMITED COLLECTION ITEMS TERMINATED BY '\002' means that Hive will use the ^B character to separate *collection items*.

Finally, the character \003 is the octal code for ^C. The clause ROW FORMAT DELIMITED MAP KEYS TERMINATED BY '\003' means that Hive will use the ^C character to separate map *keys* from *values*.

The clause LINES TERMINATED BY '…' and STORED AS … do not require the ROW FORMAT DELIMITED keywords.

Actually, it turns out that Hive does not currently support any character for LINES TERMINATED BY … *other than* '\n'. So this clause has limited utility today.

You can override the field, collection, and key-value separators and still use the default text file format, so the clause STORED AS TEXTFILE is rarely used. For most of this book, we will use the default TEXTFILE file format.

There are other file format options, but we'll defer discussing them until Chapter 15. A related issue is compression of files, which we'll discuss in Chapter 11.

So, while you can specify all these clauses explicitly, using the default separators most of the time, you normally only provide the clauses for explicit overrides.

> These specifications only affect what Hive expects to see when it reads files. Except in a few limited cases, it's up to you to *write* the data files in the correct format.

For example, here is a table definition where the data will contain comma-delimited fields.

```
CREATE TABLE some_data (
  first   FLOAT,
  second  FLOAT,
  third   FLOAT
)
ROW FORMAT DELIMITED
FIELDS TERMINATED BY ',';
```

Use '\t' for tab-delimited fields.

This example does not properly handle the general case of files in CSV (*comma-separated values*) and TSV (*tab-separated values*) formats. They can include a header row with column names and column string values might be quoted and they might contain embedded commas or tabs, respectively. See Chapter 15 for details on handling these file types more generally.

This powerful customization feature makes it much easier to use Hive with files created by other tools and various ETL (extract, transform, and load) processes.

Schema on Read

When you write data to a traditional database, either through loading external data, writing the output of a query, doing UPDATE statements, etc., the database has total control over the storage. The database is the "gatekeeper." An important implication of this control is that the database can enforce the schema as data is *written*. This is called *schema on write*.

Hive has no such control over the underlying storage. There are many ways to create, modify, and even damage the data that Hive will query. Therefore, Hive can only enforce queries on *read*. This is called *schema on read*.

So what if the schema doesn't match the file contents? Hive does the best that it can to read the data. You will get lots of null values if there aren't enough fields in each record to match the schema. If some fields are numbers and Hive encounters nonnumeric strings, it will return nulls for those fields. Above all else, Hive tries to recover from all errors as best it can.

CHAPTER 4

HiveQL: Data Definition

HiveQL is the Hive query language. Like all SQL dialects in widespread use, it doesn't fully conform to any particular revision of the ANSI SQL standard. It is perhaps closest to MySQL's dialect, but with significant differences. Hive offers no support for row-level inserts, updates, and deletes. Hive doesn't support transactions. Hive adds extensions to provide better performance in the context of Hadoop and to integrate with custom extensions and even external programs.

Still, much of HiveQL will be familiar. This chapter and the ones that follow discuss the features of HiveQL using representative examples. In some cases, we will briefly mention details for completeness, then explore them more fully in later chapters.

This chapter starts with the so-called *data definition language* parts of HiveQL, which are used for creating, altering, and dropping databases, tables, views, functions, and indexes. We'll discuss databases and tables in this chapter, deferring the discussion of views until Chapter 7, indexes until Chapter 8, and functions until Chapter 13.

We'll also discuss the SHOW and DESCRIBE commands for listing and describing items as we go.

Subsequent chapters explore the *data manipulation language* parts of HiveQL that are used to put data into Hive tables and to extract data to the filesystem, and how to explore and manipulate data with queries, grouping, filtering, joining, etc.

Databases in Hive

The Hive concept of a database is essentially just a *catalog* or *namespace* of tables. However, they are very useful for larger clusters with multiple teams and users, as a way of avoiding table name collisions. It's also common to use databases to organize production tables into logical groups.

If you don't specify a database, the default database is used.

The simplest syntax for creating a database is shown in the following example:

```
hive> CREATE DATABASE financials;
```

Hive will throw an error if `financials` already exists. You can suppress these warnings with this variation:

```
hive> CREATE DATABASE IF NOT EXISTS financials;
```

While normally you might like to be warned if a database of the same name already exists, the `IF NOT EXISTS` clause is useful for scripts that should create a database on-the-fly, if necessary, before proceeding.

You can also use the keyword `SCHEMA` instead of `DATABASE` in all the database-related commands.

At any time, you can see the databases that already exist as follows:

```
hive> SHOW DATABASES;
default
financials

hive> CREATE DATABASE human_resources;

hive> SHOW DATABASES;
default
financials
human_resources
```

If you have a lot of databases, you can restrict the ones listed using a *regular expression*, a concept we'll explain in "LIKE and RLIKE" on page 96, if it is new to you. The following example lists only those databases that start with the letter `h` and end with any other characters (the `.*` part):

```
hive> SHOW DATABASES LIKE 'h.*';
human_resources
hive> ...
```

Hive will create a directory for each database. Tables in that database will be stored in subdirectories of the database directory. The exception is tables in the `default` database, which doesn't have its own directory.

The database directory is created under a top-level directory specified by the property `hive.metastore.warehouse.dir`, which we discussed in "Local Mode Configuration" on page 24 and "Distributed and Pseudodistributed Mode Configuration" on page 26. Assuming you are using the default value for this property, */user/hive/warehouse*, when the `financials` database is created, Hive will create the directory */user/hive/warehouse/financials.db*. Note the *.db* extension.

You can override this default location for the new directory as shown in this example:

```
hive> CREATE DATABASE financials
    > LOCATION '/my/preferred/directory';
```

You can add a descriptive comment to the database, which will be shown by the `DESCRIBE DATABASE <database>` command.

```
hive> CREATE DATABASE financials
    > COMMENT 'Holds all financial tables';

hive> DESCRIBE DATABASE financials;
financials    Holds all financial tables
  hdfs://master-server/user/hive/warehouse/financials.db
```

Note that DESCRIBE DATABASE also shows the directory location for the database. In this example, the *URI scheme* is hdfs. For a MapR installation, it would be maprfs. For an Amazon Elastic MapReduce (EMR) cluster, it would also be hdfs, but you could set hive.metastore.warehouse.dir to use Amazon S3 explicitly (i.e., by specifying s3n:// bucketname/... as the property value). You could use s3 as the scheme, but the newer s3n is preferred.

In the output of DESCRIBE DATABASE, we're showing master-server to indicate the URI *authority*, in this case a DNS name and optional port number (i.e., server:port) for the "master node" of the filesystem (i.e., where the *NameNode* service is running for HDFS). If you are running in *pseudo-distributed* mode, then the master server will be localhost. For *local* mode, the path will be a local path, *file:///user/hive/warehouse/ financials.db*.

If the authority is omitted, Hive uses the master-server name and port defined by the property fs.default.name in the Hadoop configuration files, found in the *$HADOOP_HOME/conf* directory.

To be clear, *hdfs:///user/hive/warehouse/financials.db* is equivalent to *hdfs://master-server/user/hive/warehouse/financials.db*, where master-server is your master node's DNS name and optional port.

For completeness, when you specify a *relative* path (e.g., *some/relative/path*), Hive will put this under your home directory in the distributed filesystem (e.g., *hdfs:///user/<user-name>*) for HDFS. However, if you are running in *local mode*, your current working directory is used as the parent of *some/relative/path*.

For script portability, it's typical to omit the authority, only specifying it when referring to another distributed filesystem instance (including S3 buckets).

Lastly, you can associate key-value properties with the database, although their only function currently is to provide a way of adding information to the output of DESCRIBE DATABASE EXTENDED <database>:

```
hive> CREATE DATABASE financials
    > WITH DBPROPERTIES ('creator' = 'Mark Moneybags', 'date' = '2012-01-02');

hive> DESCRIBE DATABASE financials;
financials    hdfs://master-server/user/hive/warehouse/financials.db

hive> DESCRIBE DATABASE EXTENDED financials;
financials    hdfs://master-server/user/hive/warehouse/financials.db
  {date=2012-01-02, creator=Mark Moneybags);
```

The USE command sets a database as your working database, analogous to changing working directories in a filesystem:

```
hive> USE financials;
```

Now, commands such as SHOW TABLES; will list the tables in this database.

Unfortunately, there is no command to show you which database is your current working database! Fortunately, it's always safe to repeat the USE … command; there is no concept in Hive of nesting of databases.

Recall that we pointed out a useful trick in "Variables and Properties" on page 31 for setting a property to print the current database as part of the prompt (Hive v0.8.0 and later):

```
hive> set hive.cli.print.current.db=true;

hive (financials)> USE default;

hive (default)> set hive.cli.print.current.db=false;

hive> ...
```

Finally, you can drop a database:

```
hive> DROP DATABASE IF EXISTS financials;
```

The IF EXISTS is optional and suppresses warnings if financials doesn't exist.

By default, Hive won't permit you to drop a database if it contains tables. You can either drop the tables first or append the CASCADE keyword to the command, which will cause the Hive to drop the tables in the database first:

```
hive> DROP DATABASE IF EXISTS financials CASCADE;
```

Using the RESTRICT keyword instead of CASCADE is equivalent to the default behavior, where existing tables must be dropped before dropping the database.

When a database is dropped, its directory is also deleted.

Alter Database

You can set key-value pairs in the DBPROPERTIES associated with a database using the ALTER DATABASE command. No other metadata about the database can be changed, including its name and directory location:

```
hive> ALTER DATABASE financials SET DBPROPERTIES ('edited-by' = 'Joe Dba');
```

There is no way to delete or "unset" a DBPROPERTY.

Creating Tables

The `CREATE TABLE` statement follows SQL conventions, but Hive's version offers significant extensions to support a wide range of flexibility where the data files for tables are stored, the formats used, etc. We discussed many of these options in "Text File Encoding of Data Values" on page 45 and we'll return to more advanced options later in Chapter 15. In this section, we describe the other options available for the `CREATE TABLE` statement, adapting the `employees` table declaration we used previously in "Collection Data Types" on page 43:

```
CREATE TABLE IF NOT EXISTS mydb.employees (
  name         STRING COMMENT 'Employee name',
  salary       FLOAT  COMMENT 'Employee salary',
  subordinates ARRAY<STRING> COMMENT 'Names of subordinates',
  deductions   MAP<STRING, FLOAT>
               COMMENT 'Keys are deductions names, values are percentages',
  address      STRUCT<street:STRING, city:STRING, state:STRING, zip:INT>
               COMMENT 'Home address')
COMMENT 'Description of the table'
TBLPROPERTIES ('creator'='me', 'created_at'='2012-01-02 10:00:00', ...)
LOCATION '/user/hive/warehouse/mydb.db/employees';
```

First, note that you can prefix a database name, `mydb` in this case, if you're not currently working in the target database.

If you add the option `IF NOT EXISTS`, Hive will silently ignore the statement if the table already exists. This is useful in scripts that should create a table the first time they run.

However, the clause has a gotcha you should know. If the schema specified differs from the schema in the table that already exists, Hive won't warn you. If your intention is for this table to have the new schema, you'll have to drop the old table, losing your data, and then re-create it. Consider if you should use one or more `ALTER TABLE` statements to change the existing table schema instead. See "Alter Table" on page 66 for details.

 If you use `IF NOT EXISTS` and the existing table has a different schema than the schema in the `CREATE TABLE` statement, Hive will ignore the discrepancy.

You can add a comment to any column, after the type. Like databases, you can attach a comment to the table itself and you can define one or more table *properties*. In most cases, the primary benefit of `TBLPROPERTIES` is to add additional documentation in a key-value format. However, when we examine Hive's integration with databases such as DynamoDB (see "DynamoDB" on page 225), we'll see that the `TBLPROPERTIES` can be used to express essential metadata about the database connection.

Hive automatically adds two table properties: `last_modified_by` holds the username of the last user to modify the table, and `last_modified_time` holds the epoch time in seconds of that modification.

> A planned enhancement for Hive v0.10.0 is to add a `SHOW TBLPROPERTIES table_name` command that will list just the `TBLPROPERTIES` for a table.

Finally, you can optionally specify a location for the table data (as opposed to *metadata*, which the *metastore* will always hold). In this example, we are showing the default location that Hive would use, */user/hive/warehouse/mydb.db/employees*, where */user/hive/warehouse* is the default "warehouse" location (as discussed previously), *mydb.db* is the database directory, and *employees* is the table directory.

By default, Hive always creates the table's directory under the directory for the enclosing database. The exception is the *default* database. It doesn't have a directory under */user/hive/warehouse*, so a table in the *default* database will have its directory created directly in */user/hive/warehouse* (unless explicitly overridden).

> To avoid potential confusion, it's usually better to use an *external* table if you don't want to use the default location table. See "External Tables" on page 56 for details.

You can also copy the schema (but not the data) of an existing table:

```
CREATE TABLE IF NOT EXISTS mydb.employees2
LIKE mydb.employees;
```

This version also accepts the optional `LOCATION` clause, but note that no other properties, including the schema, can be defined; they are determined from the original table.

The `SHOW TABLES` command lists the tables. With no additional arguments, it shows the tables in the current working database. Let's assume we have already created a few other tables, `table1` and `table2`, and we did so in the `mydb` database:

```
hive> USE mydb;

hive> SHOW TABLES;
employees
table1
table2
```

If we aren't in the same database, we can still list the tables in that database:

```
hive> USE default;

hive> SHOW TABLES IN mydb;
employees
```

```
table1
table2
```

If we have a lot of tables, we can limit the ones listed using a *regular expression*, a concept we'll discuss in detail in "LIKE and RLIKE" on page 96:

```
hive> USE mydb;

hive> SHOW TABLES 'empl.*';
employees
```

Not all regular expression features are supported. If you know regular expressions, it's better to test a candidate regular expression to make sure it actually works!

The regular expression in the single quote looks for all tables with names starting with empl and ending with any other characters (the .* part).

 Using the IN database_name clause and a regular expression for the table names together is not supported.

We can also use the DESCRIBE EXTENDED mydb.employees command to show details about the table. (We can drop the mydb. prefix if we're currently using the mydb database.) We have reformatted the output for easier reading and we have suppressed many details to focus on the items that interest us now:

```
hive> DESCRIBE EXTENDED mydb.employees;
name      string   Employee name
salary    float    Employee salary
subordinates       array<string>    Names of subordinates
deductions         map<string,float> Keys are deductions names, values are percentages
address struct<street:string,city:string,state:string,zip:int>  Home address

Detailed Table Information      Table(tableName:employees, dbName:mydb, owner:me,
...
location:hdfs://master-server/user/hive/warehouse/mydb.db/employees,
parameters:{creator=me, created_at='2012-01-02 10:00:00',
            last_modified_user=me, last_modified_time=1337544510,
            comment:Description of the table, ...}, ...)
```

Replacing EXTENDED with FORMATTED provides more readable but also more verbose output.

The first section shows the output of DESCRIBE without EXTENDED or FORMATTED (i.e., the schema including the comments for each column).

If you only want to see the schema for a particular column, append the column to the table name. Here, EXTENDED adds no additional output:

```
hive> DESCRIBE mydb.employees.salary;
salary    float    Employee salary
```

Returning to the extended output, note the line in the description that starts with location:. It shows the full URI path in HDFS to the directory where Hive will keep all the data for this table, as we discussed above.

 We said that the last_modified_by and last_modified_time table properties are automatically created. However, they are only *shown* in the Detailed Table Information *if* a user-specified table property has also been defined!

Managed Tables

The tables we have created so far are called *managed* tables or sometimes called *internal* tables, because Hive controls the lifecycle of their data (more or less). As we've seen, Hive stores the data for these tables in a subdirectory under the directory defined by hive.metastore.warehouse.dir (e.g., */user/hive/warehouse*), by default.

When we drop a managed table (see "Dropping Tables" on page 66), Hive deletes the data in the table.

However, managed tables are less convenient for sharing with other tools. For example, suppose we have data that is created and used primarily by *Pig* or other tools, but we want to run some queries against it, but not give Hive *ownership* of the data. We can define an *external* table that points to that data, but doesn't take ownership of it.

External Tables

Suppose we are analyzing data from the stock markets. Periodically, we ingest the data for NASDAQ and the NYSE from a source like Infochimps (*http://infochimps.com/da tasets*) and we want to study this data with many tools. (See the data sets named infochimps_dataset_4777_download_16185 and infochimps_dataset_4778_download_16677, respectively, which are actually sourced from Yahoo! Finance.) The schema we'll use next matches the schemas of both these data sources. Let's assume the data files are in the distributed filesystem directory */data/stocks*.

The following table declaration creates an *external* table that can read all the data files for this comma-delimited data in */data/stocks*:

```
CREATE EXTERNAL TABLE IF NOT EXISTS stocks (
    exchange        STRING,
    symbol          STRING,
    ymd             STRING,
    price_open      FLOAT,
    price_high      FLOAT,
    price_low       FLOAT,
    price_close     FLOAT,
    volume          INT,
    price_adj_close FLOAT)
ROW FORMAT DELIMITED FIELDS TERMINATED BY ','
LOCATION '/data/stocks';
```

The EXTERNAL keyword tells Hive this table is external and the LOCATION … clause is required to tell Hive where it's located.

Because it's external, Hive does not assume it *owns* the data. Therefore, dropping the table *does not* delete the data, although the *metadata* for the table will be deleted.

There are a few other small differences between managed and external tables, where some HiveQL constructs are not permitted for external tables. We'll discuss those when we come to them.

However, it's important to note that the differences between managed and external tables are smaller than they appear at first. Even for managed tables, you *know* where they are located, so you can use other tools, hadoop dfs commands, etc., to modify and even delete the files in the directories for managed tables. Hive may technically own these directories and files, but it doesn't have full control over them! Recall, in "Schema on Read" on page 48, we said that Hive really has no control over the integrity of the files used for storage and whether or not their contents are consistent with the table schema. Even managed tables don't give us this control.

Still, a general principle of good software design is to express intent. If the data is shared between tools, then creating an external table makes this ownership explicit.

You can tell whether or not a table is managed or external using the output of DESCRIBE EXTENDED tablename. Near the end of the Detailed Table Information output, you will see the following for managed tables:

```
... tableType:MANAGED_TABLE)
```

For external tables, you will see the following:

```
... tableType:EXTERNAL_TABLE)
```

As for managed tables, you can also copy the schema (but not the data) of an existing table:

```
CREATE EXTERNAL TABLE IF NOT EXISTS mydb.employees3
LIKE mydb.employees
LOCATION '/path/to/data';
```

 If you omit the EXTERNAL keyword and the original table is external, the new table will also be external. If you omit EXTERNAL and the original table is managed, the new table will also be managed. However, if you include the EXTERNAL keyword and the original table is managed, the new table will be external. Even in this scenario, the LOCATION clause will *still* be optional.

Partitioned, Managed Tables

The general notion of partitioning data is an old one. It can take many forms, but often it's used for distributing load horizontally, moving data physically closer to its most frequent users, and other purposes.

Hive has the notion of partitioned tables. We'll see that they have important performance benefits, and they can help organize data in a logical fashion, such as hierarchically.

We'll discuss partitioned managed tables first. Let's return to our `employees` table and imagine that we work for a very large multinational corporation. Our HR people often run queries with `WHERE` clauses that restrict the results to a particular country or to a particular *first-level subdivision* (e.g., *state* in the United States or *province* in Canada). (First-level subdivision is an actual term, used here, for example: *http://www.common datahub.com/state_source.jsp.*) We'll just use the word *state* for simplicity. We have redundant state information in the `address` field. It is distinct from the `state` partition. We could remove the `state` element from `address`. There is no ambiguity in queries, since we have to use `address.state` to project the value inside the `address`. So, let's partition the data first by country and then by state:

```
CREATE TABLE employees (
    name         STRING,
    salary       FLOAT,
    subordinates ARRAY<STRING>,
    deductions   MAP<STRING, FLOAT>,
    address      STRUCT<street:STRING, city:STRING, state:STRING, zip:INT>
)
PARTITIONED BY (country STRING, state STRING);
```

Partitioning tables changes how Hive structures the data storage. If we create this table in the `mydb` database, there will still be an *employees* directory for the table:

```
hdfs://master_server/user/hive/warehouse/mydb.db/employees
```

However, Hive will now create subdirectories reflecting the partitioning structure. For example:

```
...
.../employees/country=CA/state=AB
.../employees/country=CA/state=BC
...
.../employees/country=US/state=AL
.../employees/country=US/state=AK
...
```

Yes, those are the actual directory names. The state directories will contain zero or more files for the employees in those states.

Once created, the partition *keys* (`country` and `state`, in this case) behave like regular columns. There is one known exception, due to a bug (see "Aggregate functions" on page 85). In fact, users of the table don't need to *care* if these "columns" are partitions or not, except when they want to optimize query performance.

For example, the following query selects all employees in the state of Illinois in the United States:

```
SELECT * FROM employees
WHERE country = 'US' AND state = 'IL';
```

Note that because the `country` and `state` values are encoded in directory names, there is no reason to have this data in the data files themselves. In fact, the data just gets in the way in the files, since you have to account for it in the table schema, and this data wastes space.

Perhaps the most important reason to partition data is for faster queries. In the previous query, which limits the results to employees in Illinois, it is only necessary to scan the contents of *one* directory. Even if we have thousands of country and state directories, all but one can be ignored. For very large data sets, partitioning can dramatically improve query performance, but *only* if the partitioning scheme reflects common *range* filtering (e.g., by locations, timestamp ranges).

When we add predicates to `WHERE` clauses that filter on partition values, these predicates are called *partition filters*.

Even if you do a query across the entire US, Hive only reads the 65 directories covering the 50 states, 9 territories, and the District of Columbia, and 6 military "states" used by the armed services. You can see the full list here: *http://www.50states.com/abbrevia tions.htm*.

Of course, if you need to do a query for all employees around the globe, you can still do it. Hive will have to read every directory, but hopefully these broader disk scans will be relatively rare.

However, a query across all partitions could trigger an enormous MapReduce job if the table data and number of partitions are large. A highly suggested safety measure is putting Hive into "strict" mode, which prohibits queries of partitioned tables without a `WHERE` clause that filters on partitions. You can set the mode to "nonstrict," as in the following session:

```
hive> set hive.mapred.mode=strict;

hive> SELECT e.name, e.salary FROM employees e LIMIT 100;
FAILED: Error in semantic analysis: No partition predicate found for
 Alias "e" Table "employees"

hive> set hive.mapred.mode=nonstrict;

hive> SELECT e.name, e.salary FROM employees e LIMIT 100;
```

```
John Doe  100000.0
...
```

You can see the partitions that exist with the SHOW PARTITIONS command:

```
hive> SHOW PARTITIONS employees;
...
Country=CA/state=AB
country=CA/state=BC
...
country=US/state=AL
country=US/state=AK
...
```

If you have a lot of partitions and you want to see if partitions have been defined for particular partition keys, you can further restrict the command with an optional PARTI TION clause that specifies one or more of the partitions with specific values:

```
hive> SHOW PARTITIONS employees PARTITION(country='US');
country=US/state=AL
country=US/state=AK
...

hive> SHOW PARTITIONS employees PARTITION(country='US', state='AK');
country=US/state=AK
```

The DESCRIBE EXTENDED employees command shows the partition keys:

```
hive> DESCRIBE EXTENDED employees;
name        string,
salary      float,
...
address     struct<...>,
country     string,
state       string

Detailed Table Information...
partitionKeys:[FieldSchema(name:country, type:string, comment:null),
FieldSchema(name:state, type:string, comment:null)],
...
```

The schema part of the output lists the country and state with the other columns, because they are columns as far as queries are concerned. The Detailed Table Infor mation includes the country and state as partition keys. The comments for both of these keys are null; we could have added comments just as for regular columns.

You create partitions in managed tables by loading data into them. The following example creates a US and CA (California) partition while loading data into it from a local directory, $HOME/california-employees. You must specify a value for each partition column. Notice how we reference the HOME environment variable in HiveQL:

```
LOAD DATA LOCAL INPATH '${env:HOME}/california-employees'
INTO TABLE employees
PARTITION (country = 'US', state = 'CA');
```

The directory for this partition, *.../employees/country=US/state=CA*, will be created by Hive and all data files in *$HOME/california-employees* will be copied into it. See "Loading Data into Managed Tables" on page 71 for more information on populating tables.

External Partitioned Tables

You can use partitioning with external tables. In fact, you may find that this is your most common scenario for managing large production data sets. The combination gives you a way to "share" data with other tools, while still optimizing query performance.

You also have more flexibility in the directory structure used, as you define it yourself. We'll see a particularly useful example in a moment.

Let's consider a new example that fits this scenario well: logfile analysis. Most organizations use a standard format for log messages, recording a timestamp, severity (e.g., ERROR, WARNING, INFO), perhaps a server name and process ID, and then an arbitrary text message. Suppose our Extract, Transform, and Load (ETL) process ingests and aggregates logfiles in our environment, converting each log message to a tab-delimited record and also decomposing the timestamp into separate year, month, and day fields, and a combined hms field for the remaining hour, minute, and second parts of the timestamp, for reasons that will become clear in a moment. You could do this parsing of log messages using the string parsing functions built into Hive or Pig, for example. Alternatively, we could use smaller integer types for some of the timestamp-related fields to conserve space. Here, we are ignoring subsequent resolution.

Here's how we might define the corresponding Hive table:

```
CREATE EXTERNAL TABLE IF NOT EXISTS log_messages (
    hms             INT,
    severity        STRING,
    server          STRING,
    process_id      INT,
    message         STRING)
PARTITIONED BY (year INT, month INT, day INT)
ROW FORMAT DELIMITED FIELDS TERMINATED BY '\t';
```

We're assuming that a day's worth of log data is about the correct size for a useful partition and finer grain queries over a day's data will be fast enough.

Recall that when we created the nonpartitioned external stocks table, a LOCATION … clause was required. It isn't used for external partitioned tables. Instead, an ALTER TABLE statement is used to add *each* partition separately. It must specify a value for each partition key, the year, month, and day, in this case (see "Alter Table" on page 66 for more details on this feature). Here is an example, where we add a partition for January 2nd, 2012:

```
ALTER TABLE log_messages ADD PARTITION(year = 2012, month = 1, day = 2)
LOCATION 'hdfs://master_server/data/log_messages/2012/01/02';
```

The directory convention we use is completely up to us. Here, we follow a hierarchical directory structure, because it's a logical way to organize our data, but there is no requirement to do so. We could follow Hive's directory naming convention (e.g., .../ *exchange=NASDAQ/symbol=AAPL*), but there is no requirement to do so.

An interesting benefit of this flexibility is that we can archive old data on inexpensive storage, like Amazon's S3, while keeping newer, more "interesting" data in HDFS. For example, each day we might use the following procedure to move data older than a month to S3:

- Copy the data for the partition being moved to S3. For example, you can use the `hadoop distcp` command:

  ```
  hadoop distcp /data/log_messages/2011/12/02 s3n://ourbucket/logs/2011/12/02
  ```

- Alter the table to point the partition to the S3 location:

  ```
  ALTER TABLE log_messages PARTITION(year = 2011, month = 12, day = 2)
  SET LOCATION 's3n://ourbucket/logs/2011/01/02';
  ```

- Remove the HDFS copy of the partition using the `hadoop fs -rmr` command:

  ```
  hadoop fs -rmr /data/log_messages/2011/01/02
  ```

You don't have to be an Amazon Elastic MapReduce user to use S3 this way. S3 support is part of the Apache Hadoop distribution. You can *still* query this data, even queries that cross the month-old "boundary," where some data is read from HDFS and some data is read from S3!

By the way, Hive doesn't care if a partition directory doesn't exist for a partition or if it has no files. In both cases, you'll just get no results for a query that filters for the partition. This is convenient when you want to set up partitions before a separate process starts writing data to them. As soon as data is there, queries will return results from that data.

This feature illustrates another benefit: new data can be written to a dedicated directory with a clear distinction from older data in other directories. Also, whether you move old data to an "archive" location or delete it outright, the risk of tampering with newer data is reduced since the data subsets are in separate directories.

As for nonpartitioned external tables, Hive does not own the data and it does not delete the data if the table is dropped.

As for managed partitioned tables, you can see an external table's partitions with SHOW PARTITIONS:

```
hive> SHOW PARTITIONS log_messages;
...
year=2011/month=12/day=31
year=2012/month=1/day=1
year=2012/month=1/day=2
...
```

Similarly, the `DESCRIBE EXTENDED log_messages` shows the partition keys both as part of the schema and in the list of `partitionKeys`:

```
hive> DESCRIBE EXTENDED log_messages;
...
message         string,
year            int,
month           int,
day             int

Detailed Table Information...
partitionKeys:[FieldSchema(name:year, type:int, comment:null),
FieldSchema(name:month, type:int, comment:null),
FieldSchema(name:day, type:int, comment:null)],
...
```

This output is missing a useful bit of information, the actual location of the partition data. There is a `location` field, but it only shows Hive's default directory that would be used if the table were a managed table. However, we can get a partition's location as follows:

```
hive> DESCRIBE EXTENDED log_messages PARTITION (year=2012, month=1, day=2);
...
location:s3n://ourbucket/logs/2011/01/02,
...
```

We frequently use external partitioned tables because of the many benefits they provide, such as logical data management, performant queries, etc.

`ALTER TABLE … ADD PARTITION` is not limited to external tables. You can use it with managed tables, too, when you have (or will have) data for partitions in directories created outside of the `LOAD` and `INSERT` options we discussed above. You'll need to remember that not all of the table's data will be under the usual Hive "warehouse" directory, and this data *won't* be deleted when you drop the managed table! Hence, from a "sanity" perspective, it's questionable whether you should dare to use this feature with managed tables.

Customizing Table Storage Formats

In "Text File Encoding of Data Values" on page 45, we discussed that Hive defaults to a text file format, which is indicated by the optional clause `STORED AS TEXTFILE`, and you can overload the default values for the various delimiters when creating the table. Here we repeat the definition of the `employees` table we used in that discussion:

```
CREATE TABLE employees (
    name         STRING,
    salary       FLOAT,
    subordinates ARRAY<STRING>,
    deductions   MAP<STRING, FLOAT>,
    address      STRUCT<street:STRING, city:STRING, state:STRING, zip:INT>
)
ROW FORMAT DELIMITED
```

```
FIELDS TERMINATED BY '\001'
COLLECTION ITEMS TERMINATED BY '\002'
MAP KEYS TERMINATED BY '\003'
LINES TERMINATED BY '\n'
STORED AS TEXTFILE;
```

TEXTFILE implies that all fields are encoded using alphanumeric characters, including those from international character sets, although we observed that Hive uses non-printing characters as "terminators" (delimiters), by default. When TEXTFILE is used, each line is considered a separate record.

You can replace TEXTFILE with one of the other built-in file formats supported by Hive, including SEQUENCEFILE and RCFILE, both of which optimize disk space usage and I/O bandwidth performance using binary encoding and optional compression. These formats are discussed in more detail in Chapter 11 and Chapter 15.

Hive draws a distinction between how records are encoded into files and how columns are encoded into records. You customize these behaviors separately.

The record encoding is handled by an *input format* object (e.g., the Java code behind TEXTFILE.) Hive uses a Java *class* (compiled module) named org.apache .hadoop.mapred.TextInputFormat. If you are unfamiliar with Java, the dotted name syntax indicates a hierarchical namespace tree of *packages* that actually corresponds to the directory structure for the Java code. The last name, TextInputFormat, is a *class* in the lowest-level package mapred.

The record parsing is handled by a *serializer/deserializer* or *SerDe* for short. For TEXT FILE and the encoding we described in Chapter 3 and repeated in the example above, the SerDe Hive uses is another Java class called org.apache.hadoop.hive.serde2.lazy. LazySimpleSerDe.

For completeness, there is also an *output format* that Hive uses for writing the output of queries to files and to the console. For TEXTFILE, the Java class named org.apache.hadoop.hive.ql.io.HiveIgnoreKeyTextOutputFormat is used for output.

 Hive uses an *input format* to split input streams into *records*, an *output format* to format records into output streams (i.e., the output of queries), and a *SerDe* to parse *records* into *columns*, when reading, and encodes *columns* into *records*, when writing. We'll explore these distinctions in greater depth in Chapter 15.

Third-party input and output formats and SerDes can be specified, a feature which permits users to customize Hive for a wide range of file formats not supported natively.

Here is a complete example that uses a custom SerDe, input format, and output format for files accessible through the *Avro* protocol, which we will discuss in detail in "Avro Hive SerDe" on page 209:

```
CREATE TABLE kst
PARTITIONED BY (ds string)
ROW FORMAT SERDE 'com.linkedin.haivvreo.AvroSerDe'
WITH SERDEPROPERTIES ('schema.url'='http://schema_provider/kst.avsc')
STORED AS
INPUTFORMAT 'com.linkedin.haivvreo.AvroContainerInputFormat'
OUTPUTFORMAT 'com.linkedin.haivvreo.AvroContainerOutputFormat';
```

The ROW FORMAT SERDE ... specifies the SerDe to use. Hive provides the WITH SERDEPRO
PERTIES feature that allows users to pass configuration information to the SerDe. Hive
knows nothing about the meaning of these properties. It's up to the SerDe to decide
their meaning. Note that the name and value of each property must be a quoted string.

Finally, the STORED AS INPUTFORMAT ... OUTPUTFORMAT ... clause specifies the Java classes
to use for the input and output formats, respectively. If you specify one of these formats,
you are required to specify both of them.

Note that the DESCRIBE EXTENDED table command lists the input and output formats,
the SerDe, and any SerDe properties in the DETAILED TABLE INFORMATION. For our example, we would see the following:

```
hive> DESCRIBE EXTENDED kst
...
inputFormat:com.linkedin.haivvreo.AvroContainerInputFormat,
outputFormat:com.linkedin.haivvreo.AvroContainerOutputFormat,
...
serdeInfo:SerDeInfo(name:null,
serializationLib:com.linkedin.haivvreo.AvroSerDe,
  parameters:{schema.url=http://schema_provider/kst.avsc})
...
```

Finally, there are a few additional CREATE TABLE clauses that describe more details about
how the data is supposed to be stored. Let's extend our previous stocks table example
from "External Tables" on page 56:

```
CREATE EXTERNAL TABLE IF NOT EXISTS stocks (
    exchange        STRING,
    symbol          STRING,
    ymd             STRING,
    price_open      FLOAT,
    price_high      FLOAT,
    price_low       FLOAT,
    price_close     FLOAT,
    volume          INT,
    price_adj_close FLOAT)
CLUSTERED BY (exchange, symbol)
SORTED BY (ymd ASC)
INTO 96 BUCKETS
ROW FORMAT DELIMITED FIELDS TERMINATED BY ','
LOCATION '/data/stocks';
```

The CLUSTERED BY ... INTO ... BUCKETS clause, with an optional SORTED BY ... clause is used
to optimize certain kinds of queries, which we discuss in detail in "Bucketing Table
Data Storage" on page 125.

Dropping Tables

The familiar `DROP TABLE` command from SQL is supported:

```
DROP TABLE IF EXISTS employees;
```

The `IF EXISTS` keywords are optional. If not used and the table doesn't exist, Hive returns an error.

For *managed* tables, the table metadata *and* data are deleted.

> Actually, if you enable the Hadoop Trash feature, which is *not* on by default, the data is moved to the *.Trash* directory in the distributed filesystem for the user, which in HDFS is */user/$USER/.Trash*. To enable this feature, set the property `fs.trash.interval` to a reasonable positive number. It's the number of minutes between "trash checkpoints"; 1,440 would be 24 hours. While it's not guaranteed to work for all versions of all distributed filesystems, if you accidentally drop a managed table with important data, you may be able to re-create the table, re-create any partitions, and then move the files from *.Trash* to the correct directories (using the filesystem commands) to restore the data.

For *external* tables, the metadata is deleted *but* the data is not.

Alter Table

Most table properties can be altered with `ALTER TABLE` statements, which change *metadata* about the table but not the data itself. These statements can be used to fix mistakes in schema, move partition locations (as we saw in "External Partitioned Tables" on page 61), and do other operations.

> `ALTER TABLE` modifies table metadata *only*. The data for the table is untouched. It's up to you to ensure that any modifications are consistent with the actual data.

Renaming a Table

Use this statement to rename the table `log_messages` to `logmsgs`:

```
ALTER TABLE log_messages RENAME TO logmsgs;
```

Adding, Modifying, and Dropping a Table Partition

As we saw previously, `ALTER TABLE table ADD PARTITION ...` is used to add a new partition to a table (usually an *external* table). Here we repeat the same command shown previously with the additional options available:

```
ALTER TABLE log_messages ADD IF NOT EXISTS
PARTITION (year = 2011, month = 1, day = 1) LOCATION '/logs/2011/01/01'
PARTITION (year = 2011, month = 1, day = 2) LOCATION '/logs/2011/01/02'
PARTITION (year = 2011, month = 1, day = 3) LOCATION '/logs/2011/01/03'
...;
```

Multiple partitions can be added in the same query when using Hive v0.8.0 and later. As always, IF NOT EXISTS is optional and has the usual meaning.

 Hive v0.7.X allows you to use the syntax with multiple partition specifications, but it actually uses just the *first* partition specification, silently ignoring the others! Instead, use a separate ALTER STATEMENT statement for each partition.

Similarly, you can change a partition location, effectively moving it:

```
ALTER TABLE log_messages PARTITION(year = 2011, month = 12, day = 2)
SET LOCATION 's3n://ourbucket/logs/2011/01/02';
```

This command does not move the data from the old location, nor does it delete the old data.

Finally, you can drop a partition:

```
ALTER TABLE log_messages DROP IF EXISTS PARTITION(year = 2011, month = 12, day = 2);
```

The IF EXISTS clause is optional, as usual. For managed tables, the data for the partition is *deleted*, along with the metadata, even if the partition was created using ALTER TABLE ... ADD PARTITION. For external tables, the data is not deleted.

There are a few more ALTER statements that affect partitions discussed later in "Alter Storage Properties" on page 68 and "Miscellaneous Alter Table Statements" on page 69.

Changing Columns

You can rename a column, change its position, type, or comment:

```
ALTER TABLE log_messages
CHANGE COLUMN hms hours_minutes_seconds INT
COMMENT 'The hours, minutes, and seconds part of the timestamp'
AFTER severity;
```

You have to specify the old name, a new name, and the type, even if the name or type is not changing. The keyword COLUMN is optional as is the COMMENT clause. If you aren't moving the column, the AFTER other_column clause is not necessary. In the example shown, we move the column after the **severity** column. If you want to move the column to the first position, use FIRST instead of AFTER other_column.

As always, this command changes metadata only. If you are moving columns, the data must already match the new schema or you must change it to match by some other means.

Adding Columns

You can add new columns to the end of the existing columns, before any partition columns.

```
ALTER TABLE log_messages ADD COLUMNS (
  app_name    STRING COMMENT 'Application name',
  session_id LONG   COMMENT 'The current session id');
```

The COMMENT clauses are optional, as usual. If any of the new columns are in the wrong position, use an ALTER COLUMN table CHANGE COLUMN statement for each one to move it to the correct position.

Deleting or Replacing Columns

The following example removes *all* the existing columns and replaces them with the new columns specified:

```
ALTER TABLE log_messages REPLACE COLUMNS (
  hours_mins_secs INT    COMMENT 'hour, minute, seconds from timestamp',
  severity        STRING COMMENT 'The message severity'
  message         STRING COMMENT 'The rest of the message');
```

This statement effectively renames the original hms column and removes the server and process_id columns from the original schema definition. As for all ALTER statements, only the table metadata is changed.

The REPLACE statement can only be used with tables that use one of the native *SerDe* modules: DynamicSerDe or MetadataTypedColumnsetSerDe. Recall that the SerDe determines how records are parsed into columns (deserialization) and how a record's columns are written to storage (serialization). See Chapter 15 for more details on SerDes.

Alter Table Properties

You can add additional table properties or modify existing properties, but not remove them:

```
ALTER TABLE log_messages SET TBLPROPERTIES (
  'notes' = 'The process id is no longer captured; this column is always NULL');
```

Alter Storage Properties

There are several ALTER TABLE statements for modifying format and SerDe properties.

The following statement changes the storage format for a partition to be SEQUENCE FILE, as we discussed in "Creating Tables" on page 53 (see "Sequence Files" on page 148 and Chapter 15 for more information):

```
ALTER TABLE log_messages
PARTITION(year = 2012, month = 1, day = 1)
SET FILEFORMAT SEQUENCEFILE;
```

The PARTITION clause is required if the table is partitioned.

You can specify a new SerDe along with SerDe properties or change the properties for the existing SerDe. The following example specifies that a table will use a Java class named com.example.JSONSerDe to process a file of JSON-encoded records:

```
ALTER TABLE table_using_JSON_storage
SET SERDE 'com.example.JSONSerDe'
WITH SERDEPROPERTIES (
  'prop1' = 'value1',
  'prop2' = 'value2');
```

The SERDEPROPERTIES are passed to the SerDe module (the Java class com.example.JSON SerDe, in this case). Note that both the property names (e.g., prop1) and the values (e.g., value1) must be quoted strings.

The SERDEPROPERTIES feature is a convenient mechanism that SerDe implementations can exploit to permit user customization. We'll see a real-world example of a JSON SerDe and how it uses SERDEPROPERTIES in "JSON SerDe" on page 208.

The following example demonstrates how to add new SERDEPROPERTIES for the current SerDe:

```
ALTER TABLE table_using_JSON_storage
SET SERDEPROPERTIES (
  'prop3' = 'value3',
  'prop4' = 'value4');
```

You can alter the storage properties that we discussed in "Creating Tables" on page 53:

```
ALTER TABLE stocks
CLUSTERED BY (exchange, symbol)
SORTED BY (symbol)
INTO 48 BUCKETS;
```

The SORTED BY clause is optional, but the CLUSTER BY and INTO … BUCKETS are required. (See also "Bucketing Table Data Storage" on page 125 for information on the use of data bucketing.)

Miscellaneous Alter Table Statements

In "Execution Hooks" on page 158, we'll discuss a technique for adding execution "hooks" for various operations. The ALTER TABLE … TOUCH statement is used to trigger these hooks:

```
ALTER TABLE log_messages TOUCH
PARTITION(year = 2012, month = 1, day = 1);
```

The PARTITION clause is required for partitioned tables. A typical scenario for this statement is to trigger execution of the hooks when table storage files have been modified outside of Hive. For example, a script that has just written new files for the 2012/01/01 partition for log_message can make the following call to the Hive CLI:

```
hive -e 'ALTER TABLE log_messages TOUCH PARTITION(year = 2012, month = 1, day = 1);'
```

This statement won't create the table or partition if it doesn't already exist. Use the appropriate creation commands in that case.

The `ALTER TABLE … ARCHIVE PARTITION` statement captures the partition files into a Hadoop archive (HAR) file. This only reduces the number of files in the filesystem, reducing the load on the *NameNode*, but doesn't provide any space savings (e.g., through compression):

```
ALTER TABLE log_messages ARCHIVE
PARTITION(year = 2012, month = 1, day = 1);
```

To reverse the operation, substitute `UNARCHIVE` for `ARCHIVE`. This feature is only available for individual partitions of partitioned tables.

Finally, various protections are available. The following statements prevent the partition from being dropped and queried:

```
ALTER TABLE log_messages
PARTITION(year = 2012, month = 1, day = 1) ENABLE NO_DROP;

ALTER TABLE log_messages
PARTITION(year = 2012, month = 1, day = 1) ENABLE OFFLINE;
```

To reverse either operation, replace `ENABLE` with `DISABLE`. These operations also can't be used with nonpartitioned tables.

CHAPTER 5

HiveQL: Data Manipulation

This chapter continues our discussion of *HiveQL*, the Hive query language, focusing on the *data manipulation language* parts that are used to put data into tables and to extract data from tables to the filesystem.

This chapter uses `SELECT ... WHERE` clauses extensively when we discuss populating tables with data queried from other tables. So, why aren't we covering `SELECT ... WHERE` clauses first, instead of waiting until the next chapter, Chapter 6?

Since we just finished discussing how to create tables, we wanted to cover the next obvious topic: how to get data into these tables so you'll have something to query! We assume you already understand the basics of SQL, so these clauses won't be new to you. If they are, please refer to Chapter 6 for details.

Loading Data into Managed Tables

Since Hive has no row-level insert, update, and delete operations, the only way to put data into an table is to use one of the "bulk" load operations. Or you can just write files in the correct directories by other means.

We saw an example of how to load data into a managed table in "Partitioned, Managed Tables" on page 58, which we repeat here with an addition, the use of the `OVERWRITE` keyword:

```
LOAD DATA LOCAL INPATH '${env:HOME}/california-employees'
OVERWRITE INTO TABLE employees
PARTITION (country = 'US', state = 'CA');
```

This command will first create the directory for the partition, if it doesn't already exist, then copy the data to it.

If the target table is not partitioned, you omit the `PARTITION` clause.

It is conventional practice to specify a path that is a directory, rather than an individual file. Hive will copy all the files in the directory, which give you the flexibility of organizing the data into multiple files and changing the file naming convention, without requiring a change to your Hive scripts. Either way, the files will be copied to the appropriate location for the table and the names will be the same.

If the LOCAL keyword is used, the path is assumed to be in the local filesystem. The data is *copied* into the final location. If LOCAL is omitted, the path is assumed to be in the distributed filesystem. In this case, the data is *moved* from the path to the final location.

 LOAD DATA LOCAL ... *copies* the local data to the final location in the distributed filesystem, while LOAD DATA ... (i.e., without LOCAL) *moves* the data to the final location.

The rationale for this inconsistency is the assumption that you usually don't want duplicate copies of your data files in the distributed filesystem.

Also, because files are moved in this case, Hive requires the source and target files and directories to be in the same filesystem. For example, you can't use LOAD DATA to load (move) data from one HDFS cluster to another.

It is more robust to specify a full path, but relative paths can be used. When running in local mode, the relative path is interpreted relative to the user's working directory when the Hive CLI was started. For distributed or pseudo-distributed mode, the path is interpreted relative to the user's home directory *in the distributed filesystem*, which is */user/$USER* by default in HDFS and MapRFS.

If you specify the OVERWRITE keyword, any data already present in the target directory will be deleted first. Without the keyword, the new files are simply added to the target directory. However, if files already exist in the target directory that match filenames being loaded, the old files are overwritten.

 Versions of Hive before v0.9.0 had the following bug: when the OVER WRITE keyword was not used, an existing data file in the target directory would be overwritten if its name matched the name of a data file being written to the directory. Hence, data would be lost. This bug was fixed in the v0.9.0 release.

The PARTITION clause is required if the table is partitioned and you must specify a value for each partition key.

In the example, the data will now exist in the following directory:

    hdfs://master_server/user/hive/warehouse/mydb.db/employees/country=US/state=CA

Another limit on the file path used, the INPATH clause, is that it cannot contain any directories.

Hive does not verify that the data you are loading matches the schema for the table. However, it will verify that the file format matches the table definition. For example, if the table was created with SEQUENCEFILE storage, the loaded files must be sequence files.

Inserting Data into Tables from Queries

The INSERT statement lets you load data into a table from a query. Reusing our employ ees example from the previous chapter, here is an example for the state of Oregon, where we presume the data is already in another table called staged_employees. For reasons we'll discuss shortly, let's use different names for the country and state fields in staged_employees, calling them cnty and st, respectively:

```
INSERT OVERWRITE TABLE employees
PARTITION (country = 'US', state = 'OR')
SELECT * FROM staged_employees se
WHERE se.cnty = 'US' AND se.st = 'OR';
```

With OVERWRITE, any previous contents of the partition (or whole table if not partitioned) are replaced.

If you drop the keyword OVERWRITE or replace it with INTO, Hive appends the data rather than replaces it. This feature is only available in Hive v0.8.0 or later.

This example suggests one common scenario where this feature is useful: data has been staged in a directory, exposed to Hive as an external table, and now you want to put it into the final, partitioned table. A workflow like this is also useful if you want the target table to have a different record format than the source table (e.g., a different field delimiter).

However, if staged_employees is very large and you run 65 of these statements to cover all states, then it means you are scanning staged_employees 65 times! Hive offers an alternative INSERT syntax that allows you to scan the input data once and split it multiple ways. The following example shows this feature for creating the employees partitions for three states:

```
FROM staged_employees se
INSERT OVERWRITE TABLE employees
  PARTITION (country = 'US', state = 'OR')
  SELECT * WHERE se.cnty = 'US' AND se.st = 'OR'
INSERT OVERWRITE TABLE employees
  PARTITION (country = 'US', state = 'CA')
  SELECT * WHERE se.cnty = 'US' AND se.st = 'CA'
INSERT OVERWRITE TABLE employees
  PARTITION (country = 'US', state = 'IL')
  SELECT * WHERE se.cnty = 'US' AND se.st = 'IL';
```

We have used indentation to make it clearer how the clauses group together. Each record read from staged_employees will be evaluated with each SELECT ... WHERE ... clause. Those clauses are evaluated independently; this is *not* an IF ... THEN ... ELSE ... construct!

In fact, by using this construct, some records from the source table can be written to multiple partitions of the destination table or none of them.

If a record satisfied a given SELECT ... WHERE ... clause, it gets written to the specified table and partition. To be clear, each INSERT clause can insert into a different table, when desired, and some of those tables could be partitioned while others aren't.

Hence, some records from the input might get written to multiple output locations and others might get dropped!

You can mix INSERT OVERWRITE clauses and INSERT INTO clauses, as well.

Dynamic Partition Inserts

There's still one problem with this syntax: if you have a lot of partitions to create, you have to write a lot of SQL! Fortunately, Hive also supports a *dynamic partition* feature, where it can infer the partitions to create based on query parameters. By comparison, up until now we have considered only *static partitions*.

Consider this change to the previous example:

```
INSERT OVERWRITE TABLE employees
PARTITION (country, state)
SELECT ..., se.cnty, se.st
FROM staged_employees se;
```

Hive determines the values of the partition keys, country and state, from the last two columns in the SELECT clause. This is why we used different names in staged_employ ees, to emphasize that the relationship between the source column values and the output partition values is by *position* only and not by matching on names.

Suppose that staged_employees has data for a total of 100 country and state pairs. After running this query, employees will have 100 partitions!

You can also mix *dynamic* and *static* partitions. This variation of the previous query specifies a *static* value for the country (US) and a *dynamic* value for the state:

```
INSERT OVERWRITE TABLE employees
PARTITION (country = 'US', state)
SELECT ..., se.cnty, se.st
FROM staged_employees se
WHERE se.cnty = 'US';
```

The static partition keys must come before the dynamic partition keys.

Dynamic partitioning is not enabled by default. When it is enabled, it works in "strict" mode by default, where it expects at least some columns to be static. This helps protect against a badly designed query that generates a gigantic number of partitions. For example, you partition by timestamp and generate a separate partition for each second! Perhaps you meant to partition by day or maybe hour instead. Several other properties are also used to limit excess resource utilization. Table 5-1 describes these properties.

Table 5-1. Dynamic partitions properties

Name	Default	Description
hive.exec.dynamic.parti tion	false	Set to true to enable dynamic partitioning.
hive.exec.dynamic.parti tion.mode	strict	Set to nonstrict to enable all partitions to be determined dynamically.
hive.exec.max.dynamic.par titions.pernode	100	The maximum number of dynamic partitions that can be created by each mapper or reducer. Raises a fatal error if one mapper or reducer attempts to create more than the threshold.
hive.exec.max.dynamic.par titions	+1000	The total number of dynamic partitions that can be created by one statement with dynamic partitioning. Raises a fatal error if the limit is exceeded.
hive.exec.max.cre ated.files	100000	The maximum total number of files that can be created globally. A Hadoop counter is used to track the number of files created. Raises a fatal error if the limit is exceeded.

So, for example, our first example using dynamic partitioning for all partitions might actually look this, where we set the desired properties just before use:

```
hive> set hive.exec.dynamic.partition=true;
hive> set hive.exec.dynamic.partition.mode=nonstrict;
hive> set hive.exec.max.dynamic.partitions.pernode=1000;

hive> INSERT OVERWRITE TABLE employees
    > PARTITION (country, state)
    > SELECT ..., se.cty, se.st
    > FROM staged_employees se;
```

Creating Tables and Loading Them in One Query

You can also create a table and insert query results into it in one statement:

```
CREATE TABLE ca_employees
AS SELECT name, salary, address
FROM employees
WHERE se.state = 'CA';
```

This table contains just the name, salary, and address columns from the employee table records for employees in California. The schema for the new table is taken from the SELECT clause.

A common use for this feature is to extract a convenient subset of data from a larger, more unwieldy table.

This feature can't be used with external tables. Recall that "populating" a partition for an external table is done with an ALTER TABLE statement, where we aren't "loading" data, per se, but pointing metadata to a location where the data can be found.

Exporting Data

How do we get data out of tables? If the data files are already formatted the way you want, then it's simple enough to copy the directories or files:

```
hadoop fs -cp source_path target_path
```

Otherwise, you can use `INSERT ... DIRECTORY ...`, as in this example:

```
INSERT OVERWRITE LOCAL DIRECTORY '/tmp/ca_employees'
SELECT name, salary, address
FROM employees
WHERE se.state = 'CA';
```

`OVERWRITE` and `LOCAL` have the same interpretations as before and paths are interpreted following the usual rules. One or more files will be written to */tmp/ca_employees*, depending on the number of reducers invoked.

The specified path can also be a full URI (e.g., *hdfs://master-server/tmp/ca_employees*).

Independent of how the data is actually stored in the source table, it is written to files with all fields serialized as strings. Hive uses the same encoding in the generated output files as it uses for the tables internal storage.

As a reminder, we can look at the results from within the `hive` CLI:

```
hive> ! ls /tmp/ca_employees;
000000_0
hive> ! cat /tmp/payroll/000000_0
John Doe100000.0201 San Antonio CircleMountain ViewCA94040
Mary Smith80000.01 Infinity LoopCupertinoCA95014
...
```

Yes, the filename is `000000_0`. If there were two or more reducers writing output, we would have additional files with similar names (e.g., `000001_0`).

The fields appear to be joined together without delimiters because the ^A and ^B separators aren't rendered.

Just like inserting data to tables, you can specify multiple inserts to directories:

```
FROM staged_employees se
INSERT OVERWRITE DIRECTORY '/tmp/or_employees'
  SELECT * WHERE se.cty = 'US' and se.st = 'OR'
INSERT OVERWRITE DIRECTORY '/tmp/ca_employees'
  SELECT * WHERE se.cty = 'US' and se.st = 'CA'
INSERT OVERWRITE DIRECTORY '/tmp/il_employees'
  SELECT * WHERE se.cty = 'US' and se.st = 'IL';
```

There are some limited options for customizing the output of the data (other than writing a custom `OUTPUTFORMAT`, as discussed in "Customizing Table Storage Formats" on page 63). To format columns, the built-in functions include those for formatting strings, such as converting case, padding output, and more. See "Other built-in functions" on page 88 for more details.

The field delimiter for the table can be problematic. For example, if it uses the default ^A delimiter. If you export table data frequently, it might be appropriate to use comma or tab delimiters.

Another workaround is to define a "temporary" table with the storage configured to match the desired output format (e.g., tab-delimited fields). Then write a query result to that table and use INSERT OVERWRITE DIRECTORY, selecting from the temporary table. Unlike many relational databases, there is no temporary table feature in Hive. You have to manually drop any tables you create that aren't intended to be permanent.

CHAPTER 6

HiveQL: Queries

After learning the many ways we can define and format tables, let's learn how to run queries. Of course, we have assumed all along that you have some prior knowledge of SQL. We've used some queries already to illustrate several concepts, such as loading query data into other tables in Chapter 5. Now we'll fill in most of the details. Some special topics will be covered in subsequent chapters.

We'll move quickly through details that are familiar to users with prior SQL experience and focus on what's unique to HiveQL, including syntax and feature differences, as well as performance implications.

SELECT ... FROM Clauses

SELECT is the *projection operator* in SQL. The FROM clause identifies from which table, view, or nested query we select records (see Chapter 7).

For a given record, SELECT specifies the columns to keep, as well as the outputs of function calls on one or more columns (e.g., the *aggregation* functions like count(*)).

Recall again our partitioned employees table:

```
CREATE TABLE employees (
    name         STRING,
    salary       FLOAT,
    subordinates ARRAY<STRING>,
    deductions   MAP<STRING, FLOAT>,
    address      STRUCT<street:STRING, city:STRING, state:STRING, zip:INT>
)
PARTITIONED BY (country STRING, state STRING);
```

Let's assume we have the same contents we showed in "Text File Encoding of Data Values" on page 45 for four employees in the US state of Illinois (abbreviated IL). Here are queries of this table and the output they produce:

```
hive> SELECT name, salary FROM employees;
John Doe    100000.0
Mary Smith   80000.0
```

```
Todd Jones    70000.0
Bill King     60000.0
```

The following two queries are identical. The second version uses a table alias e, which is not very useful in this query, but becomes necessary in queries with JOINs (see "JOIN Statements" on page 98) where several different tables are used:

```
hive> SELECT   name,   salary FROM employees;
hive> SELECT e.name, e.salary FROM employees e;
```

When you select columns that are one of the collection types, Hive uses JSON (Java-Script Object Notation) syntax for the output. First, let's select the subordinates, an ARRAY, where a comma-separated list surrounded with [...] is used. Note that STRING elements of the collection are quoted, while the primitive STRING name column is not:

```
hive> SELECT name, subordinates FROM employees;
John Doe    ["Mary Smith","Todd Jones"]
Mary Smith  ["Bill King"]
Todd Jones  []
Bill King   []
```

The deductions is a MAP, where the JSON representation for maps is used, namely a comma-separated list of key:value pairs, surrounded with {...}:

```
hive> SELECT name, deductions FROM employees;
John Doe    {"Federal Taxes":0.2,"State Taxes":0.05,"Insurance":0.1}
Mary Smith  {"Federal Taxes":0.2,"State Taxes":0.05,"Insurance":0.1}
Todd Jones  {"Federal Taxes":0.15,"State Taxes":0.03,"Insurance":0.1}
Bill King   {"Federal Taxes":0.15,"State Taxes":0.03,"Insurance":0.1}
```

Finally, the address is a STRUCT, which is also written using the JSON map format:

```
hive> SELECT name, address FROM employees;
John Doe    {"street":"1 Michigan Ave.","city":"Chicago","state":"IL","zip":60600}
Mary Smith  {"street":"100 Ontario St.","city":"Chicago","state":"IL","zip":60601}
Todd Jones  {"street":"200 Chicago Ave.","city":"Oak Park","state":"IL","zip":60700}
Bill King   {"street":"300 Obscure Dr.","city":"Obscuria","state":"IL","zip":60100}
```

Next, let's see how to reference elements of collections.

First, ARRAY indexing is 0-based, as in Java. Here is a query that selects the first element of the subordinates array:

```
hive> SELECT name, subordinates[0] FROM employees;
John Doe    Mary Smith
Mary Smith  Bill King
Todd Jones  NULL
Bill King   NULL
```

Note that referencing a nonexistent element returns NULL. Also, the extracted STRING values are no longer quoted!

To reference a MAP element, you also use ARRAY[...] syntax, but with key values instead of integer indices:

```
hive> SELECT name, deductions["State Taxes"] FROM employees;
John Doe    0.05
```

```
Mary Smith   0.05
Todd Jones   0.03
Bill King    0.03
```

Finally, to reference an element in a STRUCT, you use "dot" notation, similar to the table_alias.column mentioned above:

```
hive> SELECT name, address.city FROM employees;
John Doe    Chicago
Mary Smith  Chicago
Todd Jones  Oak Park
Bill King   Obscuria
```

These same referencing techniques are also used in WHERE clauses, which we discuss in "WHERE Clauses" on page 92.

Specify Columns with Regular Expressions

We can even use *regular expressions* to select the columns we want. The following query selects the symbol column and all columns from stocks whose names start with the prefix price:[1]

```
hive> SELECT symbol, `price.*` FROM stocks;
AAPL    195.69  197.88  194.0   194.12  194.12
AAPL    192.63  196.0   190.85  195.46  195.46
AAPL    196.73  198.37  191.57  192.05  192.05
AAPL    195.17  200.2   194.42  199.23  199.23
AAPL    195.91  196.32  193.38  195.86  195.86
...
```

We'll talk more about Hive's use of regular expressions in the section "LIKE and RLIKE" on page 96.

Computing with Column Values

Not only can you select columns in a table, but you can manipulate column values using function calls and arithmetic expressions.

For example, let's select the employees' names converted to uppercase, their salaries, federal taxes percentage, and the value that results if we subtract the federal taxes portion from their salaries and round to the nearest integer. We could call a built-in function map_values to extract all the values from the deductions map and then add them up with the built-in sum function.

The following query is long enough that we'll split it over two lines. Note the secondary prompt that Hive uses, an indented greater-than sign (>):

```
hive> SELECT upper(name), salary, deductions["Federal Taxes"],
    > round(salary * (1 - deductions["Federal Taxes"])) FROM employees;
```

1. At the time of this writing, the Hive Wiki shows an incorrect syntax for specifying columns using regular expressions.

```
JOHN DOE     100000.0  0.2   80000
MARY SMITH    80000.0  0.2   64000
TODD JONES    70000.0  0.15  59500
BILL KING     60000.0  0.15  51000
```

Let's discuss arithmetic operators and then discuss the use of functions in expressions.

Arithmetic Operators

All the typical arithmetic operators are supported. Table 6-1 describes the specific details.

Table 6-1. Arithmetic operators

Operator	Types	Description
A + B	Numbers	Add A and B.
A - B	Numbers	Subtract B from A.
A * B	Numbers	Multiply A and B.
A / B	Numbers	Divide A with B. If the operands are integer types, the quotient of the division is returned.
A % B	Numbers	The remainder of dividing A with B.
A & B	Numbers	Bitwise AND of A and B.
A | B	Numbers	Bitwise OR of A and B.
A ^ B	Numbers	Bitwise XOR of A and B.
~A	Numbers	Bitwise NOT of A.

Arithmetic operators take any numeric type. No type coercion is performed if the two operands are of the same numeric type. Otherwise, if the types differ, then the value of the *smaller* of the two types is promoted to *wider* type of the other value. (*Wider* in the sense that a type with more bytes can hold a wider range of values.) For example, for INT and BIGINT operands, the INT is promoted to BIGINT. For INT and FLOAT operands, the INT is promoted to FLOAT. Note that our query contained (1 - deductions[…]). Since the deductions are FLOATS, the 1 was promoted to FLOAT.

You have to be careful about data overflow or underflow when doing arithmetic. Hive follows the rules for the underlying Java types, where no attempt is made to automatically convert a result to a wider type if one exists, when overflow or underflow will occur. Multiplication and division are most likely to trigger this problem.

It pays to be aware of the ranges of your numeric data values, whether or not those values approach the upper or lower range limits of the types you are using in the corresponding schema, and what kinds of calculations people might do with the data.

If you are concerned about overflow or underflow, consider using wider types in the schema. The drawback is the extra memory each data value will occupy.

You can also convert values to wider types in specific expressions, called *casting*. See Table 6-2 below and "Casting" on page 109 for details.

Finally, it is sometimes useful to *scale* data values, such as dividing by powers of 10, using log values, and so on. Scaling can also improve the accuracy and numerical stability of algorithms used in certain *machine learning* calculations, for example.

Using Functions

Our tax-deduction example also uses a built-in mathematical function, round(), for finding the nearest integer for a DOUBLE value.

Mathematical functions

Table 6-2 describes the built-in mathematical functions, as of Hive v0.8.0, for working with single columns of data.

Table 6-2. Mathematical functions

Return type	Signature	Description
BIGINT	round(d)	Return the BIGINT for the rounded value of DOUBLE d.
DOUBLE	round(d, N)	Return the DOUBLE for the value of d, a DOUBLE, rounded to N decimal places.
BIGINT	floor(d)	Return the largest BIGINT that is <= d, a DOUBLE.
BIGINT	ceil(d), ceiling(DOUBLE d)	Return the smallest BIGINT that is >= d.
DOUBLE	rand(), rand(seed)	Return a pseudorandom DOUBLE that changes for each row. Passing in an integer seed makes the return value deterministic.
DOUBLE	exp(d)	Return e to the d, a DOUBLE.
DOUBLE	ln(d)	Return the natural logarithm of d, a DOUBLE.
DOUBLE	log10(d)	Return the base-10 logarithm of d, a DOUBLE.
DOUBLE	log2(d)	Return the base-2 logarithm of d, a DOUBLE.
DOUBLE	log(base, d)	Return the base-base logarithm of d, where base and d are DOUBLEs.
DOUBLE	pow(d, p), power(d, p)	Return d raised to the power p, where d and p are DOUBLEs.
DOUBLE	sqrt(d)	Return the square root of d, a DOUBLE.
STRING	bin(i)	Return the STRING representing the binary value of i, a BIGINT.
STRING	hex(i)	Return the STRING representing the hexadecimal value of i, a BIGINT.
STRING	hex(str)	Return the STRING representing the hexadecimal value of s, where each two characters in the STRING s is converted to its hexadecimal representation.

Return type	Signature	Description
STRING	unhex(i)	The inverse of hex(str).
STRING	conv(i, from_base, to_base)	Return the STRING in base to_base, an INT, representing the value of i, a BIGINT, in base from_base, an INT.
STRING	conv(str, from_base, to_base)	Return the STRING in base to_base, an INT, representing the value of str, a STRING, in base from_base, an INT.
DOUBLE	abs(d)	Return the DOUBLE that is the absolute value of d, a DOUBLE.
INT	pmod(i1, i2)	Return the positive module INT for two INTs, i1 mod i2.
DOUBLE	pmod(d1, d2)	Return the positive module DOUBLE for two DOUBLEs, d1 mod d2.
DOUBLE	sin(d)	Return the DOUBLE that is the *sin* of d, a DOUBLE, in *radians*.
DOUBLE	asin(d)	Return the DOUBLE that is the *arcsin* of d, a DOUBLE, in *radians*.
DOUBLE	cos(d)	Return the DOUBLE that is the *cosine* of d, a DOUBLE, in *radians*.
DOUBLE	acos(d)	Return the DOUBLE that is the *arccosine* of d, a DOUBLE, in *radians*.
DOUBLE	tan(d)	Return the DOUBLE that is the *tangent* of d, a DOUBLE, in *radians*.
DOUBLE	atan(d)	Return the DOUBLE that is the *arctangent* of d, a DOUBLE, in *radians*.
DOUBLE	degrees(d)	Return the DOUBLE that is the value of d, a DOUBLE, converted from radians to degrees.
DOUBLE	radians(d)	Return the DOUBLE that is the value of d, a DOUBLE, converted from degrees to radians.
INT	positive(i)	Return the INT value of i (i.e., it's effectively the expression \ +i).
DOUBLE	positive(d)	Return the DOUBLE value of d (i.e., it's effectively the expression \+d).
INT	negative(i)	Return the negative of the INT value of i (i.e., it's effectively the expression -i).
DOUBLE	negative(d)	Return the negative of the DOUBLE value of d; effectively, the expression -d.
FLOAT	sign(d)	Return the FLOAT value 1.0 if d, a DOUBLE, is positive; return the FLOAT value -1.0 if d is negative; otherwise return 0.0.
DOUBLE	e()	Return the DOUBLE that is the value of the constant e, 2.718281828459045.
DOUBLE	pi()	Return the DOUBLE that is the value of the constant pi, 3.141592653589793.

Note the functions floor, round, and ceil ("ceiling") for converting DOUBLE to BIGINT, which is floating-point numbers to integer numbers. These functions are the preferred technique, rather than using the *cast* operator we mentioned above.

Also, there are functions for converting integers to strings in different bases (e.g., hexadecimal).

Aggregate functions

A special kind of function is the *aggregate* function that returns a single value resulting from some computation over many rows. More precisely, this is the *User Defined Aggregate Function*, as we'll see in "Aggregate Functions" on page 164. Perhaps the two best known examples are count, which counts the number of rows (or values for a specific column), and avg, which returns the average value of the specified column values.

Here is a query that counts the number of our example employees and averages their salaries:

```
hive> SELECT count(*), avg(salary) FROM employees;
4  77500.0
```

We'll see other examples when we discuss GROUP BY in the section "GROUP BY Clauses" on page 97.

Table 6-3 lists Hive's built-in aggregate functions.

Table 6-3. Aggregate functions

Return type	Signature	Description
BIGINT	count(*)	Return the total number of retrieved rows, including rows containing NULL values.
BIGINT	count(expr)	Return the number of rows for which the supplied expression is not NULL.
BIGINT	count(DISTINCT expr[, expr_.])	Return the number of rows for which the supplied expression(s) are unique and not NULL.
DOUBLE	sum(col)	Return the sum of the values.
DOUBLE	sum(DISTINCT col)	Return the sum of the distinct values.
DOUBLE	avg(col)	Return the average of the values.
DOUBLE	avg(DISTINCT col)	Return the average of the distinct values.
DOUBLE	min(col)	Return the minimum value of the values.
DOUBLE	max(col)	Return the maximum value of the values.
DOUBLE	variance(col), var_pop(col)	Return the variance of a set of numbers in a collection: col.
DOUBLE	var_samp(col)	Return the sample variance of a set of numbers.
DOUBLE	stddev_pop(col)	Return the standard deviation of a set of numbers.
DOUBLE	stddev_samp(col)	Return the sample standard deviation of a set of numbers.
DOUBLE	covar_pop(col1, col2)	Return the covariance of a set of numbers.
DOUBLE	covar_samp(col1, col2)	Return the sample covariance of a set of numbers.

Return type	Signature	Description
DOUBLE	corr(col1, col2)	Return the correlation of two sets of numbers.
DOUBLE	percentile(int_expr, p)	Return the percentile of int_expr at p (range: [0,1]), where p is a DOUBLE.
ARRAY<DOUBLE>	percentile(int_expr, [p1, ...])	Return the percentiles of int_expr at p (range: [0,1]), where p is a DOUBLE array.
DOUBLE	percentile_approx(int_expr, p , NB)	Return the approximate percentiles of int_expr at p (range: [0,1]), where p is a DOUBLE and NB is the number of histogram bins for estimating (default: 10,000 if not specified).
DOUBLE	percentile_approx(int_expr, [p1, ...] , NB)	Return the approximate percentiles of int_expr at p (range: [0,1]), where p is a DOUBLE array and NB is the number of histogram bins for estimating (default: 10,000 if not specified).
ARRAY<STRUCT {'x','y'}>	histogram_numeric(col, NB)	Return an array of NB histogram bins, where the x value is the center and the y value is the height of the bin.
ARRAY	collect_set(col)	Return a set with the duplicate elements from collection col removed.

You can usually improve the performance of aggregation by setting the following property to true, hive.map.aggr, as shown here:

```
hive> SET hive.map.aggr=true;

hive> SELECT count(*), avg(salary) FROM employees;
```

This setting will attempt to do "top-level" aggregation in the map phase, as in this example. (An aggregation that isn't top-level would be aggregation after performing a GROUP BY.) However, this setting will require more memory.

As Table 6-3 shows, several functions accept DISTINCT ... expressions. For example, we could count the unique stock symbols this way:

```
hive> SELECT count(DISTINCT symbol) FROM stocks;
0
```

 Wait, *zero*?? There is a bug when trying to use count(DISTINCT col) when col is a *partition column*. The answer should be 743 for NASDAQ and NYSE, at least as of early 2010 in the infochimps.org data set we used.

Note that the Hive wiki currently claims that you can't use more than one function(DIS TINCT ...) expression in a query. For example, the following is supposed to be disallowed, but it actually works:

```
hive> SELECT count(DISTINCT ymd), count(DISTINCT volume) FROM stocks;
12110    26144
```

So, there are 12,110 trading days of data, over 40 years worth.

Table generating functions

The "inverse" of aggregate functions are so-called *table generating functions*, which take single columns and expand them to multiple columns or rows. We will discuss them extensively in "Table Generating Functions" on page 165, but to complete the contents of this section, we will discuss them briefly now and list the few built-in table generating functions available in Hive.

To explain by way of an example, the following query converts the subordinate array in each employees record into zero or more new records. If an employee record has an empty subordinates array, then no new records are generated. Otherwise, one new record per subordinate is generated:

```
hive> SELECT explode(subordinates) AS sub FROM employees;
Mary Smith
Todd Jones
Bill King
```

We used a *column alias*, sub, defined using the AS sub clause. When using table generating functions, column aliases are *required* by Hive. There are many other particular details that you must understand to use these functions correctly. We'll wait until "Table Generating Functions" on page 165 to discuss the details.

Table 6-4 lists the built-in table generating functions.

Table 6-4. Table generating functions

Return type	Signature	Description
N rows	explode(array)	Return 0 to many rows, one row for each element from the input array.
N rows	explode(map)	(v0.8.0 and later) Return 0 to many rows, one row for each map key-value pair, with a field for each map key and a field for the map value.
tuple	json_tuple(jsonStr, p1, p2, …, pn)	Like get_json_object, but it takes multiple names and returns a tuple. All the input parameters and output column types are STRING.
tuple	parse_url_tuple(url, part name1, partname2, …, partnameN) where N >= 1	Extract N parts from a URL. It takes a URL and the part names to extract, returning a tuple. All the input parameters and output column types are STRING. The valid partnames are case-sensitive and should only contain a minimum of white space: HOST, PATH, QUERY, REF, PROTOCOL, AUTHORITY, FILE, USERINFO, QUERY:<KEY_NAME>.
N rows	stack(n, col1, …, colM)	Convert M columns into N rows of size M/N each.

Here is an example that uses `parse_url_tuple` where we assume a `url_table` exists that contains a column of URLs called `url`:

```
SELECT parse_url_tuple(url, 'HOST', 'PATH', 'QUERY') as (host, path, query)
FROM url_table;
```

Compare `parse_url_tuple` with `parse_url` in Table 6-5 below.

Other built-in functions

Table 6-5 describes the rest of the built-in functions for working with strings, maps, arrays, JSON, and timestamps, with or without the recently introduced `TIMESTAMP` type (see "Primitive Data Types" on page 41).

Table 6-5. Other built-in functions

Return type	Signature	Description
BOOLEAN	test in(val1, val2, …)	Return true if `test` equals one of the values in the list.
INT	length(s)	Return the length of the string.
STRING	reverse(s)	Return a reverse copy of the string.
STRING	concat(s1, s2, …)	Return the string resulting from s1 joined with s2, etc. For example, `concat('ab', 'cd')` results in `'abcd'`. You can pass an arbitrary number of string arguments and the result will contain all of them joined together.
STRING	concat_ws(separator, s1, s2, …)	Like concat, but using the specified separator.
STRING	substr(s, start_index)	Return the substring of s starting from the `start_index` position, where 1 is the index of the first character, until the end of s. For example, `substr('abcd', 3)` results in `'cd'`.
STRING	substr(s, int start, int length)	Return the substring of s starting from the `start` position with the given length, e.g., `substr('abc defgh', 3, 2)` results in `'cd'`.
STRING	upper(s)	Return the string that results from converting all characters of s to upper case, e.g., `upper('hIvE')` results in `'HIVE'`.
STRING	ucase(s)	A synonym for `upper()`.
STRING	lower(s)	Return the string that results from converting all characters of s to lower case, e.g., `lower('hIvE')` results in `'hive'`.
STRING	lcase(s)	A synonym for `lower()`.
STRING	trim(s)	Return the string that results from removing whitespace from both ends of s, e.g., `trim(' hive ')` results in `'hive'`.

Return type	Signature	Description
STRING	ltrim(s)	Return the string resulting from trimming spaces from the beginning (lefthand side) of s, e.g., ltrim(' hive ') results in 'hive '.
STRING	rtrim(s)	Return the string resulting from trimming spaces from the end (righthand side) of s, e.g., rtrim(' hive ') results in ' hive'.
STRING	regexp_replace(s, regex, replacement)	Return the string resulting from replacing all substrings in s that match the Java *regular expression* re with replacement.[a] If replacement is blank, the matches are effectively deleted, e.g., regexp_replace('hive', '[ie]', 'z') returns 'hzvz'.
STRING	regexp_extract(subject, regex_pattern, index)	Returns the substring for the index's match using the regex_pattern.
STRING	parse_url(url, partname, key)	Extracts the specified part from a URL. It takes a URL and the partname to extract. The valid partnames are case-sensitive: HOST, PATH, QUERY, REF, PROTOCOL, AUTHORITY, FILE, USERINFO, QUERY:<key>. The optional key is used for the last QUERY:<key> request. Compare with parse_url_tuple described in Table 6-4.
int	size(map<K.V>)	Return the number of elements in the map.
int	size(array<T>)	Return the number of elements in the array.
value of *type*	cast(<expr> as <type>)	Convert ("cast") the result of the expression expr to *type*, e.g., cast('1' as BIGINT) will convert the string '1' to its integral representation. A NULL is returned if the conversion does not succeed.
STRING	from_unixtime(int unixtime)	Convert the number of seconds from the Unix epoch (1970-01-01 00:00:00 UTC) to a string representing the timestamp of that moment in the current system time zone in the format of '1970-01-01 00:00:00'.
STRING	to_date(timestamp)	Return the date part of a timestamp string, e.g., to_date("1970-01-01 00:00:00") returns '1970-01-01'.
INT	year(timestamp)	Return the year part as an INT of a timestamp string, e.g., year("1970-11-01 00:00:00") returns 1970.
INT	month(timestamp)	Return the month part as an INT of a timestamp string, e.g., month("1970-11-01 00:00:00") returns 11.
INT	day(timestamp)	Return the day part as an INT of a timestamp string, e.g., day("1970-11-01 00:00:00") returns 1.
STRING	get_json_object(json_string, path)	Extract the JSON object from a JSON string based on the given JSON path, and return the JSON string of the

Return type	Signature	Description
		extracted object. NULL is returned if the input JSON string is invalid.
STRING	space(n)	Returns n spaces.
STRING	repeat(s, n)	Repeats s n times.
STRING	ascii(s)	Returns the integer value for the first ASCII character in the string s.
STRING	lpad(s, len, pad)	Returns s exactly len length, prepending instances of the string pad on its left, if necessary, to reach len characters. If s is longer than len, it is truncated.
STRING	rpad(s, len, pad)	Returns s exactly len length, appending instances of the string pad on its right, if necessary, to reach len characters. If s is longer than len, it is truncated.
ARRAY<STRING>	split(s, pattern)	Returns an array of substrings of s, split on occurrences of pattern.
INT	find_in_set(s, commaSeparated String)	Returns the index of the comma-separated string where s is found, or NULL if it is not found.
INT	locate(substr, str, pos])	Returns the index of str after pos where substr is found.
INT	instr(str, substr)	Returns the index of str where substr is found.
MAP<STRING,STRING>	str_to_map(s, delim1, delim2)	Creates a map by parsing s, using delim1 as the separator between key-value pairs and delim2 as the key-value separator.
ARRAY<ARRAY<STRING>>	sentences(s, lang, locale)	Splits s into arrays of sentences, where each sentence is an array of words. The lang and country arguments are optional; if omitted, the default locale is used.
ARRAY<STRUCT<STRING,DOUBLE>>	ngrams(array<array<string>>, N, K, pf)	Estimates the top-K n-grams in the text. pf is the precision factor.
ARRAY<STRUCT<STRING,DOUBLE>>	con text_ngrams(array<array<string>>,array<string>,int K, int pf)	Like ngrams, but looks for n-grams that begin with the second array of words in each outer array.
BOOLEAN	in_file(s, filename)	Returns true if s appears in the file named filename.

[a] See http://docs.oracle.com/javase/tutorial/essential/regex/ for more on Java regular expression syntax.

Note that the time-related functions (near the end of the table) take integer or string arguments. As of Hive v0.8.0, these functions also take TIMESTAMP arguments, but they will continue to take integer or string arguments for backwards compatibility.

LIMIT Clause

The results of a typical query can return a large number of rows. The LIMIT clause puts an upper limit on the number of rows returned:

```
hive> SELECT upper(name), salary, deductions["Federal Taxes"],
    > round(salary * (1 - deductions["Federal Taxes"])) FROM employees
    > LIMIT 2;
JOHN DOE    100000.0  0.2    80000
MARY SMITH  80000.0   0.2    64000
```

Column Aliases

You can think of the previous example query as returning a new relation with new columns, some of which are anonymous results of manipulating columns in employees. It's sometimes useful to give those anonymous columns a name, called a *column alias*. Here is the previous query with column aliases for the third and fourth columns returned by the query, fed_taxes and salary_minus_fed_taxes, respectively:

```
hive> SELECT upper(name), salary, deductions["Federal Taxes"] as fed_taxes,
    > round(salary * (1 - deductions["Federal Taxes"])) as salary_minus_fed_taxes
    > FROM employees LIMIT 2;
JOHN DOE    100000.0  0.2    80000
MARY SMITH  80000.0   0.2    64000
```

Nested SELECT Statements

The column alias feature is especially useful in *nested select statements*. Let's use the previous example as a nested query:

```
hive> FROM (
    >   SELECT upper(name), salary, deductions["Federal Taxes"] as fed_taxes,
    >   round(salary * (1 - deductions["Federal Taxes"])) as salary_minus_fed_taxes
    >   FROM employees
    > ) e
    > SELECT e.name, e.salary_minus_fed_taxes
    > WHERE e.salary_minus_fed_taxes > 70000;
JOHN DOE    100000.0  0.2    80000
```

The previous result set is aliased as e, from which we perform a second query to select the name and the salary_minus_fed_taxes, where the latter is greater than 70,000. (We'll cover WHERE clauses in "WHERE Clauses" on page 92 below.)

CASE ... WHEN ... THEN Statements

The CASE … WHEN … THEN clauses are like if statements for individual columns in query results. For example:

```
hive> SELECT name, salary,
    >   CASE
    >     WHEN salary < 50000.0 THEN 'low'
```

```
>        WHEN salary >= 50000.0 AND salary <   70000.0 THEN 'middle'
>        WHEN salary >= 70000.0 AND salary < 100000.0 THEN 'high'
>        ELSE 'very high'
>     END AS bracket FROM employees;
John Doe          100000.0    very high
Mary Smith         80000.0    high
Todd Jones         70000.0    high
Bill King          60000.0    middle
Boss Man          200000.0    very high
Fred Finance      150000.0    very high
Stacy Accountant   60000.0    middle
...
```

When Hive Can Avoid MapReduce

If you have been running the queries in this book so far, you have probably noticed that a MapReduce job is started in most cases. Hive implements some kinds of queries without using MapReduce, in so-called *local mode*, for example:

```
SELECT * FROM employees;
```

In this case, Hive can simply read the records from employees and dump the formatted output to the console.

This even works for WHERE clauses that only filter on partition keys, with or without LIMIT clauses:

```
SELECT * FROM employees
WHERE country = 'US' AND state = 'CA'
LIMIT 100;
```

Furthermore, Hive will attempt to run other operations in local mode if the hive.exec.mode.local.auto property is set to true:

```
set hive.exec.mode.local.auto=true;
```

Otherwise, Hive uses MapReduce to run all other queries.

 Trust us, you want to add set hive.exec.mode.local.auto=true; to your *$HOME/.hiverc* file.

WHERE Clauses

While SELECT clauses select columns, WHERE clauses are filters; they select which records to return. Like SELECT clauses, we have already used many simple examples of WHERE clauses before defining the clause, on the assumption you have seen them before. Now we'll explore them in a bit more detail.

WHERE clauses use *predicate expressions*, applying *predicate operators*, which we'll describe in a moment, to columns. Several predicate expressions can be joined with AND and OR clauses. When the predicate expressions evaluate to true, the corresponding rows are retained in the output.

We just used the following example that restricts the results to employees in the state of California:

```
SELECT * FROM employees
WHERE country = 'US' AND state = 'CA';
```

The predicates can reference the same variety of computations over column values that can be used in SELECT clauses. Here we adapt our previously used query involving *Federal Taxes*, filtering for those rows where the salary minus the federal taxes is greater than 70,000:

```
hive> SELECT name, salary, deductions["Federal Taxes"],
    >    salary * (1 - deductions["Federal Taxes"])
    > FROM employees
    > WHERE round(salary * (1 - deductions["Federal Taxes"])) > 70000;
John Doe     100000.0  0.2   80000.0
```

This query is a bit ugly, because the complex expression on the second line is duplicated in the WHERE clause. The following variation eliminates the duplication, using a column alias, but unfortunately it's not valid:

```
hive>  SELECT name, salary, deductions["Federal Taxes"],
    >    salary * (1 - deductions["Federal Taxes"]) as salary_minus_fed_taxes
    >  FROM employees
    >  WHERE round(salary_minus_fed_taxes) > 70000;
FAILED: Error in semantic analysis: Line 4:13 Invalid table alias or
column reference 'salary_minus_fed_taxes': (possible column names are:
name, salary, subordinates, deductions, address)
```

As the error message says, we can't reference column aliases in the WHERE clause. However, we can use a nested SELECT statement:

```
hive> SELECT e.* FROM
    > (SELECT name, salary, deductions["Federal Taxes"] as ded,
    >    salary * (1 - deductions["Federal Taxes"]) as salary_minus_fed_taxes
    >  FROM employees) e
    > WHERE round(e.salary_minus_fed_taxes) > 70000;
John Doe       100000.0     0.2     80000.0
Boss Man       200000.0     0.3     140000.0
Fred Finance   150000.0     0.3     105000.0
```

Predicate Operators

Table 6-6 describes the predicate operators, which are also used in JOIN … ON and HAVING clauses.

Table 6-6. Predicate operators

Operator	Types	Description
A = B	Primitive types	True if A equals B. False otherwise.
A <> B, A != B	Primitive types	NULL if A or B is NULL; true if A is not equal to B; false otherwise.
A < B	Primitive types	NULL if A or B is NULL; true if A is less than B; false otherwise.
A <= B	Primitive types	NULL if A or B is NULL; true if A is less than or equal to B; false otherwise.
A > B	Primitive types	NULL if A or B is NULL; true if A is greater than B; false otherwise.
A >= B	Primitive types	NULL if A or B is NULL; true if A is greater than or equal to B; false otherwise.
A IS NULL	All types	True if A evaluates to NULL; false otherwise.
A IS NOT NULL	All types	False if A evaluates to NULL; true otherwise.
A LIKE B	String	True if A matches the SQL simplified *regular expression* specification given by B; false otherwise. B is interpreted as follows: ' x%' means A must begin with the prefix ' x', '%x' means A must end with the suffix ' x', and '%x%' means A must begin with, end with, or contain the substring ' x'. Similarly, the underscore '_' matches a single character. B must match the whole string A.
A RLIKE B, A REGEXP B	String	True if A matches the *regular expression* given by B; false otherwise. Matching is done by the JDK regular expression library and hence it follows the rules of that library. For example, the regular expression must match the entire string A, not just a subset. See below for more information about regular expressions.

We'll discuss LIKE and RLIKE in detail below ("LIKE and RLIKE" on page 96). First, let's point out an issue with comparing floating-point numbers that you should understand.

Gotchas with Floating-Point Comparisons

A common gotcha arises when you compare floating-point numbers of different types (i.e., FLOAT versus DOUBLE). Consider the following query of the employees table, which is designed to return the employee's name, salary, and federal taxes deduction, but only if that tax deduction exceeds 0.2 (20%) of his or her salary:

```
hive> SELECT name, salary, deductions['Federal Taxes']
    > FROM employees WHERE deductions['Federal Taxes'] > 0.2;
John Doe        100000.0        0.2
Mary Smith       80000.0        0.2
```

```
Boss Man        200000.0     0.3
Fred Finance    150000.0     0.3
```

Wait! Why are records with `deductions['Federal Taxes'] = 0.2` being returned?

Is it a Hive bug? There is a bug filed against Hive for this issue, but it actually reflects the behavior of the internal representation of floating-point numbers when they are compared and it *affects almost all software written in most languages on all modern digital computers* (see *https://issues.apache.org/jira/browse/HIVE-2586*).

When you write a floating-point literal value like 0.2, Hive uses a `DOUBLE` to hold the value. We defined the `deductions` map values to be `FLOAT`, which means that Hive will implicitly convert the tax deduction value to `DOUBLE` to do the comparison. This should work, right?

Actually, it doesn't work. Here's why. The number 0.2 can't be represented exactly in a `FLOAT` or `DOUBLE`. (See *http://docs.oracle.com/cd/E19957-01/806-3568/ncg_goldberg .html* for an in-depth discussion of floating-point number issues.) In this particular case, the closest exact value is just slightly greater than 0.2, with a few nonzero bits at the least significant end of the number.

To simplify things a bit, let's say that 0.2 is actually 0.2000001 for `FLOAT` and 0.200000000001 for `DOUBLE`, because an 8-byte `DOUBLE` has more significant digits (after the decimal point). When the `FLOAT` value from the table is converted to `DOUBLE` by Hive, it produces the `DOUBLE` value 0.200000100000, which is greater than 0.200000000001. That's why the query results appear to use >= not >!

This issue is not unique to Hive nor Java, in which Hive is implemented. Rather, it's a general problem for all systems that use the IEEE standard for encoding floating-point numbers!

However, there are two workarounds we can use in Hive.

First, if we read the data from a `TEXTFILE` (see Chapter 15), which is what we have been assuming so far, then Hive reads the string "0.2" from the data file and converts it to a real number. We could use `DOUBLE` instead of `FLOAT` in our schema. Then we would be comparing a `DOUBLE` for the `deductions['Federal Taxes']` with a double for the literal 0.2. However, this change will increase the memory footprint of our queries. Also, we can't simply change the schema like this if the data file is a binary file format like `SEQUENCEFILE` (discussed in Chapter 15).

The second workaround is to explicitly cast the 0.2 literal value to `FLOAT`. Java has a nice way of doing this: you append the letter f or F to the end of the number (e.g., 0.2f). Unfortunately, Hive doesn't support this syntax; we have to use the `cast` operator.

Here is a modified query that casts the 0.2 literal value to `FLOAT`. With this change, the expected results are returned by the query:

```
hive> SELECT name, salary, deductions['Federal Taxes'] FROM employees
    > WHERE deductions['Federal Taxes'] > cast(0.2 AS FLOAT);
```

```
Boss Man        200000.0      0.3
Fred Finance    150000.0      0.3
```

Note the syntax inside the **cast** operator: *number* `AS FLOAT`.

Actually, there is also a third solution: avoid floating-point numbers for anything involving money.

 Use extreme caution when comparing floating-point numbers. Avoid all implicit casts from smaller to wider types.

LIKE and RLIKE

Table 6-6 describes the `LIKE` and `RLIKE` predicate operators. You have probably seen `LIKE` before, a standard SQL operator. It lets us match on strings that begin with or end with a particular substring, or when the substring appears anywhere within the string.

For example, the following three queries select the employee names and addresses where the street ends with `Ave.`, the city begins with 0, and the street contains `Chicago`:

```
hive> SELECT name, address.street FROM employees WHERE address.street LIKE '%Ave.';
John Doe        1 Michigan Ave.
Todd Jones      200 Chicago Ave.

hive> SELECT name, address.city FROM employees WHERE address.city LIKE '0%';
Todd Jones      Oak Park
Bill King       Obscuria

hive> SELECT name, address.street FROM employees WHERE address.street LIKE '%Chi%';
Todd Jones      200 Chicago Ave.
```

A Hive extension is the `RLIKE` clause, which lets us use Java *regular expressions*, a more powerful minilanguage for specifying matches. The rich details of regular expression syntax and features are beyond the scope of this book. The entry for `RLIKE` in Table 6-6 provides links to resources with more details on regular expressions. Here, we demonstrate their use with an example, which finds all the employees whose street contains the word `Chicago` or `Ontario`:

```
hive> SELECT name, address.street
    > FROM employees WHERE address.street RLIKE '.*(Chicago|Ontario).*';
Mary Smith      100 Ontario St.
Todd Jones      200 Chicago Ave.
```

The string after the `RLIKE` keyword has the following interpretation. A period (.) matches any character and a star (*) means repeat the "thing to the left" (period, in the two cases shown) zero to many times. The expression (x|y) means match *either* x *or* y.

Hence, there might be no characters before "Chicago" or "Ontario" and there might be no characters after them. Of course, we could have written this particular example with two `LIKE` clauses:

```
SELECT name, address FROM employees
WHERE address.street LIKE '%Chicago%' OR address.street LIKE '%Ontario%';
```

General regular expression matches will let us express much richer matching criteria that would become very unwieldy with joined LIKE clauses such as these.

For more details about regular expressions as implemented by Hive using Java, see the documentation for the Java regular expression syntax at *http://docs.oracle.com/javase/6/docs/api/java/util/regex/Pattern.html* or see *Regular Expression Pocket Reference* by Tony Stubblebine (O'Reilly), *Regular Expressions Cookbook* (*http://shop.oreilly.com/product/0636920023630.do*) by Jan Goyvaerts and Steven Levithan (O'Reilly), or *Mastering Regular Expressions, 3rd Edition*, by Jeffrey E.F. Friedl (O'Reilly).

GROUP BY Clauses

The GROUP BY statement is often used in conjunction with aggregate functions to group the result set by one or more columns and then perform an aggregation over each group.

Let's return to the stocks table we defined in "External Tables" on page 56. The following query groups stock records for Apple by year, then averages the closing price for each year:

```
hive> SELECT year(ymd), avg(price_close) FROM stocks
    > WHERE exchange = 'NASDAQ' AND symbol = 'AAPL'
    > GROUP BY year(ymd);
1984    25.578625440597534
1985    20.193676221040867
1986    32.46102808021274
1987    53.88968399108163
1988    41.540079275138766
1989    41.65976212516664
1990    37.56268799823263
1991    52.49553383386182
1992    54.80338610251119
1993    41.02671956450572
1994    34.0813495847914
...
```

HAVING Clauses

The HAVING clause lets you constrain the groups produced by GROUP BY in a way that could be expressed with a subquery, using a syntax that's easier to express. Here's the previous query with an additional HAVING clause that limits the results to years where the average closing price was greater than $50.0:

```
hive> SELECT year(ymd), avg(price_close) FROM stocks
    > WHERE exchange = 'NASDAQ' AND symbol = 'AAPL'
    > GROUP BY year(ymd)
       > HAVING avg(price_close) > 50.0;
1987    53.88968399108163
1991    52.49553383386182
1992    54.80338610251119
1999    57.77071460844979
2000    71.74892876261757
2005    52.401745992993554
...
```

Without the HAVING clause, this query would require a nested SELECT statement:

```
hive> SELECT s2.year, s2.avg FROM
    > (SELECT year(ymd) AS year, avg(price_close) AS avg FROM stocks
    > WHERE exchange = 'NASDAQ' AND symbol = 'AAPL'
    > GROUP BY year(ymd)) s2
    > WHERE s2.avg > 50.0;
1987    53.88968399108163
...
```

JOIN Statements

Hive supports the classic SQL JOIN statement, but only *equi-joins* are supported.

Inner JOIN

In an inner JOIN, records are discarded unless join criteria finds matching records in every table being joined. For example, the following query compares Apple (symbol AAPL) and IBM (symbol IBM). The *stocks* table is joined against itself, a *self-join*, where the dates, ymd (year-month-day) values must be equal in both tables. We say that the ymd columns are the *join keys* in this query:

```
hive> SELECT a.ymd, a.price_close, b.price_close
    > FROM stocks a JOIN stocks b ON a.ymd = b.ymd
    > WHERE a.symbol = 'AAPL' AND b.symbol = 'IBM';
2010-01-04    214.01   132.45
2010-01-05    214.38   130.85
2010-01-06    210.97   130.0
2010-01-07    210.58   129.55
2010-01-08    211.98   130.85
2010-01-11    210.11   129.48
...
```

The ON clause specifies the conditions for joining records between the two tables. The WHERE clause limits the lefthand table to AAPL records and the righthand table to IBM records. You can also see that using table aliases for the two occurrences of stocks is essential in this query.

As you may know, IBM is an older company than Apple. It has been a publicly traded stock for much longer than Apple. However, since this is an inner JOIN, no IBM records will be returned older than September 7, 1984, which was the first day that Apple was publicly traded!

Standard SQL allows a non-equi-join on the join keys, such as the following example that shows Apple versus IBM, but with *all* older records for Apple paired up with each day of IBM data. It would be a lot of data (Example 6-1)!

Example 6-1. Query that will not work in Hive
```
SELECT a.ymd, a.price_close, b.price_close
FROM stocks a JOIN stocks b
ON a.ymd <= b.ymd
WHERE a.symbol = 'AAPL' AND b.symbol = 'IBM';
```

This is not valid in Hive, primarily because it is difficult to implement these kinds of joins in MapReduce. It turns out that *Pig* offers a *cross product* feature that makes it possible to implement this join, even though Pig's native join feature doesn't support it, either.

Also, Hive does not currently support using OR between predicates in ON clauses.

To see a nonself join, let's introduce the corresponding dividends data, also available from infochimps.org (*www.infochimps.org*), as described in "External Tables" on page 56:
```
CREATE EXTERNAL TABLE IF NOT EXISTS dividends (
  ymd           STRING,
  dividend      FLOAT
)
PARTITIONED BY (exchange STRING, symbol STRING)
ROW FORMAT DELIMITED FIELDS TERMINATED BY ',';
```

Here is an inner JOIN between stocks and dividends for Apple, where we use the ymd and symbol columns as join keys:
```
hive> SELECT s.ymd, s.symbol, s.price_close, d.dividend
    > FROM stocks s JOIN dividends d ON s.ymd = d.ymd AND s.symbol = d.symbol
    > WHERE s.symbol = 'AAPL';
1987-05-11    AAPL    77.0     0.015
1987-08-10    AAPL    48.25    0.015
1987-11-17    AAPL    35.0     0.02
...
1995-02-13    AAPL    43.75    0.03
1995-05-26    AAPL    42.69    0.03
1995-08-16    AAPL    44.5     0.03
1995-11-21    AAPL    38.63    0.03
```

Yes, Apple paid a dividend years ago and only recently announced it would start doing so again! Note that because we have an inner JOIN, we only see records approximately every three months, the typical schedule of dividend payments, which are announced when reporting quarterly results.

You can join more than two tables together. Let's compare Apple, IBM, and GE side by side:

```
hive> SELECT a.ymd, a.price_close, b.price_close , c.price_close
    > FROM stocks a JOIN stocks b ON a.ymd = b.ymd
    >                 JOIN stocks c ON a.ymd = c.ymd
    > WHERE a.symbol = 'AAPL' AND b.symbol = 'IBM' AND c.symbol = 'GE';
2010-01-04      214.01  132.45  15.45
2010-01-05      214.38  130.85  15.53
2010-01-06      210.97  130.0   15.45
2010-01-07      210.58  129.55  16.25
2010-01-08      211.98  130.85  16.6
2010-01-11      210.11  129.48  16.76
...
```

Most of the time, Hive will use a separate MapReduce job for each pair of things to join. In this example, it would use one job for tables a and b, then a second job to join the output of the first join with c.

Why not join b and c first? Hive goes from left to right.

However, this example actually benefits from an optimization we'll discuss next.

Join Optimizations

In the previous example, every ON clause uses a.ymd as one of the join keys. In this case, Hive can apply an optimization where it joins all three tables in a *single* MapReduce job. The optimization would also be used if b.ymd were used in both ON clauses.

When joining three or more tables, if every ON clause uses the same join key, a single MapReduce job will be used.

Hive also assumes that the *last* table in the query is the *largest*. It attempts to buffer the other tables and then stream the last table through, while performing joins on individual records. Therefore, you should structure your join queries so the largest table is last.

Recall our previous join between stocks and dividends. We actually made the mistake of using the smaller dividends table last:

```
SELECT s.ymd, s.symbol, s.price_close, d.dividend
FROM stocks s JOIN dividends d ON s.ymd = d.ymd AND s.symbol = d.symbol
WHERE s.symbol = 'AAPL';
```

We should switch the positions of stocks and dividends:

```
SELECT s.ymd, s.symbol, s.price_close, d.dividend
FROM dividends d JOIN stocks s ON s.ymd = d.ymd AND s.symbol = d.symbol
WHERE s.symbol = 'AAPL';
```

It turns out that these data sets are too small to see a noticeable performance difference, but for larger data sets, you'll want to exploit this optimization.

Fortunately, you don't have to put the largest table last in the query. Hive also provides a "hint" mechanism to tell the query optimizer which table should be streamed:

```
SELECT /*+ STREAMTABLE(s) */ s.ymd, s.symbol, s.price_close, d.dividend
FROM stocks s JOIN dividends d ON s.ymd = d.ymd AND s.symbol = d.symbol
WHERE s.symbol = 'AAPL';
```

Now Hive will attempt to stream the stocks table, even though it's not the last table in the query.

There is another important optimization called *map-side joins* that we'll return to in "Map-side Joins" on page 105.

LEFT OUTER JOIN

The left-outer join is indicated by adding the LEFT OUTER keywords:

```
hive> SELECT s.ymd, s.symbol, s.price_close, d.dividend
    > FROM stocks s LEFT OUTER JOIN dividends d ON s.ymd = d.ymd AND s.symbol = d.symbol
    > WHERE s.symbol = 'AAPL';
...
1987-05-01    AAPL    80.0     NULL
1987-05-04    AAPL    79.75    NULL
1987-05-05    AAPL    80.25    NULL
1987-05-06    AAPL    80.0     NULL
1987-05-07    AAPL    80.25    NULL
1987-05-08    AAPL    79.0     NULL
1987-05-11    AAPL    77.0     0.015
1987-05-12    AAPL    75.5     NULL
1987-05-13    AAPL    78.5     NULL
1987-05-14    AAPL    79.25    NULL
1987-05-15    AAPL    78.25    NULL
1987-05-18    AAPL    75.75    NULL
1987-05-19    AAPL    73.25    NULL
1987-05-20    AAPL    74.5     NULL
...
```

In this join, *all* the records from the lefthand table that match the WHERE clause are returned. If the righthand table doesn't have a record that matches the ON criteria, NULL is used for each column selected from the righthand table.

Hence, in this result set, we see that the every Apple stock record is returned and the d.dividend value is usually NULL, except on days when a dividend was paid (May 11th, 1987, in this output).

OUTER JOIN Gotcha

Before we discuss the other outer joins, let's discuss a gotcha you should understand.

Recall what we said previously about speeding up queries by adding partition filters in the WHERE clause. To speed up our previous query, we might choose to add predicates that select on the exchange in both tables:

```
hive> SELECT s.ymd, s.symbol, s.price_close, d.dividend
    > FROM stocks s LEFT OUTER JOIN dividends d ON s.ymd = d.ymd AND s.symbol = d.symbol
    > WHERE s.symbol = 'AAPL'
    > AND s.exchange = 'NASDAQ' AND d.exchange = 'NASDAQ';
1987-05-11    AAPL    77.0    0.015
1987-08-10    AAPL    48.25   0.015
1987-11-17    AAPL    35.0    0.02
1988-02-12    AAPL    41.0    0.02
1988-05-16    AAPL    41.25   0.02
...
```

However, the output has changed, even though we thought we were just adding an optimization! We're back to having approximately four stock records per year and we have non-NULL entries for all the dividend values. In other words, we are back to the original inner join!

This is actually common behavior for all outer joins in most SQL implementations. It occurs because the JOIN clause is evaluated first, then the results are passed through the WHERE clause. By the time the WHERE clause is reached, d.exchange is NULL most of the time, so the "optimization" actually filters out all records except those on the day of dividend payments.

One solution is straightforward; remove the clauses in the WHERE clause that reference the dividends table:

```
hive> SELECT s.ymd, s.symbol, s.price_close, d.dividend
    > FROM stocks s LEFT OUTER JOIN dividends d ON s.ymd = d.ymd AND s.symbol = d.symbol
    > WHERE s.symbol = 'AAPL' AND s.exchange = 'NASDAQ';
...
1987-05-07    AAPL    80.25   NULL
1987-05-08    AAPL    79.0    NULL
1987-05-11    AAPL    77.0    0.015
1987-05-12    AAPL    75.5    NULL
1987-05-13    AAPL    78.5    NULL
...
```

This isn't very satisfactory. You might wonder if you can move the predicates from the WHERE clause into the ON clause, at least the partition filters. *This does not work for outer joins*, despite documentation on the Hive Wiki that claims it should work (*https://cwiki .apache.org/confluence/display/Hive/LanguageManual+Joins*).

```
hive> SELECT s.ymd, s.symbol, s.price_close, d.dividend
    > FROM stocks s LEFT OUTER JOIN dividends d
    > ON s.ymd = d.ymd AND s.symbol = d.symbol
    > AND s.symbol = 'AAPL' AND s.exchange = 'NASDAQ' AND d.exchange = 'NASDAQ';
...
1962-01-02    GE     74.75    NULL
1962-01-02    IBM    572.0    NULL
1962-01-03    GE     74.0     NULL
1962-01-03    IBM    577.0    NULL
```

```
1962-01-04    GE     73.12    NULL
1962-01-04    IBM    571.25   NULL
1962-01-05    GE     71.25    NULL
1962-01-05    IBM    560.0    NULL
...
```

The partition filters are *ignored* for OUTER JOINTS. However, using such filter predicates in ON clauses for inner joins *does* work!

Fortunately, there is solution that works for all joins; use nested SELECT statements:

```
hive> SELECT s.ymd, s.symbol, s.price_close, d.dividend FROM
    > (SELECT * FROM stocks WHERE symbol = 'AAPL' AND exchange = 'NASDAQ') s
    > LEFT OUTER JOIN
    > (SELECT * FROM dividends WHERE symbol = 'AAPL' AND exchange = 'NASDAQ') d
    > ON s.ymd = d.ymd;
...
1988-02-10    AAPL    41.0     NULL
1988-02-11    AAPL    40.63    NULL
1988-02-12    AAPL    41.0     0.02
1988-02-16    AAPL    41.25    NULL
1988-02-17    AAPL    41.88    NULL
...
```

The nested SELECT statement performs the required "push down" to apply the partition filters before data is joined.

 WHERE clauses are evaluated after joins are performed, so WHERE clauses should use predicates that only filter on column values that won't be NULL. Also, contrary to Hive documentation, partition filters don't work in ON clauses for OUTER JOINS, although they *do* work for INNER JOINS!

RIGHT OUTER JOIN

Right-outer joins return all records in the righthand table that match the WHERE clause. NULL is used for fields of missing records in the lefthand table.

Here we switch the places of stocks and dividends and perform a righthand join, but leave the SELECT statement unchanged:

```
hive> SELECT s.ymd, s.symbol, s.price_close, d.dividend
    > FROM dividends d RIGHT OUTER JOIN stocks s ON d.ymd = s.ymd AND d.symbol = s.symbol
    > WHERE s.symbol = 'AAPL';
...
1987-05-07    AAPL    80.25    NULL
1987-05-08    AAPL    79.0     NULL
1987-05-11    AAPL    77.0     0.015
1987-05-12    AAPL    75.5     NULL
1987-05-13    AAPL    78.5     NULL
...
```

FULL OUTER JOIN

Finally, a full-outer join returns all records from all tables that match the WHERE clause. NULL is used for fields in missing records in either table.

If we convert the previous query to a full-outer join, we'll actually get the same results, since there is never a case where a dividend record exists without a matching stock record:

```
hive> SELECT s.ymd, s.symbol, s.price_close, d.dividend
    > FROM dividends d FULL OUTER JOIN stocks s ON d.ymd = s.ymd AND d.symbol = s.symbol
    > WHERE s.symbol = 'AAPL';
...
1987-05-07    AAPL    80.25    NULL
1987-05-08    AAPL    79.0     NULL
1987-05-11    AAPL    77.0     0.015
1987-05-12    AAPL    75.5     NULL
1987-05-13    AAPL    78.5     NULL
...
```

LEFT SEMI-JOIN

A *left semi-join* returns records from the lefthand table if records are found in the right-hand table that satisfy the ON predicates. It's a special, optimized case of the more general inner join. Most SQL dialects support an IN ... EXISTS construct to do the same thing. For instance, the following query in Example 6-2 attempts to return stock records only on the days of dividend payments, but it doesn't work in Hive.

Example 6-2. Query that will not work in Hive

```
SELECT s.ymd, s.symbol, s.price_close FROM stocks s
WHERE s.ymd, s.symbol IN
(SELECT d.ymd, d.symbol FROM dividends d);
```

Instead, you use the following LEFT SEMI JOIN syntax:

```
hive> SELECT s.ymd, s.symbol, s.price_close
    > FROM stocks s LEFT SEMI JOIN dividends d ON s.ymd = d.ymd AND s.symbol = d.symbol;
...
1962-11-05    IBM    361.5
1962-08-07    IBM    373.25
1962-05-08    IBM    459.5
1962-02-06    IBM    551.5
```

Note that the SELECT and WHERE clauses can't reference columns from the righthand table.

Right semi-joins are not supported in Hive.

The reason semi-joins are more efficient than the more general inner join is as follows. For a given record in the lefthand table, Hive can stop looking for matching records in the righthand table as soon as *any* match is found. At that point, the selected columns from the lefthand table record can be projected.

Cartesian Product JOINs

A Cartesian product is a join where all the tuples in the left side of the join are paired with all the tuples of the right table. If the left table has 5 rows and the right table has 6 rows, 30 rows of output will be produced:

```
SELECTS * FROM stocks JOIN dividends;
```

Using the table of stocks and dividends, it is hard to find a reason for a join of this type, as the dividend of one stock is not usually paired with another. Additionally, Cartesian products create a lot of data. Unlike other join types, Cartesian products are not executed in parallel, and they are not optimized in any way using MapReduce.

It is *critical* to point out that using the wrong join syntax will cause a long, slow-running Cartesian product query. For example, the following query will be optimized to an inner join in many databases, but *not* in Hive:

```
hive > SELECT * FROM stocks JOIN dividends
     > WHERE stock.symbol = dividends.symbol and stock.symbol='AAPL';
```

In Hive, this query computes the *full* Cartesian product before applying the WHERE clause. It could take a very long time to finish. When the property hive.mapred.mode is set to strict, Hive prevents users from inadvertently issuing a Cartesian product query. We'll discuss the features of strict mode more extensively in Chapter 10.

 Cartesian product queries can be useful. For example, suppose there is a table of user preferences, a table of news articles, and an algorithm that predicts which articles a user would like to read. A Cartesian product is required to generate the set of all users and all pages.

Map-side Joins

If all but one table is small, the largest table can be streamed through the mappers while the small tables are cached in memory. Hive can do all the joining map-side, since it can look up every possible match against the small tables in memory, thereby eliminating the reduce step required in the more common join scenarios. Even on smaller data sets, this optimization is noticeably faster than the normal join. Not only does it eliminate reduce steps, it sometimes reduces the number of map steps, too.

The joins between stocks and dividends can exploit this optimization, as the dividends data set is small enough to be cached.

Before Hive v0.7, it was necessary to add a hint to the query to enable this optimization. Returning to our inner join example:

```
SELECT /*+ MAPJOIN(d) */ s.ymd, s.symbol, s.price_close, d.dividend
FROM stocks s JOIN dividends d ON s.ymd = d.ymd AND s.symbol = d.symbol
WHERE s.symbol = 'AAPL';
```

Running this query versus the original on a fast MacBook Pro laptop yielded times of approximately 23 seconds versus 33 seconds for the original unoptimized query, which is roughly 30% faster using our sample stock data.

The hint still works, but it's now deprecated as of Hive v0.7. However, you still have to set a property, `hive.auto.convert.join`, to true before Hive will attempt the optimization. It's false by default:

```
hive> set hive.auto.convert.join=true;

hive> SELECT s.ymd, s.symbol, s.price_close, d.dividend
    > FROM stocks s JOIN dividends d ON s.ymd = d.ymd AND s.symbol = d.symbol
    > WHERE s.symbol = 'AAPL';
```

Note that you can also configure the threshold size for table files considered small enough to use this optimization. Here is the default definition of the property (in bytes):

```
hive.mapjoin.smalltable.filesize=25000000
```

If you always want Hive to attempt this optimization, set one or both of these properties in your *$HOME/.hiverc* file.

Hive does not support the optimization for right- and full-outer joins.

This optimization can also be used for larger tables under certain conditions when the data for every table is *bucketed*, as discussed in "Bucketing Table Data Storage" on page 125. Briefly, the data must be bucketed on the keys used in the ON clause and the number of buckets for one table must be a multiple of the number of buckets for the other table. When these conditions are met, Hive can join individual buckets between tables in the map phase, because it does not need to fetch the entire contents of one table to match against each bucket in the other table.

However, this optimization is not turned on by default. It must be enabled by setting the property `hive.optimize.bucketmapjoin`:

```
set hive.optimize.bucketmapjoin=true;
```

If the bucketed tables actually have the same number of buckets and the data is sorted by the join/bucket keys, then Hive can perform an even faster sort-merge join. Once again, properties must be set to enable the optimization:

```
set hive.input.format=org.apache.hadoop.hive.ql.io.BucketizedHiveInputFormat;
set hive.optimize.bucketmapjoin=true;
set hive.optimize.bucketmapjoin.sortedmerge=true;
```

ORDER BY and SORT BY

The ORDER BY clause is familiar from other SQL dialects. It performs a *total ordering* of the query result set. This means that *all* the data is passed through a single reducer, which may take an unacceptably long time to execute for larger data sets.

Hive adds an alternative, SORT BY, that orders the data only within each reducer, thereby performing a *local ordering*, where each reducer's output will be sorted. Better performance is traded for total ordering.

In both cases, the syntax differs only by the use of the ORDER or SORT keyword. You can specify any columns you wish and specify whether or not the columns are ascending using the ASC keyword (the default) or descending using the DESC keyword.

Here is an example using ORDER BY:

```
SELECT s.ymd, s.symbol, s.price_close
FROM stocks s
ORDER BY s.ymd ASC, s.symbol DESC;
```

Here is the same example using SORT BY instead:

```
SELECT s.ymd, s.symbol, s.price_close
FROM stocks s
SORT BY s.ymd ASC, s.symbol DESC;
```

The two queries look almost identical, but if more than one reducer is invoked, the output will be sorted differently. While each reducer's output files will be sorted, the data will probably overlap with the output of other reducers.

Because ORDER BY can result in excessively long run times, Hive will require a LIMIT clause with ORDER BY if the property hive.mapred.mode is set to strict. By default, it is set to nonstrict.

DISTRIBUTE BY with SORT BY

DISTRIBUTE BY controls how map output is divided among reducers. All data that flows through a MapReduce job is organized into key-value pairs. Hive must use this feature internally when it converts your queries to MapReduce jobs.

Usually, you won't need to worry about this feature. The exceptions are queries that use the *Streaming* feature (see Chapter 14) and some stateful UDAFs (*User-Defined Aggregate Functions*; see "Aggregate Functions" on page 164). There is one other scenario where these clauses are useful.

By default, MapReduce computes a hash on the keys output by mappers and tries to evenly distribute the key-value pairs among the available reducers using the hash values. Unfortunately, this means that when we use SORT BY, the contents of one reducer's output will overlap significantly with the output of the other reducers, as far as sorted order is concerned, even though the data is sorted *within* each reducer's output.

Say we want the data for each stock symbol to be captured together. We can use DISTRIBUTE BY to ensure that the records for each stock symbol go to the same reducer, then use SORT BY to order the data the way we want. The following query demonstrates this technique:

```
hive> SELECT s.ymd, s.symbol, s.price_close
    > FROM stocks s
    > DISTRIBUTE BY s.symbol
    > SORT BY  s.symbol ASC, s.ymd ASC;
1984-09-07  AAPL  26.5
1984-09-10  AAPL  26.37
1984-09-11  AAPL  26.87
1984-09-12  AAPL  26.12
1984-09-13  AAPL  27.5
1984-09-14  AAPL  27.87
1984-09-17  AAPL  28.62
1984-09-18  AAPL  27.62
1984-09-19  AAPL  27.0
1984-09-20  AAPL  27.12
...
```

Of course, the ASC keywords could have been omitted as they are the defaults. The ASC keyword is placed here for reasons that will be described shortly.

DISTRIBUTE BY works similar to GROUP BY in the sense that it controls how reducers receive rows for processing, while SORT BY controls the sorting of data inside the reducer.

Note that Hive requires that the DISTRIBUTE BY clause come before the SORT BY clause.

CLUSTER BY

In the previous example, the s.symbol column was used in the DISTRIBUTE BY clause, and the s.symbol and the s.ymd columns in the SORT BY clause. Suppose that the same columns are used in both clauses *and* all columns are sorted by ascending order (the default). In this case, the CLUSTER BY clause is a shor-hand way of expressing the same query.

For example, let's modify the previous query to drop sorting by s.ymd and use CLUSTER BY on s.symbol:

```
hive> SELECT s.ymd, s.symbol, s.price_close
    > FROM stocks s
    > CLUSTER BY s.symbol;
2010-02-08  AAPL  194.12
2010-02-05  AAPL  195.46
2010-02-04  AAPL  192.05
2010-02-03  AAPL  199.23
2010-02-02  AAPL  195.86
2010-02-01  AAPL  194.73
2010-01-29  AAPL  192.06
2010-01-28  AAPL  199.29
```

```
2010-01-27  AAPL  207.88
...
```

Because the sort requirements are removed for the s.ymd, the output reflects the original order of the stock data, which is sorted descending.

Using DISTRIBUTE BY ... SORT BY or the shorthand CLUSTER BY clauses is a way to exploit the parallelism of SORT BY, yet achieve a total ordering across the output files.

Casting

We briefly mentioned in "Primitive Data Types" on page 41 that Hive will perform some *implicit* conversions, called *casts*, of numeric data types, as needed. For example, when doing comparisons between two numbers of different types. This topic is discussed more fully in "Predicate Operators" on page 93 and "Gotchas with Floating-Point Comparisons" on page 94.

Here we discuss the cast() function that allows you to *explicitly* convert a value of one type to another.

Recall our employees table uses a FLOAT for the salary column. Now, imagine for a moment that STRING was used for that column instead. How could we work with the values as FLOATS?

The following example casts the values to FLOAT before performing a comparison:

```
SELECT name, salary FROM employees
WHERE cast(salary AS FLOAT) < 100000.0;
```

The syntax of the cast function is cast(value AS TYPE). What would happen in the example if a salary value was not a valid string for a floating-point number? In this case, Hive returns NULL.

Note that the preferred way to convert floating-point numbers to integers is to use the round() or floor() functions listed in Table 6-2, rather than to use the cast operator.

Casting BINARY Values

The new BINARY type introduced in Hive v0.8.0 only supports casting BINARY to STRING. However, if you know the value is a number, you can nest cast() invocations, as in this example where column b is a BINARY column:

```
SELECT (2.0*cast(cast(b as string) as double)) from src;
```

You can also cast STRING to BINARY.

Queries that Sample Data

For very large data sets, sometimes you want to work with a representative sample of a query result, not the whole thing. Hive supports this goal with queries that sample tables organized into buckets.

In the following example, assume the numbers table has one number column with values 1–10.

We can sample using the rand() function, which returns a random number. In the first two queries, two distinct numbers are returned for each query. In the third query, no results are returned:

```
hive> SELECT * from numbers TABLESAMPLE(BUCKET 3 OUT OF 10 ON rand()) s;
2
4

hive> SELECT * from numbers TABLESAMPLE(BUCKET 3 OUT OF 10 ON rand()) s;
7
10

hive> SELECT * from numbers TABLESAMPLE(BUCKET 3 OUT OF 10 ON rand()) s;
```

If we bucket on a column instead of rand(), then identical results are returned on multiple runs:

```
hive> SELECT * from numbers TABLESAMPLE(BUCKET 3 OUT OF 10 ON number) s;
2

hive> SELECT * from numbers TABLESAMPLE(BUCKET 5 OUT OF 10 ON number) s;
4

hive> SELECT * from numbers TABLESAMPLE(BUCKET 3 OUT OF 10 ON number) s;
2
```

The denominator in the bucket clause represents the number of buckets into which data will be hashed. The numerator is the bucket number selected:

```
hive> SELECT * from numbers TABLESAMPLE(BUCKET 1 OUT OF 2 ON number) s;
2
4
6
8
10

hive> SELECT * from numbers TABLESAMPLE(BUCKET 2 OUT OF 2 ON number) s;
1
3
5
7
9
```

Block Sampling

Hive offers another syntax for sampling a percentage of blocks of an input path as an alternative to sampling based on rows:

```
hive> SELECT * FROM numbersflat TABLESAMPLE(0.1 PERCENT) s;
```

 This sampling is not known to work with all file formats. Also, the smallest unit of sampling is a single HDFS block. Hence, for tables less than the typical block size of 128 MB, all rows will be retuned.

Percentage-based sampling offers a variable to control the seed information for block-based tuning. Different seeds produce different samples:

```
<property>
  <name>hive.sample.seednumber</name>
  <value>0</value>
  <description>A number used for percentage sampling. By changing this
  number, user will change the subsets of data sampled.</description>
</property>
```

Input Pruning for Bucket Tables

From a first look at the TABLESAMPLE syntax, an astute user might come to the conclusion that the following query would be equivalent to the TABLESAMPLE operation:

```
hive> SELECT * FROM numbersflat WHERE number % 2 = 0;
2
4
6
8
10
```

It is true that for most table types, sampling scans through the entire table and selects every Nth row. However, if the columns specified in the TABLESAMPLE clause match the columns in the CLUSTERED BY clause, TABLESAMPLE queries only scan the required hash partitions of the table:

```
hive> CREATE TABLE numbers_bucketed (number int) CLUSTERED BY (number) INTO 3 BUCKETS;

hive> SET hive.enforce.bucketing=true;

hive> INSERT OVERWRITE TABLE numbers_bucketed SELECT number FROM numbers;

hive> dfs -ls /user/hive/warehouse/mydb.db/numbers_bucketed;
/user/hive/warehouse/mydb.db/numbers_bucketed/000000_0
/user/hive/warehouse/mydb.db/numbers_bucketed/000001_0
/user/hive/warehouse/mydb.db/numbers_bucketed/000002_0
```

```
hive> dfs -cat /user/hive/warehouse/mydb.db/numbers_bucketed/000001_0;
1
7
10
4
```

Because this table is clustered into three buckets, the following query can be used to sample only one of the buckets efficiently:

```
hive> SELECT * FROM numbers_bucketed TABLESAMPLE (BUCKET 2 OUT OF 3 ON NUMBER) s;
1
7
10
4
```

UNION ALL

UNION ALL combines two or more tables. Each subquery of the union query must pro-duce the same number of columns, and for each column, its type must match all the column types in the same position. For example, if the second column is a FLOAT, then the second column of all the other query results must be a FLOAT.

Here is an example the merges log data:

```
SELECT log.ymd, log.level, log.message
  FROM (
    SELECT l1.ymd, l1.level,
      l1.message, 'Log1' AS source
    FROM log1 l1
  UNION ALL
    SELECT l2.ymd, l2.level,
      l2.message, 'Log2' AS source
    FROM log1 l2
  ) log
SORT BY log.ymd ASC;
```

UNION may be used when a clause selects from the same source table. Logically, the same results could be achieved with a single SELECT and WHERE clause. This technique increases readability by breaking up a long complex WHERE clause into two or more UNION queries. However, unless the source table is indexed, the query will have to make multiple passes over the same source data. For example:

```
FROM (
  FROM src SELECT src.key, src.value WHERE src.key < 100
  UNION ALL
  FROM src SELECT src.* WHERE src.key > 110
) unioninput
INSERT OVERWRITE DIRECTORY '/tmp/union.out' SELECT unioninput.*
```

CHAPTER 7

HiveQL: Views

A *view* allows a query to be saved and treated like a table. It is a logical construct, as it does not store data like a table. In other words, *materialized views* are not currently supported by Hive.

When a query references a view, the information in its definition is combined with the rest of the query by Hive's query planner. Logically, you can imagine that Hive executes the view and then uses the results in the rest of the query.

Views to Reduce Query Complexity

When a query becomes long or complicated, a view may be used to hide the complexity by dividing the query into smaller, more manageable pieces; similar to writing a function in a programming language or the concept of layered design in software. Encapsulating the complexity makes it easier for end users to construct complex queries from reusable parts. For example, consider the following query with a nested subquery:

```
FROM (
  SELECT * FROM people JOIN cart
    ON (cart.people_id=people.id) WHERE firstname='john'
) a SELECT a.lastname WHERE a.id=3;
```

It is common for Hive queries to have many levels of nesting. In the following example, the nested portion of the query is turned into a view:

```
CREATE VIEW shorter_join AS
SELECT * FROM people JOIN cart
ON (cart.people_id=people.id) WHERE firstname='john';
```

Now the view is used like any other table. In this query we added a WHERE clause to the SELECT statement. This exactly emulates the original query:

```
SELECT lastname FROM shorter_join WHERE id=3;
```

Views that Restrict Data Based on Conditions

A common use case for views is restricting the result rows based on the value of one or more columns. Some databases allow a view to be used as a security mechanism. Rather than give the user access to the raw table with sensitive data, the user is given access to a view with a WHERE clause that restricts the data. Hive does not currently support this feature, as the user must have access to the entire underlying raw table for the view to work. However, the concept of a view created to limit data access can be used to protect information from the casual query:

```
hive> CREATE TABLE userinfo (
    >   firstname string, lastname string, ssn string, password string);
hive> CREATE VIEW safer_user_info AS
    > SELECT firstname,lastname FROM userinfo;
```

Here is another example where a view is used to restrict data based on a WHERE clause. In this case, we wish to provide a view on an employee table that only exposes employees from a specific department:

```
hive> CREATE TABLE employee (firstname string, lastname string,
    >   ssn string, password string, department string);
hive> CREATE VIEW techops_employee AS
    > SELECT firstname,lastname,ssn FROM userinfo WERE department='techops';
```

Views and Map Type for Dynamic Tables

Recall from Chapter 3 that Hive supports arrays, maps, and structs datatypes. These datatypes are not common in traditional databases as they break first normal form. Hive's ability to treat a line of text as a map, rather than a fixed set of columns, combined with the view feature, allows you to define multiple *logical* tables over one *physical* table.

For example, consider the following sample data file that treats an entire row as a map rather than a list of fixed columns. Rather than using Hive's default values for separators, this file uses ^A (Control-A) as the collection item separator (i.e., between key-value pairs in this case, where the collection is a map) and ^B (Control-B) as the separator between keys and values in the map. The long lines wrap in the following listing, so we added a blank line between them for better clarity:

time^B1298598398404^Atype^Brequest^Astate^Bny^Acity^Bwhite plains^Apart\^Bmuffler

time^B1298598398432^Atype^Bresponse^Astate^Bny^Acity^Btarry-town^Apart\^Bmuffler

time^B1298598399404^Atype^Brequest^Astate^Btx^Acity^Baus-tin^Apart^Bheadlight

Now we create our table:

```
CREATE EXTERNAL TABLE dynamictable(cols map<string,string>)
ROW FORMAT DELIMITED
  FIELDS TERMINATED BY '\004'
  COLLECTION ITEMS TERMINATED BY '\001'
  MAP KEYS TERMINATED BY '\002'
STORED AS TEXTFILE;
```

Because there is only one field per row, the `FIELDS TERMINATED BY` value actually has no effect.

Now we can create a view that extracts only rows with type equal to requests and get the city, state, and part into a view called orders:

```
CREATE VIEW orders(state, city, part) AS
SELECT cols["state"], cols["city"], cols["part"]
FROM dynamictable
WHERE cols["type"] = "request";
```

A second view is created named shipments. This view returns the time and part column from rows where the type is response:

```
CREATE VIEW shipments(time, part) AS
SELECT cols["time"], cols["parts"]
FROM dynamictable
WHERE cols["type"] = "response";
```

For another example of this feature, see *http://dev.bizo.com/2011/02/columns-in-hive .html#!/2011/02/columns-in-hive.html*.

View Odds and Ends

We said that Hive evaluates the view and then uses the results to evaluate the query. However, as part of Hive's query optimization, the clauses of both the query and view may be combined together into a single actual query.

Nevertheless, the conceptual view still applies when the view and a query that uses it both contain an `ORDER BY` clause or a `LIMIT` clause. The view's clauses are evaluated *before* the using query's clauses.

For example, if the view has a `LIMIT 100` clause and the query has a `LIMIT 200` clause, you'll get at most 100 results.

While defining a view doesn't "materialize" any data, the view is frozen to any subsequent changes to any tables and columns that the view uses. Hence, a query using a view can fail if the referenced tables or columns no longer exist.

There are a few other clauses you can use when creating views. Modifying our last example:

```
CREATE VIEW IF NOT EXISTS shipments(time, part)
COMMENT 'Time and parts for shipments.'
TBLPROPERTIES ('creator' = 'me')
AS SELECT ...;
```

As for tables, the IF NOT EXISTS and COMMENT ... clauses are optional, and have the same meaning they have for tables.

A view's name must be unique compared to all other table and view names in the same database.

You can also add a COMMENT for any or all of the new column names. The comments are not "inherited" from the definition of the original table.

Also, if the AS SELECT contains an expression without an alias—e.g., size(cols) (the number of items in cols)—then Hive will use _CN as the name, where N is a number starting with 0. The view definition will fail if the AS SELECT clause is invalid.

Before the AS SELECT clause, you can also define TBLPROPERTIES, just like for tables. In the example, we defined a property for the "creator" of the view.

The CREATE TABLE ... LIKE ... construct discussed in "Creating Tables" on page 53 can also be used to copy a view, that is with a view as part of the LIKE expression:

```
CREATE TABLE shipments2
LIKE shipments;
```

You can also use the optional EXTERNAL keyword and LOCATION ... clause, as before.

 The behavior of this statement is different as of Hive v0.8.0 and previous versions of Hive. For v0.8.0, the command creates a new *table*, not a new *view*. It uses defaults for the *SerDe* and file formats. For earlier versions, a new *view* is created.

A view is dropped in the same way as a table:

```
DROP VIEW IF EXISTS shipments;
```

As usual, IF EXISTS is optional.

A view will be shown using SHOW TABLES (there is no SHOW VIEWS), however DROP TABLE cannot be used to delete a view.

As for tables, DESCRIBE shipments and DESCRIBE EXTENDED shipments displays the usual data for the shipment view. With the latter, there will be a tableType value in the Detailed Table Information indicating the "table" is a VIRTUAL_VIEW.

You cannot use a view as a target of an INSERT or LOAD command.

Finally, views are read-only. You can only alter the metadata TBLPROPERTIES for a view:

```
ALTER VIEW shipments SET TBLPROPERTIES ('created_at' = 'some_timestamp');
```

CHAPTER 8

HiveQL: Indexes

Hive has limited indexing capabilities. There are no keys in the usual relational database sense, but you can build an index on columns to speed some operations. The index data for a table is stored in another table.

Also, the feature is relatively new, so it doesn't have a lot of options yet. However, the indexing process is designed to be customizable with plug-in Java code, so teams can extend the feature to meet their needs.

Indexing is also a good alternative to partitioning when the logical partitions would actually be too numerous and small to be useful. Indexing can aid in pruning some blocks from a table as input for a MapReduce job. Not all queries can benefit from an index—the EXPLAIN syntax and Hive can be used to determine if a given query is aided by an index.

Indexes in Hive, like those in relational databases, need to be evaluated carefully. Maintaining an index requires extra disk space and building an index has a processing cost. The user must weigh these costs against the benefits they offer when querying a table.

Creating an Index

Let's create an index for our managed, partitioned employees table we described in "Partitioned, Managed Tables" on page 58. Here is the table definition we used previously, for reference:

```
CREATE TABLE employees (
    name          STRING,
    salary        FLOAT,
    subordinates  ARRAY<STRING>,
    deductions    MAP<STRING, FLOAT>,
    address       STRUCT<street:STRING, city:STRING, state:STRING, zip:INT>
)
PARTITIONED BY (country STRING, state STRING);
```

Let's index on the country partition only:

```
CREATE INDEX employees_index
ON TABLE employees (country)
AS 'org.apache.hadoop.hive.ql.index.compact.CompactIndexHandler'
WITH DEFERRED REBUILD
IDXPROPERTIES ('creator = 'me', 'created_at' = 'some_time')
IN TABLE employees_index_table
PARTITIONED BY (country, name)
COMMENT 'Employees indexed by country and name.';
```

In this case, we did not partition the index table to the same level of granularity as the original table. We could choose to do so. If we omitted the PARTITIONED BY clause completely, the index would span all partitions of the original table.

The AS ... clause specifies the *index handler*, a Java class that implements indexing. Hive ships with a few representative implementations; the CompactIndexHandler shown was in the first release of this feature. Third-party implementations can optimize certain scenarios, support specific file formats, and more. We'll provide more information on implementing your own index handler in "Implementing a Custom Index Handler" on page 119.

We'll discuss the meaning of WITH DEFERRED REBUILD in the next section.

It's not a requirement for the index handler to save its data in a new table, but if it does, the IN TABLE ... clause is used. It supports many of the options available when creating other tables. Specifically, the example doesn't use the optional ROW FORMAT, STORED AS, STORED BY, LOCATION, and TBLPROPERTIES clauses that we discussed in Chapter 4. All would appear before the final COMMENT clause shown.

Currently, indexing external tables and views is supported except for data residing in S3.

Bitmap Indexes

Hive v0.8.0 adds a built-in bitmap index handler. Bitmap indexes are commonly used for columns with few distinct values. Here is our previous example rewritten to use the bitmap index handler:

```
CREATE INDEX employees_index
ON TABLE employees (country)
AS 'BITMAP'
WITH DEFERRED REBUILD
IDXPROPERTIES ('creator = 'me', 'created_at' = 'some_time')
IN TABLE employees_index_table
PARTITIONED BY (country, name)
COMMENT 'Employees indexed by country and name.';
```

Rebuilding the Index

If you specified WITH DEFERRED REBUILD, the new index starts empty. At any time, the index can be built the first time or rebuilt using the ALTER INDEX statement:

```
ALTER INDEX employees_index
ON TABLE employees
PARTITION (country = 'US')
REBUILD;
```

If the `PARTITION` clause is omitted, the index is rebuilt for all partitions.

There is no built-in mechanism to trigger an automatic rebuild of the index if the underlying table or a particular partition changes. However, if you have a workflow that updates table partitions with data, one where you might already use the `ALTER TABLE ...` `TOUCH PARTITION(...)` feature described in "Miscellaneous Alter Table Statements" on page 69, that same workflow could issue the `ALTER INDEX ... REBUILD` command for a corresponding index.

The rebuild is *atomic* in the sense that if the rebuild fails, the index is left in the previous state before the rebuild was started.

Showing an Index

The following command will show all the indexes defined for any column in the indexed table:

```
SHOW FORMATTED INDEX ON employees;
```

`FORMATTED` is optional. It causes column titles to be added to the output. You can also replace `INDEX` with `INDEXES`, as the output may list multiple indexes.

Dropping an Index

Dropping an index also drops the index table, if any:

```
DROP INDEX IF EXISTS employees_index ON TABLE employees;
```

Hive won't let you attempt to drop the index table directly with `DROP TABLE`. As always, `IF EXISTS` is optional and serves to suppress errors if the index doesn't exist.

If the table that was indexed is dropped, the index itself and its table is dropped. Similarly, if a partition of the original table is dropped, the corresponding partition index is also dropped.

Implementing a Custom Index Handler

The full details for implementing a custom index handler are given on the Hive Wiki page, *https://cwiki.apache.org/confluence/display/Hive/IndexDev#CREATE_INDEX*, where the initial design of indexing is documented. Of course, you can use the source code for `org.apache.hadoop.hive.ql.index.compact.CompactIndexHandler` as an example.

When the index is created, the Java code you implement for the index handler has to do some initial validation and define the schema for the index table, if used. It also has to implement the rebuilding process where it reads the table to be indexed and writes to the index storage (e.g., the index table). The handler must clean up any nontable storage it uses for the index when the index is dropped, relying on Hive to drop the index table, as needed. Finally, the handler must participate in optimizing queries.

CHAPTER 9

Schema Design

Hive looks and acts like a relational database. Users have a familiar nomenclature such as tables and columns, as well as a query language that is remarkably similar to SQL dialects they have used before. However, Hive is implemented and used in ways that are very different from conventional relational databases. Often, users try to carry over paradigms from the relational world that are actually Hive *anti-patterns*. This section highlights some Hive patterns you should use and some anti-patterns you should avoid.

Table-by-Day

Table-by-day is a pattern where a table named supply is appended with a timestamp such as supply_2011_01_01, supply_2011_01_02, etc. Table-by-day is an anti-pattern in the database world, but due to common implementation challenges of ever-growing data sets, it is still widely used:

```
hive> CREATE TABLE supply_2011_01_02 (id int, part string, quantity int);

hive> CREATE TABLE supply_2011_01_03 (id int, part string, quantity int);

hive> CREATE TABLE supply_2011_01_04 (id int, part string, quantity int);

hive> .... load data ...

hive> SELECT part,quantity supply_2011_01_02
    > UNION ALL
    > SELECT part,quantity from supply_2011_01_03
    > WHERE quantity < 4;
```

With Hive, a partitioned table should be used instead. Hive uses expressions in the WHERE clause to select input only from the partitions needed for the query. This query will run efficiently, and it is clean and easy on the eyes:

```
hive> CREATE TABLE supply (id int, part string, quantity int)
    > PARTITIONED BY (int day);

hive> ALTER TABLE supply add PARTITION (day=20110102);
```

```
hive> ALTER TABLE supply add PARTITION (day=20110103);

hive> ALTER TABLE supply add PARTITION (day=20110102);

hive> .... load data ...

hive> SELECT part,quantity FROM supply
    > WHERE day>=20110102 AND day<20110103 AND quantity < 4;
```

Over Partitioning

The partitioning feature is very useful in Hive. This is because Hive typically performs full scans over all input to satisfy a query (we'll leave Hive's indexing out for this discussion). However, a design that creates too many partitions may optimize some queries, but be detrimental for other important queries:

```
hive> CREATE TABLE weblogs (url string, time long )
    > PARTITIONED BY (day int, state string, city string);

hive> SELECT * FROM weblogs WHERE day=20110102;
```

HDFS was designed for many millions of large files, not billions of small files. The first drawback of having too many partitions is the large number of Hadoop files and directories that are created unnecessarily. Each partition corresponds to a directory that usually contains multiple files. If a given table contains thousands of partitions, it may have tens of thousands of files, possibly created every day. If the retention of this table is multiplied over years, it will eventually exhaust the capacity of the *NameNode* to manage the filesystem metadata. The *NameNode* must keep all metadata for the filesystem in memory. While each file requires a small number of bytes for its metadata (approximately 150 bytes/file), the net effect is to impose an upper limit on the total number of files that can be managed in an HDFS installation. Other filesystems, like MapR and Amazon S3 don't have this limitation.

MapReduce processing converts a job into multiple tasks. In the default case, each task is a new JVM instance, requiring the overhead of start up and tear down. For small files, a separate task will be used for each file. In pathological scenarios, the overhead of JVM start up and tear down can exceed the actual processing time!

Hence, an ideal partition scheme should not result in too many partitions and their directories, and the files in each directory should be large, some multiple of the filesystem block size.

A good strategy for time-range partitioning, for example, is to determine the approximate size of your data accumulation over different granularities of time, and start with the granularity that results in "modest" growth in the number of partitions over time, while each partition contains files at least on the order of the filesystem block size or multiples thereof. This balancing keeps the partitions large, which optimizes throughput for the general case query. Consider when the next level of granularity is appropriate, especially if query `WHERE` clauses typically select ranges of smaller granularities:

```
hive> CREATE TABLE weblogs (url string, time long, state string, city string )
    > PARTITIONED BY (day int);
hive> SELECT * FROM weblogs WHERE day=20110102;
```

Another solution is to use two levels of partitions along different dimensions. For example, the first partition might be by day and the second-level partition might be by geographic region, like the state:

```
hive> CREATE TABLE weblogs (url string, time long, city string )
    > PARTITIONED BY (day int, state string);
hive> SELECT * FROM weblogs WHERE day=20110102;
```

However, since some states will probably result in lots more data than others, you could see imbalanced map tasks, as processing the larger states takes a lot longer than processing the smaller states.

If you can't find good, comparatively sized partition choices, consider using *bucketing* as described in "Bucketing Table Data Storage" on page 125.

Unique Keys and Normalization

Relational databases typically use unique keys, indexes, and normalization to store data sets that fit into memory or mostly into memory. Hive, however, does not have the concept of primary keys or automatic, sequence-based key generation. Joins should be avoided in favor of denormalized data, when feasible. The complex types, `Array`, `Map`, and `Struct`, help by allowing the storage of one-to-many data inside a single row. This is not to say normalization should never be utilized, but star-schema type designs are nonoptimal.

The primary reason to avoid normalization is to minimize disk seeks, such as those typically required to navigate foreign key relations. Denormalizing data permits it to be scanned from or written to large, contiguous sections of disk drives, which optimizes I/O performance. However, you pay the penalty of denormalization, data duplication and the greater risk of inconsistent data.

For example, consider our running example, the `employees` table. Here it is again with some changes for clarity:

```
CREATE TABLE employees (
  name         STRING,
  salary       FLOAT,
  subordinates ARRAY<STRING>,
  deductions   MAP<STRING, FLOAT>
  address      STRUCT<street:STRING, city:STRING, state:STRING, zip:INT>);
```

The data model of this example breaks the traditional design rules in a few ways.

First, we are informally using name as the primary key, although we all know that names are often not unique! Ignoring that issue for now, a relational model would have a single foreign key relation from an employee record to the manager record, using the name key. We represented this relation the other way around: each employee has an ARRAY of names of subordinates.

Second, the value for each deduction is unique to the employee, but the map keys are duplicated data, even if you substitute "flags" (say, integers) for the actual key strings. A normal relational model would have a separate, two-column table for the deduction name (or flag) and value, with a one-to-many relationship between the employees and this deductions table.

Finally, chances are that at least some employees live at the same address, but we are duplicating the address for each employee, rather than using a one-to-one relationship to an addresses table.

It's up to us to manage referential integrity (or deal with the consequences), and to fix the duplicates of a particular piece of data that has changed. Hive does not give us a convenient way to UPDATE single records.

Still, when you have 10s of terabytes to many petabytes of data, optimizing speed makes these limitations worth accepting.

Making Multiple Passes over the Same Data

Hive has a special syntax for producing multiple aggregations from a single pass through a source of data, rather than rescanning it for each aggregation. This change can save considerable processing time for large input data sets. We discussed the details previously in Chapter 5.

For example, each of the following two queries creates a table from the same source table, history:

```
hive> INSERT OVERWRITE TABLE sales
    > SELECT * FROM history WHERE action='purchased';
hive> INSERT OVERWRITE TABLE credits
    > SELECT * FROM history WHERE action='returned';
```

This syntax is correct, but inefficient. The following rewrite achieves the same thing, but using a single pass through the source history table:

```
hive> FROM history
    > INSERT OVERWRITE sales   SELECT * WHERE action='purchased'
    > INSERT OVERWRITE credits SELECT * WHERE action='returned';
```

The Case for Partitioning Every Table

Many ETL processes involve multiple processing steps. Each step may produce one or more temporary tables that are only needed until the end of the next job. At first it may appear that partitioning these temporary tables is unnecessary. However, imagine a scenario where a mistake in step's query or raw data forces a rerun of the ETL process for several days of input. You will likely need to run the catch-up process a day at a time in order to make sure that one job does not overwrite the temporary table before other tasks have completed.

For example, this following design creates an intermediate table by the name of distinct_ip_in_logs to be used by a subsequent processing step:

```
$ hive -hiveconf dt=2011-01-01
hive> INSERT OVERWRITE table distinct_ip_in_logs
    > SELECT distinct(ip) as ip from weblogs
    > WHERE hit_date='${hiveconf:dt}';

hive> CREATE TABLE state_city_for_day (state string,city string);

hive> INSERT OVERWRITE state_city_for_day
    > SELECT distinct(state,city) FROM distinct_ip_in_logs
    > JOIN geodata ON (distinct_ip_in_logs.ip=geodata.ip);
```

This approach works, however computing a single day causes the record of the previous day to be removed via the INSERT OVERWRITE clause. If two instances of this process are run at once for different days they could stomp on each others' results.

A more robust approach is to carry the partition information all the way through the process. This makes synchronization a nonissue. Also, as a side effect, this approach allows you to compare the intermediate data day over day:

```
$ hive -hiveconf dt=2011-01-01
hive> INSERT OVERWRITE table distinct_ip_in_logs
    > PARTITION (hit_date=${dt})
    > SELECT distinct(ip) as ip from weblogs
    > WHERE hit_date='${hiveconf:dt}';

hive> CREATE TABLE state_city_for_day (state string,city string)
    > PARTITIONED BY (hit_date string);

hive> INSERT OVERWRITE table state_city_for_day PARTITION(${hiveconf:df})
    > SELECT distinct(state,city) FROM distinct_ip_in_logs
    > JOIN geodata ON (distinct_ip_in_logs.ip=geodata.ip)
    > WHERE (hit_date='${hiveconf:dt}');
```

A drawback of this approach is that you will need to manage the intermediate table and delete older partitions, but these tasks are easy to automate.

Bucketing Table Data Storage

Partitions offer a convenient way to segregate data and to optimize queries. However, not all data sets lead to sensible partitioning, especially given the concerns raised earlier about appropriate sizing.

Bucketing is another technique for decomposing data sets into more manageable parts.

For example, suppose a table using the date `dt` as the top-level partition and the `user_id` as the second-level partition leads to too many small partitions. Recall that if you use dynamic partitioning to create these partitions, by default Hive limits the maximum number of dynamic partitions that may be created to prevent the extreme case where so many partitions are created they overwhelm the filesystem's ability to manage them and other problems. So, the following commands might fail:

```
hive> CREATE TABLE weblog (url STRING, source_ip STRING)
    > PARTITIONED BY (dt STRING, user_id INT);

hive> FROM raw_weblog
    > INSERT OVERWRITE TABLE page_view PARTITION(dt='2012-06-08', user_id)
    > SELECT server_name, url, source_ip, dt, user_id;
```

Instead, if we bucket the `weblog` table and use `user_id` as the bucketing column, the value of this column will be hashed by a user-defined number into buckets. Records with the same `user_id` will always be stored in the same bucket. Assuming the number of users is much greater than the number of buckets, each bucket will have many users:

```
hive> CREATE TABLE weblog (user_id INT, url STRING, source_ip STRING)
    > PARTITIONED BY (dt STRING)
    > CLUSTERED BY (user_id) INTO 96 BUCKETS;
```

However, *it is up to you* to insert data correctly into the table! The specification in `CREATE TABLE` only defines metadata, but has no effect on commands that actually populate the table.

This is how to populate the table correctly, when using an `INSERT … TABLE` statement. First, we set a property that forces Hive to choose the correct number of reducers corresponding to the target table's bucketing setup. Then we run a query to populate the partitions. For example:

```
hive> SET hive.enforce.bucketing = true;

hive> FROM raw_logs
    > INSERT OVERWRITE TABLE weblog
    > PARTITION (dt='2009-02-25')
    > SELECT user_id, url, source_ip WHERE dt='2009-02-25';
```

If we didn't use the `hive.enforce.bucketing` property, we would have to set the number of reducers to match the number of buckets, using `set mapred.reduce.tasks=96`. Then the `INSERT` query would require a `CLUSTER BY` clause after the `SELECT` clause.

 As for all table metadata, specifying bucketing doesn't ensure that the table is properly populated. Follow the previous example to ensure that you correctly populate bucketed tables.

Bucketing has several advantages. The number of buckets is fixed so it does not fluctuate with data. Buckets are ideal for sampling. If two tables are bucketed by `user_id`,

Hive can create a logically correct sampling. Bucketing also aids in doing efficient map-side joins, as we discussed in "Map-side Joins" on page 105.

Adding Columns to a Table

Hive allows the definition of a schema over raw data files, unlike many databases that force the conversion and importation of data following a specific format. A benefit of this separation of concerns is the ability to adapt a table definition easily when new columns are added to the data files.

Hive offers the SerDe abstraction, which enables the extraction of data from input. The SerDe also enables the output of data, though the output feature is not used as frequently because Hive is used primarily as a query mechanism. A SerDe usually parses from left to right, splitting rows by specified delimiters into columns. The SerDes tend to be very forgiving. For example, if a row has fewer columns than expected, the missing columns will be returned as null. If the row has more columns than expected, they will be ignored. Adding new columns to the schema involves a single ALTER TABLE ADD COL UMN command. This is very useful as log formats tend to only add more information to a message:

```
hive> CREATE TABLE weblogs (version LONG, url STRING)
    > PARTITIONED BY (hit_date int)
    > ROW FORMAT DELIMITED FIELDS TERMINATED BY '\t';

hive> ! cat log1.txt
1   /mystuff
1   /toys

hive> LOAD DATA LOCAL INPATH 'log1.txt' int weblogs partition(20110101);

hive> SELECT * FROM weblogs;
1   /mystuff   20110101
1   /toys      20110101
```

Over time a new column may be added to the underlying data. In the following example the column user_id is added to the data. Note that some older raw data files may not have this column:

```
hive> ! cat log2.txt
2   /cars    bob
2   /stuff   terry

hive> ALTER TABLE weblogs ADD COLUMNS (user_id string);

hive> LOAD DATA LOCAL INPATH 'log2.txt' int weblogs partition(20110102);

hive> SELECT * from weblogs
1   /mystuff   20110101   NULL
1   /toys      20110101   NULL
2   /cars      20110102   bob
2   /stuff     20110102   terry
```

Note that with this approach, columns cannot be added in the beginning or the middle.

Using Columnar Tables

Hive typically uses row-oriented storage, however Hive also has a columnar SerDe that stores information in a hybrid row-column orientated form. While this format can be used for any type of data there are some data sets that it is optimal for.

Repeated Data

Given enough rows, fields like `state` and `age` will have the same data repeated many times. This type of data benefits from column-based storage.

state	uid	age
NY	Bob	40
NJ	Sara	32
NY	Peter	14
NY	Sandra	4

Many Columns

The table below has a large number of columns.

state	uid	age	server	tz	many_more ...
NY	Bob	40	web1	est	stuff
NJ	Sara	32	web1	est	stuff
NY	Peter	14	web3	pst	stuff
NY	Sandra	4	web45	pst	stuff

Queries typically only use a single column or a small set of columns. Column-based storage will make analyzing the table data faster:

```
hive> SELECT distinct(state) from weblogs;
NY
NJ
```

You can reference the section "RCFile" on page 202 to see how to use this format.

(Almost) Always Use Compression!

In almost all cases, compression makes data smaller on disk, which usually makes queries faster by reducing I/O overhead. Hive works seamlessly with many compression types. The only compelling reason to not use compression is when the data produced is intended for use by an external system, and an uncompressed format, such as text, is the most compatible.

But compression and decompression consumes CPU resources. MapReduce jobs tend to be I/O bound, so the extra CPU overhead is usually not a problem. However, for workflows that are CPU intensive, such as some machine-learning algorithms, compression may actually reduce performance by stealing valuable CPU resources from more essential operations.

See Chapter 11 for more on how to use compression.

CHAPTER 10

Tuning

HiveQL is a declarative language where users issue declarative queries and Hive figures out how to translate them into MapReduce jobs. Most of the time, you don't need to understand how Hive works, freeing you to focus on the problem at hand. While the sophisticated process of query parsing, planning, optimization, and execution is the result of many years of hard engineering work by the Hive team, most of the time you can remain oblivious to it.

However, as you become more experienced with Hive, learning about the theory behind Hive, and the low-level implementation details, will let you use Hive more effectively, especially where performance optimizations are concerned.

This chapter covers several different topics related to tuning Hive performance. Some tuning involves adjusting numeric configuration parameters ("turning the knobs"), while other tuning steps involve enabling or disabling specific features.

Using EXPLAIN

The first step to learning how Hive works (after reading this book...) is to use the EXPLAIN feature to learn how Hive translates queries into MapReduce jobs.

Consider the following example:

```
hive> DESCRIBE onecol;
number  int

hive> SELECT * FROM onecol;
5
5
4

hive> SELECT SUM(number) FROM onecol;
14
```

Now, put the EXPLAIN keyword in front of the last query to see the query plan and other information. The query will not be executed.

```
hive> EXPLAIN SELECT SUM(number) FROM onecol;
```

The output requires some explaining and practice to understand.

First, the *abstract syntax tree* is printed. This shows how Hive parsed the query into tokens and literals, as part of the first step in turning the query into the ultimate result:

```
ABSTRACT SYNTAX TREE:
(TOK_QUERY
  (TOK_FROM (TOK_TABREF (TOK_TABNAME onecol)))
  (TOK_INSERT (TOK_DESTINATION (TOK_DIR TOK_TMP_FILE))
  (TOK_SELECT
    (TOK_SELEXPR
      (TOK_FUNCTION sum (TOK_TABLE_OR_COL number))))))
```

(The indentation of the actual output was changed to fit the page.)

For those not familiar with parsers and tokenizers, this can look overwhelming. However, even if you are a novice in this area, you can study the output to get a sense for what Hive is doing with the SQL statement. (As a first step, ignore the TOK_ prefixes.)

Even though our query will write its output to the console, Hive will actually write the output to a temporary file first, as shown by this part of the output:

```
'(TOK_INSERT (TOK_DESTINATION (TOK_DIR TOK_TMP_FILE))'
```

Next, we can see references to our column name number, our table name onecol, and the sum function.

A Hive job consists of one or more *stages*, with dependencies between different stages. As you might expect, more complex queries will usually involve more stages and more stages usually requires more processing time to complete.

A stage could be a MapReduce job, a sampling stage, a merge stage, a limit stage, or a stage for some other task Hive needs to do. By default, Hive executes these stages one at a time, although later we'll discuss parallel execution in "Parallel Execution" on page 136.

Some stages will be short, like those that move files around. Other stages may also finish quickly if they have little data to process, even though they require a map or reduce task:

```
STAGE DEPENDENCIES:
  Stage-1 is a root stage
  Stage-0 is a root stage
```

The STAGE PLAN section is verbose and complex. Stage-1 is the bulk of the processing for this job and happens via a MapReduce job. A TableScan takes the input of the table and produces a single output column number. The Group By Operator applies the sum(number) and produces an output column _col0 (a synthesized name for an anonymous result). All this is happening on the map side of the job, under the Map Operator Tree:

```
STAGE PLANS:
  Stage: Stage-1
    Map Reduce
      Alias -> Map Operator Tree:
        onecol
          TableScan
            alias: onecol
            Select Operator
              expressions:
                    expr: number
                    type: int
              outputColumnNames: number
              Group By Operator
                aggregations:
                      expr: sum(number)
                bucketGroup: false
                mode: hash
                outputColumnNames: _col0
                Reduce Output Operator
                  sort order:
                  tag: -1
                  value expressions:
                        expr: _col0
                        type: bigint
```

On the reduce side, under the Reduce Operator Tree, we see the same Group by Opera
tor but this time it is applying sum on _col0. Finally, in the reducer we see the File
Output Operator, which shows that the output will be text, based on the string output
format: HiveIgnoreKeyTextOutputFormat:

```
        Reduce Operator Tree:
          Group By Operator
            aggregations:
                  expr: sum(VALUE._col0)
            bucketGroup: false
            mode: mergepartial
            outputColumnNames: _col0
            Select Operator
              expressions:
                    expr: _col0
                    type: bigint
              outputColumnNames: _col0
              File Output Operator
                compressed: false
                GlobalTableId: 0
                table:
                    input format: org.apache.hadoop.mapred.TextInputFormat
                    output format:
                        org.apache.hadoop.hive.ql.io.HiveIgnoreKeyTextOutputFormat
```

Because this job has no LIMIT clause, Stage-0 is a no-op stage:

```
Stage: Stage-0
  Fetch Operator
    limit: -1
```

Understanding the intricate details of how Hive parses and plans every query is not useful all of the time. However, it is a nice to have for analyzing complex or poorly performing queries, especially as we try various tuning steps. We can observe what effect these changes have at the "logical" level, in tandem with performance measurements.

EXPLAIN EXTENDED

Using EXPLAIN EXTENDED produces even more output. In an effort to "go green," we won't show the entire output, but we will show you the Reduce Operator Tree to demonstrate the different output:

```
Reduce Operator Tree:
      Group By Operator
        aggregations:
              expr: sum(VALUE._col0)
        bucketGroup: false
        mode: mergepartial
        outputColumnNames: _col0
        Select Operator
          expressions:
                expr: _col0
                type: bigint
          outputColumnNames: _col0
          File Output Operator
            compressed: false
            GlobalTableId: 0
            directory: file:/tmp/edward/hive_2012-[long number]/-ext-10001
            NumFilesPerFileSink: 1
            Stats Publishing Key Prefix:
                file:/tmp/edward/hive_2012-[long number]/-ext-10001/
            table:
                input format: org.apache.hadoop.mapred.TextInputFormat
                output format:
                    org.apache.hadoop.hive.ql.io.HiveIgnoreKeyTextOutputFormat
                properties:
                  columns _col0
                  columns.types bigint
                  escape.delim \
                  serialization.format 1
            TotalFiles: 1
            GatherStats: false
            MultiFileSpray: false
```

We encourage you to compare the two outputs for the Reduce Operator Tree.

Limit Tuning

The LIMIT clause is commonly used, often by people working with the CLI. However, in many cases a LIMIT clause still executes the entire query, then only returns a handful

---

of results. Because this behavior is generally wasteful, it should be avoided when possible. Hive has a configuration property to enable sampling of source data for use with LIMIT:

```
<property>
  <name>hive.limit.optimize.enable</name>
  <value>true</value>
  <description>Whether to enable to optimization to
    try a smaller subset of data for simple LIMIT first.</description>
</property>
```

Once the hive.limit.optimize.enable is set to true, two variables control its operation, hive.limit.row.max.size and hive.limit.optimize.limit.file:

```
<property>
  <name>hive.limit.row.max.size</name>
  <value>100000</value>
  <description>When trying a smaller subset of data for simple LIMIT,
    how much size we need to guarantee each row to have at least.
  </description>
</property>

<property>
  <name>hive.limit.optimize.limit.file</name>
  <value>10</value>
  <description>When trying a smaller subset of data for simple LIMIT,
    maximum number of files we can sample.</description>
</property>
```

A drawback of this feature is the risk that useful input data will never get processed. For example, any query that requires a reduce step, such as most JOIN and GROUP BY operations, most calls to *aggregate* functions, etc., will have very different results. Perhaps this difference is okay in many cases, but it's important to understand.

Optimized Joins

We discussed optimizing join performance in "Join Optimizations" on page 100 and "Map-side Joins" on page 105. We won't reproduce the details here, but just remind yourself that it's important to know which table is the largest and put it *last* in the JOIN clause, or use the /* streamtable(table_name) */ directive.

If all but one table is small enough, typically to fit in memory, then Hive can perform a *map-side join*, eliminating the need for reduce tasks and even some map tasks. Sometimes even tables that do not fit in memory are good candidates because removing the reduce phase outweighs the cost of bringing semi-large tables into each map tasks.

Local Mode

Many Hadoop jobs need the full scalability benefits of Hadoop to process large data sets. However, there are times when the input to Hive is very small. In these cases, the overhead of launching tasks for queries consumes a significant percentage of the overall job execution time. In many of these cases, Hive can leverage the lighter weight of the *local mode* to perform all the tasks for the job on a single machine and sometimes in the same process. The reduction in execution times can be dramatic for small data sets.

You can explicitly enable local mode temporarily, as in this example:

```
hive> set oldjobtracker=${hiveconf:mapred.job.tracker};

hive> set mapred.job.tracker=local;

hive> set mapred.tmp.dir=/home/edward/tmp;

hive> SELECT * from people WHERE firstname=bob;
...

hive> set mapred.job.tracker=${oldjobtracker};
```

You can also tell Hive to automatically apply this optimization by setting hive.exec.mode.local.auto to true, perhaps in your *$HOME/.hiverc*.

To set this property permanently for all users, change the value in your *$HIVE_HOME/ conf/hive-site.xml*:

```
<property>
  <name>hive.exec.mode.local.auto</name>
  <value>true</value>
  <description>
    Let hive determine whether to run in local mode automatically
  </description>
</property>
```

Parallel Execution

Hive converts a query into one or more stages. Stages could be a MapReduce stage, a sampling stage, a merge stage, a limit stage, or other possible tasks Hive needs to do. By default, Hive executes these stages one at a time. However, a particular job may consist of some stages that are not dependent on each other and could be executed in parallel, possibly allowing the overall job to complete more quickly. However, if more stages are run simultaneously, the job may complete much faster.

Setting hive.exec.parallel to true enables parallel execution. Be careful in a shared cluster, however. If a job is running more stages in parallel, it will increase its cluster utilization:

```
<property>
  <name>hive.exec.parallel</name>
  <value>true</value>
  <description>Whether to execute jobs in parallel</description>
</property>
```

Strict Mode

Strict mode is a setting in Hive that prevents users from issuing queries that could have unintended and undesirable effects.

Setting the property `hive.mapred.mode` to `strict` disables three types of queries.

First, queries on partitioned tables are not permitted unless they include a *partition filter* in the `WHERE` clause, limiting their scope. In other words, you're prevented from queries that will scan all partitions. The rationale for this limitation is that partitioned tables often hold very large data sets that may be growing rapidly. An unrestricted partition could consume unacceptably large resources over such a large table:

```
hive> SELECT DISTINCT(planner_id) FROM fracture_ins WHERE planner_id=5;
FAILED: Error in semantic analysis: No Partition Predicate Found for
Alias "fracture_ins" Table "fracture_ins"
```

The following enhancement adds a partition filter—the table partitions—to the `WHERE` clause:

```
hive> SELECT DISTINCT(planner_id) FROM fracture_ins
    > WHERE planner_id=5 AND hit_date=20120101;
... normal results ...
```

The second type of restricted query are those with `ORDER BY` clauses, but no `LIMIT` clause. Because `ORDER BY` sends all results to a single reducer to perform the ordering, forcing the user to specify a `LIMIT` clause prevents the reducer from executing for an extended period of time:

```
hive> SELECT * FROM fracture_ins WHERE hit_date>2012 ORDER BY planner_id;
FAILED: Error in semantic analysis: line 1:56 In strict mode,
limit must be specified if ORDER BY is present planner_id
```

To issue this query, add a `LIMIT` clause:

```
hive> SELECT * FROM fracture_ins WHERE hit_date>2012 ORDER BY planner_id
    > LIMIT 100000;
... normal results ...
```

The third and final type of query prevented is a *Cartesian product*. Users coming from the relational database world may expect that queries that perform a `JOIN` not with an `ON` clause but with a `WHERE` clause will have the query optimized by the query planner, effectively converting the `WHERE` clause into an `ON` clause. Unfortunately, Hive does not perform this optimization, so a runaway query will occur if the tables are large:

```
hive> SELECT * FROM fracture_act JOIN fracture_ads
    > WHERE fracture_act.planner_id = fracture_ads.planner_id;
FAILED: Error in semantic analysis: In strict mode, cartesian product
is not allowed. If you really want to perform the operation,
+set hive.mapred.mode=nonstrict+
```

Here is a properly constructed query with `JOIN` and `ON` clauses:

```
hive> SELECT * FROM fracture_act JOIN fracture_ads
    > ON (fracture_act.planner_id = fracture_ads.planner_id);
... normal results ...
```

Tuning the Number of Mappers and Reducers

Hive is able to parallelize queries by breaking the query into one or more MapReduce jobs. Each of which might have multiple mapper and reducer tasks, at least some of which can run in parallel. Determining the optimal number of mappers and reducers depends on many variables, such as the size of the input and the operation being performed on the data.

A balance is required. Having too many mapper or reducer tasks causes excessive overhead in starting, scheduling, and running the job, while too few tasks means the inherent parallelism of the cluster is underutilized.

When running a Hive query that has a reduce phase, the CLI prints information about how the number of reducers can be tuned. Let's see an example that uses a GROUP BY query, because they always require a reduce phase. In contrast, many other queries are converted into map-only jobs:

```
hive> SELECT pixel_id, count FROM fracture_ins WHERE hit_date=20120119
    > GROUP BY pixel_id;
Total MapReduce jobs = 1
Launching Job 1 out of 1
Number of reduce tasks not specified. Estimated from input data size: 3
In order to change the average load for a reducer (in bytes):
  set hive.exec.reducers.bytes.per.reducer=<number>
In order to limit the maximum number of reducers:
  set hive.exec.reducers.max=<number>
In order to set a constant number of reducers:
  set mapred.reduce.tasks=<number>
...
```

Hive is determining the number of reducers from the input size. This can be confirmed using the dfs -count command, which works something like the Linux du -s command; it computes a total size for all the data under a given directory:

```
[edward@etl02 ~]$ hadoop dfs -count /user/media6/fracture/ins/* | tail -4
  1   8  2614608737 hdfs://.../user/media6/fracture/ins/hit_date=20120118
  1   7  2742992546 hdfs://.../user/media6/fracture/ins/hit_date=20120119
  1  17  2656878252 hdfs://.../user/media6/fracture/ins/hit_date=20120120
  1   2   362657644 hdfs://.../user/media6/fracture/ins/hit_date=20120121
```

(We've reformatted the output and elided some details for space.)

The default value of hive.exec.reducers.bytes.per.reducer is 1 GB. Changing this value to 750 MB causes Hive to estimate four reducers for this job:

```
hive> set hive.exec.reducers.bytes.per.reducer=750000000;

hive> SELECT pixel_id,count(1) FROM fracture_ins WHERE hit_date=20120119
    > GROUP BY pixel_id;
```

```
Total MapReduce jobs = 1
Launching Job 1 out of 1
Number of reduce tasks not specified. Estimated from input data size: 4
...
```

This default typically yields good results. However, there are cases where a query's map phase will create significantly more data than the input size. In the case of excessive map phase data, the input size of the default might be selecting too few reducers. Likewise the map function might filter a large portion of the data from the data set and then fewer reducers may be justified.

A quick way to experiment is by setting the number of reducers to a fixed size, rather than allowing Hive to calculate the value. If you remember, the Hive default estimate is three reducers. Set `mapred.reduce.tasks` to different numbers and determine if more or fewer reducers results in faster run times. Remember that benchmarking like this is complicated by external factors such as other users running jobs simultaneously. Hadoop has a few seconds overhead to start up and schedule map and reduce tasks. When executing performance tests, it's important to keep these factors in mind, especially if the jobs are small.

The `hive.exec.reducers.max` property is useful for controlling resource utilization on shared clusters when dealing with large jobs. A Hadoop cluster has a fixed number of map and reduce "slots" to allocate to tasks. One large job could reserve all of the slots and block other jobs from starting. Setting `hive.exec.reducers.max` can stop a query from taking too many reducer resources. It is a good idea to set this value in your *$HIVE_HOME/conf/hive-site.xml*. A suggested formula is to set the value to the result of this calculation:

```
(Total Cluster Reduce Slots * 1.5) / (avg number of queries running)
```

The 1.5 multiplier is a fudge factor to prevent underutilization of the cluster.

JVM Reuse

JVM reuse is a Hadoop tuning parameter that is very relevant to Hive performance, especially scenarios where it's hard to avoid small files and scenarios with lots of tasks, most which have short execution times.

The default configuration of Hadoop will typically launch map or reduce tasks in a forked JVM. The JVM start-up may create significant overhead, especially when launching jobs with hundreds or thousands of tasks. Reuse allows a JVM instance to be reused up to N times for the same job. This value is set in Hadoop's *mapred-site.xml* (in *$HADOOP_HOME/conf*):

```
<property>
  <name>mapred.job.reuse.jvm.num.tasks</name>
  <value>10</value>
  <description>How many tasks to run per jvm. If set to -1, there is no limit.
```

```
    </description>
  </property>
```

A drawback of this feature is that JVM reuse will keep reserved task slots open until the job completes, in case they are needed for reuse. If an "unbalanced" job has some reduce tasks that run considerably longer than the others, the reserved slots will sit idle, unavailable for other jobs, until the last task completes.

Indexes

Indexes may be used to accelerate the calculation speed of a GROUP BY query.

Hive contains an implementation of bitmap indexes since v0.8.0. The main use case for bitmap indexes is when there are comparatively few values for a given column. See "Bitmap Indexes" on page 118 for more information.

Dynamic Partition Tuning

As explained in "Dynamic Partition Inserts" on page 74, dynamic partition INSERT statements enable a succinct SELECT statement to create many new partitions for insertion into a partitioned table.

This is a very powerful feature, however if the number of partitions is high, a large number of output handles must be created on the system. This is a somewhat uncommon use case for Hadoop, which typically creates a few files at once and streams large amounts of data to them.

Out of the box, Hive is configured to prevent dynamic partition inserts from creating more than 1,000 or so partitions. While it can be bad for a table to have too many partitions, it is generally better to tune this setting to the larger value and allow these queries to work.

First, it is always good to set the dynamic partition mode to strict in your *hive-site.xml*, as discussed in "Strict Mode" on page 137. When strict mode is on, at least one partition has to be static, as demonstrated in "Dynamic Partition Inserts" on page 74:

```
<property>
  <name>hive.exec.dynamic.partition.mode</name>
  <value>strict</value>
  <description>In strict mode, the user must specify at least one
static partition in case the user accidentally overwrites all
partitions.</description>
</property>
```

Then, increase the other relevant properties to allow queries that will create a large number of dynamic partitions, for example:

```
<property>
  <name>hive.exec.max.dynamic.partitions</name>
```

```
  <value>300000</value>
  <description>Maximum number of dynamic partitions allowed to be
created in total.</description>
</property>

<property>
  <name>hive.exec.max.dynamic.partitions.pernode</name>
  <value>10000</value>
  <description>Maximum number of dynamic partitions allowed to be
created in each mapper/reducer node.</description>
</property>
```

Another setting controls how many files a *DataNode* will allow to be open at once. It must be set in the *DataNode's $HADOOP_HOME/conf/hdfs-site.xml*.

In Hadoop v0.20.2, the default value is 256, which is too low. The value affects the number of maximum threads and resources, so setting it to a very high number is not recommended. Note also that in Hadoop v0.20.2, changing this variable requires restarting the *DataNode* to take effect:

```
<property>
  <name>dfs.datanode.max.xcievers</name>
  <value>8192</value>
</property>
```

Speculative Execution

Speculative execution is a feature of Hadoop that launches a certain number of duplicate tasks. While this consumes more resources computing duplicate copies of data that may be discarded, the goal of this feature is to improve overall job progress by getting individual task results faster, and detecting then black-listing slow-running *TaskTrackers*.

Hadoop speculative execution is controlled in the *$HADOOP_HOME/conf/mapred-site.xml* file by the following two variables:

```
<property>
  <name>mapred.map.tasks.speculative.execution</name>
  <value>true</value>
  <description>If true, then multiple instances of some map tasks
  may be executed in parallel.</description>
</property>

<property>
  <name>mapred.reduce.tasks.speculative.execution</name>
  <value>true</value>
  <description>If true, then multiple instances of some reduce tasks
  may be executed in parallel.</description>
</property>
```

However, Hive provides its own variable to control reduce-side speculative execution:

```
<property>
  <name>hive.mapred.reduce.tasks.speculative.execution</name>
  <value>true</value>
  <description>Whether speculative execution for
  reducers should be turned on. </description>
</property>
```

It is hard to give a concrete recommendation about tuning these speculative execution variables. If you are very sensitive to deviations in runtime, you may wish to turn these features on. However, if you have long-running map or reduce tasks due to large amounts of input, the waste could be significant.

Single MapReduce MultiGROUP BY

Another special optimization attempts to combine multiple GROUP BY operations in a query into a single MapReduce job. For this optimization to work, a common set of GROUP BY keys is required:

```
<property>
  <name>hive.multigroupby.singlemr</name>
  <value>false</value>
  <description>Whether to optimize multi group by query to generate single M/R
  job plan. If the multi group by query has common group by keys, it will be
  optimized to generate single M/R job.</description>
</property>
```

Virtual Columns

Hive provides two virtual columns: one for the input filename for split and the other for the block offset in the file. These are helpful when diagnosing queries where Hive is producing unexpected or null results. By projecting these "columns," you can see which file and row is causing problems:

```
hive> set hive.exec.rowoffset=true;

hive> SELECT INPUT__FILE__NAME, BLOCK__OFFSET__INSIDE__FILE, line
    > FROM hive_text WHERE line LIKE '%hive%' LIMIT 2;
har://file/user/hive/warehouse/hive_text/folder=docs/
data.har/user/hive/warehouse/hive_text/folder=docs/README.txt    2243
        http://hive.apache.org/

har://file/user/hive/warehouse/hive_text/folder=docs/
data.har/user/hive/warehouse/hive_text/folder=docs/README.txt    3646
- Hive 0.8.0 ignores the hive-default.xml file, though we continue
```

(We wrapped the long output and put a blank line between the two output rows.)

A third virtual column provides the row offset of the file. It must be enabled explicitly:

```
<property>
  <name>hive.exec.rowoffset</name>
  <value>true</value>
```

```
    <description>Whether to provide the row offset virtual column</description>
  </property>
```

Now it can be used in queries:

```
hive> SELECT INPUT__FILE__NAME, BLOCK__OFFSET__INSIDE__FILE,
    >   ROW__OFFSET__INSIDE__BLOCK
    > FROM hive_text WHERE line LIKE '%hive%' limit 2;
file:/user/hive/warehouse/hive_text/folder=docs/README.txt      2243    0
file:/user/hive/warehouse/hive_text/folder=docs/README.txt      3646    0
```

Other File Formats and Compression

One of Hive's unique features is that Hive does not force data to be converted to a specific format. Hive leverages Hadoop's InputFormat APIs to read data from a variety of sources, such as text files, sequence files, or even custom formats. Likewise, the OutputFormat API is used to write data to various formats.

While Hadoop offers linear scalability in file storage for uncompressed data, storing data in compressed form has many benefits. Compression typically saves significant disk storage; for example, text-based files may compress 40% or more. Compression also can increase throughput and performance. This may seem counterintuitive because compressing and decompressing data incurs extra CPU overhead, however, the I/O savings resulting from moving fewer bytes into memory can result in a net performance gain.

Hadoop jobs tend to be *I/O bound*, rather than CPU bound. If so, compression will improve performance. However, if your jobs are CPU bound, then compression will probably lower your performance. The only way to really know is to experiment with different options and measure the results.

Determining Installed Codecs

Based on your Hadoop version, different codecs will be available to you. The set feature in Hive can be used to display the value of hiveconf or Hadoop configuration values. The codecs available are in a comma-separated list named io.compression.codec:

```
# hive -e "set io.compression.codecs"
io.compression.codecs=org.apache.hadoop.io.compress.GzipCodec,
org.apache.hadoop.io.compress.DefaultCodec,
org.apache.hadoop.io.compress.BZip2Codec,
org.apache.hadoop.io.compress.SnappyCodec
```

Choosing a Compression Codec

Using compression has the advantage of minimizing the disk space required for files and the overhead of disk and network I/O. However, compressing and decompressing files increases the CPU overhead. Therefore, compression is best used for I/O-bound jobs, where there is extra CPU capacity, or when disk space is at a premium.

All recent versions of Hadoop have built-in support for the GZip and BZip2 compression schemes, including native Linux libraries that accelerate compression and decompression for these formats. Bundled support for Snappy compression was recently added, but if your version of Hadoop doesn't support it, you can add the appropriate libraries yourself.[1] Finally, LZO compression is often used.[2]

So, why do we need different compression schemes? Each scheme makes a trade-off between speed and minimizing the size of the compressed output. BZip2 creates the smallest compressed output, but with the highest CPU overhead. GZip is next in terms of compressed size versus speed. Hence, if disk space utilization and I/O overhead are concerns, both are attractive choices.

LZO and Snappy create larger files but are much faster, especially for decompression. They are good choices if disk space and I/O overhead are less important than rapid decompression of frequently read data.

Another important consideration is whether or not the compression format is *splittable*. MapReduce wants to split very large input files into *splits* (often one split per filesystem block, i.e., a multiple of 64 MB), where each split is sent to a separate map process. This can only work if Hadoop knows the record boundaries in the file. In text files, each line is a record, but these boundaries are obscured by GZip and Snappy. However, BZip2 and LZO provide block-level compression, where each block has complete records, so Hadoop can split these files on block boundaries.

The desire for splittable files doesn't rule out GZip and Snappy. When you create your data files, you could partition them so that they are approximately the desired size. Typically the number of output files is equal to the number of reducers. If you are using N reducers you typically get N output files. Be careful, if you have a large nonsplittable file, a single task will have to read the entire file beginning to end.

There's much more we could say about compression, but instead we'll refer you to *Hadoop: The Definitive Guide* by Tom White (O'Reilly) for more details, and we'll focus now on how to tell Hive what format you're using.

From Hive's point of view, there are two aspects to the file format. One aspect is how the file is delimited into rows (records). Text files use \n (linefeed) as the default row delimiter. When you aren't using the default text file format, you tell Hive the name of

---

1. See *http://code.google.com/p/hadoop-snappy/*.

2. See *http://wiki.apache.org/hadoop/UsingLzoCompression*.

---

an `InputFormat` and an `OutputFormat` to use. Actually, you will specify the names of Java classes that implement these formats. The `InputFormat` knows how to read splits and partition them into records, and the `OutputFormat` knows how to write these splits back to files or console output.

The second aspect is how records are partitioned into fields (or columns). Hive uses ^A by default to separate fields in text files. Hive uses the name *SerDe*, which is short for *serializer/deserializer* for the "module" that partitions incoming records (the deserializer) and also knows how to write records in this format (the serializer). This time you will specify a single Java class that performs both jobs.

All this information is specified as part of the table definition when you create the table. After creation, you query the table as you normally would, agnostic to the underlying format. Hence, if you're a user of Hive, but not a Java developer, don't worry about the Java aspects. The developers on your team will help you specify this information when needed, after which you'll work as you normally do.

Enabling Intermediate Compression

Intermediate compression shrinks the data shuffled between the map and reduce tasks for a job. For intermediate compression, choosing a codec that has lower CPU cost is typically more important than choosing a codec that results in the most compression. The property `hive.exec.compress.intermediate` defaults to `false` and should be set to `true` by default:

```
<property>
  <name>hive.exec.compress.intermediate</name>
  <value>true</value>
  <description> This controls whether intermediate files produced by Hive between
  multiple map-reduce jobs are compressed. The compression codec and other options
  are determined from hadoop config variables mapred.output.compress* </description>
</property>
```

> The property that controls intermediate compression for other Hadoop jobs is `mapred.compress.map.output`.

Hadoop compression has a `DefaultCodec`. Changing the codec involves setting the `mapred.map.output.compression.codec` property. This is a Hadoop variable and can be set in the *$HADOOP_HOME/conf/mapred-site.xml* or the *$HADOOP_HOME/conf/hive-site.xml*. `SnappyCodec` is a good choice for intermediate compression because it combines good compression performance with low CPU cost:

```
<property>
  <name>mapred.map.output.compression.codec</name>
  <value>org.apache.hadoop.io.compress.SnappyCodec</value>
  <description> This controls whether intermediate files produced by Hive
```

```
between multiple map-reduce jobs are compressed. The compression codec
and other options are determined from hadoop config variables
mapred.output.compress* </description>
</property>
```

Final Output Compression

When Hive writes output to a table, that content can also be compressed. The property
`hive.exec.compress.output` controls this feature. You may wish to leave this value set
to `false` in the global configuration file, so that the default output is uncompressed
clear text. Users can turn on final compression by setting the property to true on a
query-by-query basis or in their scripts:

```
<property>
  <name>hive.exec.compress.output</name>
  <value>false</value>
  <description> This controls whether the final outputs of a query
  (to a local/hdfs file or a Hive table) is compressed. The compression
  codec and other options are determined from hadoop config variables
  mapred.output.compress* </description>
</property>
```

 The property that controls final compression for other Hadoop jobs is
`mapred.output.compress`.

If `hive.exec.compress.output` is set `true`, a codec can be chosen. GZip compression is
a good choice for output compression because it typically reduces the size of files significantly, but remember that GZipped files aren't splittable by subsequent MapReduce
jobs:

```
<property>
  <name>mapred.output.compression.codec</name>
  <value>org.apache.hadoop.io.compress.GzipCodec</value>
  <description>If the job outputs are compressed, how should they be compressed?
  </description>
</property>
```

Sequence Files

Compressing files results in space savings but one of the downsides of storing raw
compressed files in Hadoop is that often these files are not splittable. Splittable files
can be broken up and processed in parts by multiple mappers in parallel. Most compressed files are not splittable because you can only start reading from the beginning.

The sequence file format supported by Hadoop breaks a file into blocks and then optionally compresses the blocks in a splittable way.

To use sequence files from Hive, add the `STORED AS SEQUENCEFILE` clause to a `CREATE TABLE` statement:

```
CREATE TABLE a_sequence_file_table STORED AS SEQUENCEFILE;
```

Sequence files have three different compression options: `NONE`, `RECORD`, and `BLOCK`. `RECORD` is the default. However, `BLOCK` compression is usually more efficient and it still provides the desired splittability. Like many other compression properties, this one is not Hive-specific. It can be defined in Hadoop's *mapred-site.xml* file, in Hive's *hive-site.xml*, or as needed in scripts or before individual queries:

```
<property>
  <name>mapred.output.compression.type</name>
  <value>BLOCK</value>
  <description>If the job outputs are to compressed as SequenceFiles,
  how should they be compressed? Should be one of NONE, RECORD or BLOCK.
  </description>
</property>
```

Compression in Action

We have introduced a number of compression-related properties in Hive, and different permutations of these options result in different output. Let's use these properties in some examples and show what they produce. Remember that variables set by the CLI persist across the rest of the queries in the session, so between examples you should revert the settings or simply restart the Hive session:

```
hive> SELECT * FROM a;
4       5
3       2

hive> DESCRIBE a;
a       int
b       int
```

First, let's enable intermediate compression. This won't affect the final output, however the job counters will show less physical data transferred for the job, since the shuffle sort data was compressed:

```
hive> set hive.exec.compress.intermediate=true;
hive> CREATE TABLE intermediate_comp_on
    > ROW FORMAT DELIMITED FIELDS TERMINATED BY '\t'
    > AS SELECT * FROM a;
Moving data to: file:/user/hive/warehouse/intermediate_comp_on
Table default.intermediate_comp_on stats: [num_partitions: 0, num_files: 1,
num_rows: 2, total_size: 8, raw_data_size: 6]
...
```

As expected, intermediate compression did not affect the final output, which remains uncompressed:

```
hive> dfs -ls /user/hive/warehouse/intermediate_comp_on;
Found 1 items
```

```
/user/hive/warehouse/intermediate_comp_on/000000_0

hive> dfs -cat /user/hive/warehouse/intermediate_comp_on/000000_0;
4     5
3     2
```

We can also chose an intermediate compression codec other then the default codec. In
this case we chose GZIP, although Snappy is normally a better option. The first line is
wrapped for space:

```
hive> set mapred.map.output.compression.codec
    =org.apache.hadoop.io.compress.GZipCodec;
hive> set hive.exec.compress.intermediate=true;

hive> CREATE TABLE intermediate_comp_on_gz
    > ROW FORMAT DELIMITED FIELDS TERMINATED BY '\t'
    > AS SELECT * FROM a;
Moving data to: file:/user/hive/warehouse/intermediate_comp_on_gz
Table default.intermediate_comp_on_gz stats:
[num_partitions: 0, num_files: 1, num_rows: 2, total_size: 8, raw_data_size: 6]

hive> dfs -cat /user/hive/warehouse/intermediate_comp_on_gz/000000_0;
4     5
3     2
```

Next, we can enable output compression:

```
hive> set hive.exec.compress.output=true;

hive> CREATE TABLE final_comp_on
    > ROW FORMAT DELIMITED FIELDS TERMINATED BY '\t'
    > AS SELECT * FROM a;
Moving data to: file:/tmp/hive-edward/hive_2012-01-15_11-11-01_884_.../-ext-10001
Moving data to: file:/user/hive/warehouse/final_comp_on
Table default.final_comp_on stats:
[num_partitions: 0, num_files: 1, num_rows: 2, total_size: 16, raw_data_size: 6]

hive> dfs -ls /user/hive/warehouse/final_comp_on;
Found 1 items
/user/hive/warehouse/final_comp_on/000000_0.deflate
```

The output table statistics show that the total_size is 16, but the raw_data_size is 6.
The extra space is overhead for the deflate algorithm. We can also see the output file
is named *.deflate*.

Trying to cat the file is not suggested, as you get binary output. However, Hive can
query this data normally:

```
hive> dfs -cat /user/hive/warehouse/final_comp_on/000000_0.deflate;
... UGLYBINARYHERE ...

hive> SELECT * FROM final_comp_on;
4     5
3     2
```

This ability to seamlessly work with compressed files is not Hive-specific; Hadoop's TextInputFormat is at work here. While the name is confusing in this case, TextInput Format understands file extensions such as *.deflate* or *.gz* and decompresses these files on the fly. Hive is unaware if the underlying files are uncompressed or compressed using any of the supported compression schemes.

Let's change the codec used by output compression to see the results (another line wrap for space):

```
hive> set hive.exec.compress.output=true;
hive> set mapred.output.compression.codec
  =org.apache.hadoop.io.compress.GzipCodec;

hive> CREATE TABLE final_comp_on_gz
    > ROW FORMAT DELIMITED FIELDS TERMINATED BY '\t'
    > AS SELECT * FROM a;
Moving data to: file:/user/hive/warehouse/final_comp_on_gz
Table default.final_comp_on_gz stats:
[num_partitions: 0, num_files: 1, num_rows: 2, total_size: 28, raw_data_size: 6]

hive> dfs -ls /user/hive/warehouse/final_comp_on_gz;
Found 1 items
/user/hive/warehouse/final_comp_on_gz/000000_0.gz
```

As you can see, the output folder now contains zero or more *.gz* files. Hive has a quick hack to execute local commands like zcat from inside the Hive shell. The ! tells Hive to fork and run the external command and block until the system returns a result. zcat is a command-line utility that decompresses and displays output:

```
hive> ! /bin/zcat /user/hive/warehouse/final_comp_on_gz/000000_0.gz;
4       5
3       2
hive> SELECT * FROM final_comp_on_gz;
OK
4       5
3       2
Time taken: 0.159 seconds
```

Using output compression like this results in binary compressed files that are small and, as a result, operations on them are very fast. However, recall that the number of output files is a side effect of how many mappers or reducers processed the data. In the worst case scenario, you can end up with one large binary file in a directory that is not splittable. This means that subsequent steps that have to read this data cannot work in parallel. The answer to this problem is to use sequence files:

```
hive> set mapred.output.compression.type=BLOCK;
hive> set hive.exec.compress.output=true;
hive> set mapred.output.compression.codec=org.apache.hadoop.io.compress.GzipCodec;

hive> CREATE TABLE final_comp_on_gz_seq
    > ROW FORMAT DELIMITED FIELDS TERMINATED BY '\t'
    > STORED AS SEQUENCEFILE
    > AS SELECT * FROM a;
```

```
Moving data to: file:/user/hive/warehouse/final_comp_on_gz_seq
Table default.final_comp_on_gz_seq stats:
[num_partitions: 0, num_files: 1, num_rows: 2, total_size: 199, raw_data_size: 6]

hive> dfs -ls /user/hive/warehouse/final_comp_on_gz_seq;
Found 1 items
/user/hive/warehouse/final_comp_on_gz_seq/000000_0
```

Sequence files are binary. But it is a nice exercise to see the header. To confirm the results are what was intended (output wrapped):

```
hive> dfs -cat /user/hive/warehouse/final_comp_on_gz_seq/000000_0;
SEQ[]org.apache.hadoop.io.BytesWritable[]org.apache.hadoop.io.BytesWritable[]
  org.apache.hadoop.io.compress.GzipCodec[]
```

Because of the meta-information embedded in the sequence file and in the Hive metastore, Hive can query the table without any specific settings. Hadoop also offers the dfs -text command to strip the header and compression away from sequence files and return the raw result:

```
hive> dfs -text /user/hive/warehouse/final_comp_on_gz_seq/000000_0;
        4       5
        3       2
hive> select * from final_comp_on_gz_seq;
OK
4       5
3       2
```

Finally, let's use intermediate and output compression at the same time and set different compression codecs for each while saving the final output to sequence files! These settings are commonly done for production environments where data sets are large and such settings improve performance:

```
hive> set mapred.map.output.compression.codec
  =org.apache.hadoop.io.compress.SnappyCodec;
hive> set hive.exec.compress.intermediate=true;
hive> set mapred.output.compression.type=BLOCK;
hive> set hive.exec.compress.output=true;
hive> set mapred.output.compression.codec
  =org.apache.hadoop.io.compress.GzipCodec;

hive> CREATE TABLE final_comp_on_gz_int_compress_snappy_seq
    > ROW FORMAT DELIMITED FIELDS TERMINATED BY '\t'
    > STORED AS SEQUENCEFILE AS SELECT * FROM a;
```

Archive Partition

Hadoop has a format for storage known as HAR, which stands for *Hadoop ARchive*. A HAR file is like a TAR file that lives in the HDFS filesystem as a single file. However, internally it can contain multiple files and directories. In some use cases, older directories and files are less commonly accessed than newer files. If a particular partition contains thousands of files it will require significant overhead to manage it in the HDFS

NameNode. By archiving the partition it is stored as a single, large file, but it can still be accessed by hive. The trade-off is that HAR files will be less efficient to query. Also, HAR files are not compressed, so they don't save any space.

In the following example, we'll use Hive's own documentation as data.

First, create a partitioned table and load it with the text data from the Hive package:

```
hive> CREATE TABLE hive_text (line STRING) PARTITIONED BY (folder STRING);

hive> ! ls $HIVE_HOME;
LICENSE
README.txt
RELEASE_NOTES.txt

hive> ALTER TABLE hive_text ADD PARTITION (folder='docs');

hive> LOAD DATA INPATH '${env:HIVE_HOME}/README.txt'
    > INTO TABLE hive_text PARTITION (folder='docs');
Loading data to table default.hive_text partition (folder=docs)

hive> LOAD DATA INPATH '${env:HIVE_HOME}/RELEASE_NOTES.txt'
    > INTO TABLE hive_text PARTITION (folder='docs');
Loading data to table default.hive_text partition (folder=docs)

hive> SELECT * FROM hive_text WHERE line LIKE '%hive%' LIMIT 2;
  http://hive.apache.org/        docs
- Hive 0.8.0 ignores the hive-default.xml file, though we continue        docs
```

Some versions of Hadoop, such as Hadoop v0.20.2, will require the JAR containing the Hadoop archive tools to be placed on the Hive *auxlib*:

```
$ mkdir $HIVE_HOME/auxlib
$ cp $HADOOP_HOME/hadoop-0.20.2-tools.jar $HIVE_HOME/auxlib/
```

Take a look at the underlying structure of the table, before we archive it. Note the location of the table's data partition, since it's a managed, partitioned table:

```
hive> dfs -ls /user/hive/warehouse/hive_text/folder=docs;
Found 2 items
/user/hive/warehouse/hive_text/folder=docs/README.txt
/user/hive/warehouse/hive_text/folder=docs/RELEASE_NOTES.txt
```

The ALTER TABLE ... ARCHIVE PARTITION statement converts the table into an archived table:

```
hive> SET hive.archive.enabled=true;
hive> ALTER TABLE hive_text ARCHIVE PARTITION (folder='docs');
intermediate.archived is
 file:/user/hive/warehouse/hive_text/folder=docs_INTERMEDIATE_ARCHIVED
intermediate.original is
 file:/user/hive/warehouse/hive_text/folder=docs_INTERMEDIATE_ORIGINAL
Creating data.har for file:/user/hive/warehouse/hive_text/folder=docs
in file:/tmp/hive-edward/hive_..._3862901820512961909/-ext-10000/partlevel
Please wait... (this may take a while)
Moving file:/tmp/hive-edward/hive_..._3862901820512961909/-ext-10000/partlevel
```

```
to file:/user/hive/warehouse/hive_text/folder=docs_INTERMEDIATE_ARCHIVED
Moving file:/user/hive/warehouse/hive_text/folder=docs
to file:/user/hive/warehouse/hive_text/folder=docs_INTERMEDIATE_ORIGINAL
Moving file:/user/hive/warehouse/hive_text/folder=docs_INTERMEDIATE_ARCHIVED
to file:/user/hive/warehouse/hive_text/folder=docs
```

(We reformatted the output slightly so it would fit, and used ... to replace two time-stamp strings in the original output.)

The underlying table has gone from two files to one Hadoop archive (HAR file):

```
hive> dfs -ls /user/hive/warehouse/hive_text/folder=docs;
Found 1 items
/user/hive/warehouse/hive_text/folder=docs/data.har
```

The ALTER TABLE ... UNARCHIVE PARTITION command extracts the files from the HAR and puts them back into HDFS:

```
ALTER TABLE hive_text UNARCHIVE PARTITION (folder='docs');
```

Compression: Wrapping Up

Hive's ability to read and write different types of compressed files is a big performance win as it saves disk space and processing overhead. This flexibility also aids in integration with other tools, as Hive can query many native file types without the need to write custom "adapters" in Java.

CHAPTER 12

Developing

Hive won't provide everything you could possibly need. Sometimes a third-party library will fill a gap. At other times, you or someone else who is a Java developer will need to write *user-defined functions* (UDFs; see Chapter 13), *SerDes* (see "Record Formats: SerDes" on page 205), input and/or output formats (see Chapter 15), or other enhancements.

This chapter explores working with the Hive source code itself, including the new *Plugin Developer Kit* introduced in Hive v0.8.0.

Changing Log4J Properties

Hive can be configured with two separate Log4J configuration files found in *$HIVE_HOME/conf*. The *hive-log4j.properties* file controls the logging of the CLI or other locally launched components. The *hive-exec-log4j.properties* file controls the logging inside the MapReduce tasks. These files do not need to be present inside the Hive installation because the default properties come built inside the Hive JARs. In fact, the actual files in the *conf* directory have the *.template* extension, so they are ignored by default. To use either of them, copy it with a name that removes the *.template* extension and edit it to taste:

```
$ cp conf/hive-log4j.properties.template conf/hive-log4j.properties
$ ... edit file ...
```

It is also possible to change the logging configuration of Hive temporarily without copying and editing the Log4J files. The hiveconf switch can be specified on start-up with definitions of any properties in the *log4.properties* file. For example, here we set the default logger to the DEBUG level and send output to the console appender:

```
$ bin/hive -hiveconf hive.root.logger=DEBUG,console
12/03/27 08:46:01 WARN conf.HiveConf: hive-site.xml not found on CLASSPATH
12/03/27 08:46:01 DEBUG conf.Configuration: java.io.IOException: config()
```

Connecting a Java Debugger to Hive

When enabling more verbose output does not help find the solution to the problem you are troubleshooting, attaching a Java debugger will give you the ability to step through the Hive code and hopefully find the problem.

Remote debugging is a feature of Java that is manually enabled by setting specific command-line properties for the JVM. The Hive shell script provides a switch and help screen that makes it easy to set these properties (some output truncated for space):

```
$ bin/hive --help --debug
Allows to debug Hive by connecting to it via JDI API
Usage: hive --debug[:comma-separated parameters list]

Parameters:

recursive=<y|n>      Should child JVMs also be started in debug mode. Default: y
port=<port_number>   Port on which main JVM listens for debug connection. Defaul...
mainSuspend=<y|n>    Should main JVM wait with execution for the debugger to con...
childSuspend=<y|n>   Should child JVMs wait with execution for the debugger to c...
swapSuspend          Swaps suspend options between main and child JVMs
```

Building Hive from Source

Running Apache releases is usually a good idea, however you may wish to use features that are not part of a release, or have an internal branch with nonpublic customizations.

Hence, you'll need to build Hive from source. The minimum requirements for building Hive are a recent Java JDK, Subversion, and ANT. Hive also contains components such as Thrift-generated classes that are not built by default. Rebuilding Hive requires a Thrift compiler, too.

The following commands check out a Hive release and builds it, produces output in the *hive-trunk/build/dist* directory:

```
$ svn co http://svn.apache.org/repos/asf/hive/trunk hive-trunk
$ cd hive-trunk
$ ant package

$ ls build/dist/
bin   examples  LICENSE  README.txt        scripts
conf  lib       NOTICE   RELEASE_NOTES.txt
```

Running Hive Test Cases

Hive has a unique built-in infrastructure for testing. Hive does have traditional *JUnit* tests, however the majority of the testing happens by running queries saved in *.q* files, then comparing the results with a previous run saved in Hive source.[1] There are multiple

---

1. That is, they are more like *feature* or *acceptance* tests.

---

directories inside the Hive source folder. "Positive" tests are those that should pass, while "negative" tests should fail.

An example of a positive test is a well-formed query. An example of a negative test is a query that is malformed or tries doing something that is not allowed by HiveQL:

```
$ ls -lah ql/src/test/queries/
total 76K
drwxrwxr-x. 7 edward edward 4.0K May 28  2011 .
drwxrwxr-x. 8 edward edward 4.0K May 28  2011 ..
drwxrwxr-x. 3 edward edward  20K Feb 21 20:08 clientnegative
drwxrwxr-x. 3 edward edward  36K Mar  8 09:17 clientpositive
drwxrwxr-x. 3 edward edward 4.0K May 28  2011 negative
drwxrwxr-x. 3 edward edward 4.0K Mar 12 09:25 positive
```

Take a look at *ql/src/test/queries/clientpositive/cast1.q*. The first thing you should know is that a src table is the first table automatically created in the test process. It is a table with two columns, key and value, where key is an INT and value is a STRING. Because Hive does not currently have the ability to do a SELECT without a FROM clause, selecting a single row from the src table is the trick used to test out functions that don't really need to retrieve table data; inputs can be "hard-coded" instead.

As you can see in the following example queries, the src table is never referenced in the SELECT clauses:

```
hive> CREATE TABLE dest1(c1 INT, c2 DOUBLE, c3 DOUBLE,
    > c4 DOUBLE, c5 INT, c6 STRING, c7 INT) STORED AS TEXTFILE;

hive> EXPLAIN
    > FROM src INSERT OVERWRITE TABLE dest1
    > SELECT 3 + 2, 3.0 + 2, 3 + 2.0, 3.0 + 2.0,
    > 3 + CAST(2.0 AS INT) + CAST(CAST(0 AS SMALLINT) AS INT),
    > CAST(1 AS BOOLEAN), CAST(TRUE AS INT) WHERE src.key = 86;

hive> FROM src INSERT OVERWRITE TABLE dest1
    > SELECT 3 + 2, 3.0 + 2, 3 + 2.0, 3.0 + 2.0,
    > 3 + CAST(2.0 AS INT) + CAST(CAST(0 AS SMALLINT) AS INT),
    > CAST(1 AS BOOLEAN), CAST(TRUE AS INT) WHERE src.key = 86;

hive> SELECT dest1.* FROM dest1;
```

The results of the script are found here: *ql/src/test/results/clientpositive/cast1.q.out*. The result file is large and printing the complete results inline will kill too many trees. However, portions of the file are worth noting.

This command invokes a positive and a negative test case for the Hive client:

```
ant test -Dtestcase=TestCliDriver -Dqfile=mapreduce1.q
ant test -Dtestcase=TestNegativeCliDriver -Dqfile=script_broken_pipe1.q
```

The two particular tests only parse queries. They do not actually run the client. They are now deprecated in favor of clientpositive and clientnegative.

You can also run multiple tests in one ant invocation to save time (the last `-Dqfile=…` string was wrapped for space; it's all one string):

```
ant test -Dtestcase=TestCliDriver -Dqfile=avro_change_schema.q,avro_joins.q,
avro_schema_error_message.q,avro_evolved_schemas.q,avro_sanity_test.q,
avro_schema_literal.q
```

Execution Hooks

PreHooks and *PostHooks* are utilities that allow user code to hook into parts of Hive and execute custom code. Hive's testing framework uses hooks to echo commands that produce no output, so that the results show up inside tests:

```
PREHOOK: query: CREATE TABLE dest1(c1 INT, c2 DOUBLE, c3 DOUBLE,
c4 DOUBLE, c5 INT, c6 STRING, c7 INT) STORED AS TEXTFILE
PREHOOK: type: CREATETABLE
POSTHOOK: query: CREATE TABLE dest1(c1 INT, c2 DOUBLE, c3 DOUBLE,
c4 DOUBLE, c5 INT, c6 STRING, c7 INT) STORED AS TEXTFILE
```

Setting Up Hive and Eclipse

Eclipse (http://www.eclipse.org/) is an open source IDE (Integrated Development Environment). The following steps allow you to use Eclipse to work with the Hive source code:

```
$ ant clean package eclipse-files
$ cd metastore
$ ant model-jar
$ cd ../ql
$ ant gen-test
```

Once built, you can import the project into Eclipse and use it as you normally would.

Create a workspace in Eclipse, as normal. Then use the File → Import command and then select General → Existing Projects into Workspace. Select the directory where Hive is installed.

When the list of available projects is shown in the wizard, you'll see one named *hive-trunk*, which you should select and click Finish.

Figure 12-1 shows how to start the *Hive Command CLI Driver* from within Eclipse.

Hive in a Maven Project

You can set up Hive as a dependency in Maven builds. The Maven repository *http://mvnrepository.com/artifact/org.apache.hive/hive-service* contains the most recent releases. This page also lists the dependencies `hive-service` requires.

Here is the top-level dependency definition for Hive v0.9.0, not including the tree of transitive dependencies, which is quite deep:

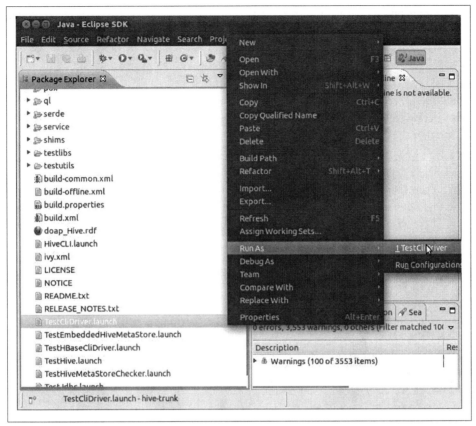

Figure 12-1. Starting the Hive Command CLI Driver from within Eclipse

```xml
<dependency>
  <groupId>org.apache.hive</groupId>
  <artifactId>hive-service</artifactId>
  <version>0.9.0</version>
</dependency>
```

The *pom.xml* file for hive_test, which we discuss next, provides a complete example of the transitive dependencies for Hive v0.9.0. You can find that file at *https://github .com/edwardcapriolo/hive_test/blob/master/pom.xml*.

Unit Testing in Hive with hive_test

The optimal way to write applications to work with Hive is to access Hive with Thrift through the HiveService. However, the Thrift service was traditionally difficult to bring up in an embedded environment due to Hive's many JAR dependencies and the metastore component.

Hive_test fetches all the Hive dependencies from *Maven*, sets up the metastore and Thrift service locally, and provides test classes to make unit testing easier. Also, because it is very lightweight and unit tests run quickly, this is in contrast to the elaborate test targets inside Hive, which have to rebuild the entire project to execute any unit test.

Hive_test is ideal for testing code such as UDFs, input formats, SerDes, or any component that only adds a pluggable feature for the language. It is not useful for internal Hive development because all the Hive components are pulled from Maven and are external to the project.

In your Maven project, create a *pom.xml* and include hive_test as a dependency, as shown here:

```
<dependency>
  <groupId>com.jointhegrid</groupId>
  <artifactId>hive_test</artifactId>
  <version>3.0.1-SNAPSHOT</version>
</dependency>
```

Then create a version of *hive-site.xml*:

```
$ cp $HIVE_HOME/conf/* src/test/resources/
$ vi src/test/resources/hive-site.xml
```

Unlike a normal *hive-site.xml*, this version should not save any data to a permanent place. This is because unit tests are not supposed to create or preserve any permanent state. javax.jdo.option.ConnectionURL is set to use a feature in *Derby* that only stores the database in main memory. The warehouse directory hive .metastore.warehouse.dir is set to a location inside */tmp* that will be deleted on each run of the unit test:

```
<configuration>

  <property>
    <name>javax.jdo.option.ConnectionURL</name>
    <value>jdbc:derby:memory:metastore_db;create=true</value>
    <description>JDBC connect string for a JDBC metastore</description>
  </property>

  <property>
    <name>hive.metastore.warehouse.dir</name>
    <value>/tmp/warehouse</value>
    <description>location of default database for the warehouse</description>
  </property>

</configuration>
```

Hive_test provides several classes that extend JUnit test cases. HiveTestService set up the environment, cleared out the warehouse directory, and launched a metastore and HiveService in-process. This is typically the component to extend for testing. However, other components, such as HiveTestEmbedded are also available:

```
package com.jointhegrid.hive_test;
```

```
import java.io.BufferedWriter;
import java.io.IOException;
import java.io.OutputStreamWriter;

import org.apache.hadoop.fs.FSDataOutputStream;
import org.apache.hadoop.fs.Path;

/* Extending HiveTestService creates and initializes
the metastore and thrift service in an embedded mode */
public class ServiceHiveTest extends HiveTestService {

  public ServiceHiveTest() throws IOException {
    super();
  }

  public void testExecute() throws Exception {

    /* Use the Hadoop filesystem API to create a
    data file */
    Path p = new Path(this.ROOT_DIR, "afile");
    FSDataOutputStream o = this.getFileSystem().create(p);
    BufferedWriter bw = new BufferedWriter(new OutputStreamWriter(o));
    bw.write("1\n");
    bw.write("2\n");
    bw.close();

    /* ServiceHive is a component that connections
    to an embedded or network HiveService based
    on the constructor used */
    ServiceHive sh = new ServiceHive();

    /* We can now interact through the HiveService
    and assert on results */
    sh.client.execute("create table atest (num int)");
    sh.client.execute("load data local inpath '"
      + p.toString() + "' into table atest");
    sh.client.execute("select count(1) as cnt from atest");
    String row = sh.client.fetchOne();
    assertEquals("2", row);
    sh.client.execute("drop table atest");

  }
}
```

The New Plugin Developer Kit

Hive v0.8.0 introduced a *Plugin Developer Kit* (PDK). Its intent is to allow developers to build and test plug-ins without the Hive source. Only Hive binary code is required.

The PDK is relatively new and has some subtle bugs of its own that can make it difficult to use. If you want to try using the PDK anyway, consult the wiki page, *https://cwiki .apache.org/Hive/plugindeveloperkit.html*, but note that this page has a few errors, at least at the time of this writing.

CHAPTER 13

Functions

User-Defined Functions (UDFs) are a powerful feature that allow users to extend HiveQL. As we'll see, you implement them in Java and once you add them to your session (interactive or driven by a script), they work just like built-in functions, even the online help. Hive has several types of user-defined functions, each of which performs a particular "class" of transformations on input data.

In an ETL workload, a process might have several processing steps. The Hive language has multiple ways to pipeline the output from one step to the next and produce multiple outputs during a single query. Users also have the ability to create their own functions for custom processing. Without this feature a process might have to include a custom MapReduce step or move the data into another system to apply the changes. Interconnecting systems add complexity and increase the chance of misconfigurations or other errors. Moving data between systems is time consuming when dealing with gigabyte- or terabyte-sized data sets. In contrast, UDFs run in the same processes as the tasks for your Hive queries, so they work efficiently and eliminate the complexity of integration with other systems. This chapter covers best practices associated with creating and using UDFs.

Discovering and Describing Functions

Before writing custom UDFs, let's familiarize ourselves with the ones that are already part of Hive. Note that it's common in the Hive community to use "UDF" to refer to any function, user-defined or built-in.

The SHOW FUNCTIONS command lists the functions currently loaded in the Hive session, both built-in and any user-defined functions that have been loaded using the techniques we will discuss shortly:

```
hive> SHOW FUNCTIONS;
abs
acos
and
array
```

```
array_contains
...
```

Functions usually have their own documentation. Use `DESCRIBE FUNCTION` to display a short description:

```
hive> DESCRIBE FUNCTION concat;
concat(str1, str2, ... strN) - returns the concatenation of str1, str2, ... strN
```

Functions may also contain extended documentation that can be accessed by adding the `EXTENDED` keyword:

```
hive> DESCRIBE FUNCTION EXTENDED concat;
concat(str1, str2, ... strN) - returns the concatenation of str1, str2, ... strN
Returns NULL if any argument is NULL.
Example:
  > SELECT concat('abc', 'def') FROM src LIMIT 1;
  'abcdef'
```

Calling Functions

To use a function, simply call it by name in a query, passing in any required arguments. Some functions take a specific number of arguments and argument types, while other functions accept a variable number of arguments with variable types. Just like keywords, the case of function names is ignored:

```
SELECT concat(column1,column2) AS x FROM table;
```

Standard Functions

The term *user-defined function* (UDF) is also used in a narrower sense to refer to any function that takes a row argument or one or more columns from a row and returns a single value. Most functions fall into this category.

Examples include many of the mathematical functions, like `round()` and `floor()`, for converting `DOUBLES` to `BIGINTS`, and `abs()`, for taking the absolute value of a number.

Other examples include string manipulation functions, like `ucase()`, which converts the string to upper case; `reverse()`, which reverses a string; and `concat()`, which joins multiple input strings into one output string.

Note that these UDFs can return a complex object, such as an array, map, or struct.

Aggregate Functions

Another type of function is an aggregate function. All aggregate functions, user-defined and built-in, are referred to generically as *user-defined aggregate functions* (UDAFs).

An aggregate function takes one or more columns from zero to many rows and returns a single result. Examples include the math functions: `sum()`, which returns a sum of all inputs; `avg()`, which computes the average of the values; `min()` and `max()`, which return the lowest and highest values, respectively:

```
hive> SELECT avg(price_close)
    > FROM stocks
    > WHERE exchange = 'NASDAQ' AND symbol = 'AAPL';
```

Aggregate methods are often combined with `GROUP BY` clauses. We saw this example in "GROUP BY Clauses" on page 97:

```
hive> SELECT year(ymd), avg(price_close) FROM stocks
    > WHERE exchange = 'NASDAQ' AND symbol = 'AAPL'
    > GROUP BY year(ymd);
1984    25.578625440597534
1985    20.193676221040867
1986    32.46102808021274
...
```

Table 6-3 in Chapter 6 lists the built-in aggregate functions in HiveQL.

Table Generating Functions

A third type of function supported by Hive is a *table generating function*. As for the other function kinds, all table generating functions, user-defined and built-in, are often referred to generically as *user-defined table generating functions* (UDTFs).

Table generating functions take zero or more inputs and produce multiple columns or rows of output. The `array` function takes a list of arguments and returns the list as a single `array` type. Suppose we start with this query using an `array`:

```
hive> SELECT array(1,2,3) FROM dual;
[1,2,3]
```

The `explode()` function is a UDTF that takes an `array` of input and iterates through the list, returning each element from the list in a separate row.

```
hive> SELECT explode(array(1,2,3)) AS element FROM src;
1
2
3
```

However, Hive only allows table generating functions to be used in limited ways. For example, we can't project out any other columns from the table, a significant limitation. Here is a query we would like to write with the `employees` table we have used before. We want to list each manager-subordinate pair.

Example 13-1. Invalid use of explode

```
hive> SELECT name, explode(subordinates) FROM employees;
FAILED: Error in semantic analysis: UDTF's are not supported outside
the SELECT clause, nor nested in expressions
```

However, Hive offers a `LATERAL VIEW` feature to allow this kind of query:

```
hive> SELECT name, sub
    > FROM employees
    > LATERAL VIEW explode(subordinates) subView AS sub;
John Doe        Mary Smith
John Doe        Todd Jones
Mary Smith      Bill King
```

Note that there are no output rows for employees who aren't managers (i.e., who have no subordinates), namely `Bill King` and `Todd Jones`. Hence, `explode` outputs zero to many new records.

The `LATERAL VIEW` wraps the output of the `explode` call. A view alias and column alias are required, `subView` and `sub`, respectively, in this case.

The list of built-in, table generating functions can be found in Table 6-4 in Chapter 6.

A UDF for Finding a Zodiac Sign from a Day

Let's tackle writing our own UDF. Imagine we have a table with each user's birth date stored as a column of a table. With that information, we would like to determine the user's Zodiac sign. This process can be implemented with a standard function (UDF in the most restrictive sense). Specifically, we assume we have a discrete input either as a date formatted as a string or as a month and a day. The function must return a discrete single column of output.

Here is a sample data set, which we'll put in a file called *littlebigdata.txt* in our home directory:

```
edward capriolo,edward@media6degrees.com,2-12-1981,209.191.139.200,M,10
bob,bob@test.net,10-10-2004,10.10.10.1,M,50
sara connor,sara@sky.net,4-5-1974,64.64.5.1,F,2
```

Load this data set into a table called `littlebigdata`:

```
hive > CREATE TABLE IF NOT EXISTS littlebigdata(
    >   name    STRING,
    >   email   STRING,
    >   bday    STRING,
    >   ip      STRING,
    >   gender  STRING,
    >   anum    INT)
    > ROW FORMAT DELIMITED FIELDS TERMINATED BY ',';

hive> LOAD DATA LOCAL INPATH '${env:HOME}/littlebigdata.txt'
    > INTO TABLE littlebigdata;
```

The input for the function will be a date and the output will be a string representing the user's Zodiac sign.

Here is a Java implementation of the UDF we need:

```
package org.apache.hadoop.hive.contrib.udf.example;

import java.util.Date;
```

```
import java.text.SimpleDateFormat;
import org.apache.hadoop.hive.ql.exec.UDF;

@Description(name = "zodiac",
    value = "_FUNC_(date) - from the input date string "+
            "or separate month and day arguments, returns the sign of the Zodiac.",
    extended = "Example:\n"
            + " > SELECT _FUNC_(date_string) FROM src;\n"
            + " > SELECT _FUNC_(month, day) FROM src;")

public class UDFZodiacSign extends UDF{

  private SimpleDateFormat df;

  public UDFZodiacSign(){
    df = new SimpleDateFormat("MM-dd-yyyy");
  }

  public String evaluate( Date bday ){
    return this.evaluate( bday.getMonth(), bday.getDay() );
  }

  public String evaluate(String bday){
    Date date = null;
    try {
      date = df.parse(bday);
    } catch (Exception ex) {
      return null;
    }
    return this.evaluate( date.getMonth()+1, date.getDay() );
  }

  public String evaluate( Integer month, Integer day ){
    if (month==1) {
      if (day < 20 ){
        return "Capricorn";
      } else {
        return "Aquarius";
      }
    }
    if (month==2){
      if (day < 19 ){
        return "Aquarius";
      } else {
        return "Pisces";
      }
    }
    /* ...other months here */
    return null;
  }
}
```

To write a UDF, start by extending the UDF class and implements and the **evaluate()**
function. During query processing, an instance of the class is instantiated for each usage
of the function in a query. The **evaluate()** is called for each input row. The result of

`evaluate()` is returned to Hive. It is legal to overload the evaluate method. Hive will pick the method that matches in a similar way to Java method overloading.

The `@Description(...)` is an optional Java *annotation*. This is how function documentation is defined and you should use these annotations to document your own UDFs. When a user invokes `DESCRIBE FUNCTION ...`, the `_FUNC_` strings will be replaced with the function name the user picks when defining a "temporary" function, as discussed below.

 The arguments and return types of the UDF's `evaluate()` function can only be types that Hive can serialize. For example, if you are working with whole numbers, a UDF can take as input a primitive `int`, an `Integer` wrapper object, or an `IntWritable`, which is the Hadoop wrapper for integers. You do not have to worry specifically about what the caller is sending because Hive will convert the types for you if they do not match. Remember that `null` is valid for any type in Hive, but in Java primitives are not objects and cannot be `null`.

To use the UDF inside Hive, compile the Java code and package the UDF bytecode class file into a JAR file. Then, in your Hive session, add the JAR to the classpath and use a `CREATE FUNCTION` statement to define a function that uses the Java class:

```
hive> ADD JAR /full/path/to/zodiac.jar;
hive> CREATE TEMPORARY FUNCTION zodiac
    > AS 'org.apache.hadoop.hive.contrib.udf.example.UDFZodiacSign';
```

Note that quotes are not required around the JAR file path and currently it needs to be a full path to the file on a *local* filesystem. Hive not only adds this JAR to the classpath, it puts the JAR file in the distributed cache so it's available around the cluster.

Now the Zodiac UDF can be used like any other function. Notice the word `TEMPORARY` found inside the `CREATE FUNCTION` statement. Functions declared will only be available in the current session. You will have to add the JAR and create the function in each session. However, if you use the same JAR files and functions frequently, you can add these statements to your *$HOME/.hiverc* file:

```
hive> DESCRIBE FUNCTION zodiac;
zodiac(date) - from the input date string or separate month and day
arguments, returns the sign of the Zodiac.

hive> DESCRIBE FUNCTION EXTENDED zodiac;
zodiac(date) - from the input date string or separate month and day
arguments, returns the sign of the Zodiac.
Example:
  > SELECT zodiac(date_string) FROM src;
  > SELECT zodiac(month, day) FROM src;

hive> SELECT name, bday, zodiac(bday) FROM littlebigdata;
edward capriolo   2-12-1981  Aquarius
```

```
bob          10-10-2004 Libra
sara connor   4-5-1974  Aries
```

To recap, our UDF allows us to do custom transformations inside the Hive language. Hive can now convert the user's birthday to the corresponding Zodiac sign while it is doing any other aggregations and transformations.

If we're finished with the function, we can drop it:

```
hive> DROP TEMPORARY FUNCTION IF EXISTS zodiac;
```

As usual, the IF EXISTS is optional. It suppresses errors if the function doesn't exist.

UDF Versus GenericUDF

In our Zodiac example we extended the UDF class. Hive offers a counterpart called GenericUDF. GenericUDF is a more complex abstraction, but it offers support for better null handling and makes it possible to handle some types of operations programmatically that a standard UDF cannot support. An example of a generic UDF is the Hive CASE ... WHEN statement, which has complex logic depending on the arguments to the statement. We will demonstrate how to use the GenericUDF class to write a user-defined function, called nvl(), which returns a default value if null is passed in.

The nvl() function takes two arguments. If the first argument is non-null, it is returned. If the first argument is null, the second argument is returned. The GenericUDF framework is a good fit for this problem. A standard UDF could be used as a solution but it would be cumbersome because it requires overloading the evaluate method to handle many different input types. GenericUDF will detect the type of input to the function programmatically and provide an appropriate response.

We begin with the usual laundry list of import statements:

```
package org.apache.hadoop.hive.ql.udf.generic;

import org.apache.hadoop.hive.ql.exec.Description;
import org.apache.hadoop.hive.ql.exec.UDFArgumentException;
import org.apache.hadoop.hive.ql.exec.UDFArgumentLengthException;
import org.apache.hadoop.hive.ql.exec.UDFArgumentTypeException;
import org.apache.hadoop.hive.ql.metadata.HiveException;
import org.apache.hadoop.hive.ql.udf.generic.GenericUDF;
import org.apache.hadoop.hive.ql.udf.generic.GenericUDFUtils;
import org.apache.hadoop.hive.serde2.objectinspector.ObjectInspector;
```

Next, we use the @Description annotation to document the UDF:

```
@Description(name = "nvl",
value = "_FUNC_(value,default_value) - Returns default value if value"
  +" is null else returns value",
extended = "Example:\n"
+ "  > SELECT _FUNC_(null,'bla') FROM src LIMIT 1;\n")
```

Now the class extends GenericUDF, a requirement to exploit the generic handling we want.

The initialize() method is called and passed an ObjectInspector for each argument. The goal of this method is to determine the return type from the arguments. The user can also throw an Exception to signal that bad types are being sent to the method. The returnOIResolver is a built-in class that determines the return type by finding the type of non-null variables and using that type:

```
public class GenericUDFNvl extends GenericUDF {
  private GenericUDFUtils.ReturnObjectInspectorResolver returnOIResolver;
  private ObjectInspector[] argumentOIs;

  @Override
  public ObjectInspector initialize(ObjectInspector[] arguments)
      throws UDFArgumentException {
    argumentOIs = arguments;
    if (arguments.length != 2) {
      throw new UDFArgumentLengthException(
          "The operator 'NVL' accepts 2 arguments.");
    }
    returnOIResolver = new GenericUDFUtils.ReturnObjectInspectorResolver(true);
    if (!(returnOIResolver.update(arguments[0]) && returnOIResolver
        .update(arguments[1]))) {
      throw new UDFArgumentTypeException(2,
          "The 1st and 2nd args of function NLV should have the same type, "
          + "but they are different: \"" + arguments[0].getTypeName()
          + "\" and \"" + arguments[1].getTypeName() + "\"");
    }
    return returnOIResolver.get();
  }
  ...
```

The evaluate method has access to the values passed to the method stored in an array of DeferredObject values. The returnOIResolver created in the initialize method is used to get values from the DeferredObjects. In this case, the function returns the first non-null value:

```
  ...
  @Override
  public Object evaluate(DeferredObject[] arguments) throws HiveException {
    Object retVal = returnOIResolver.convertIfNecessary(arguments[0].get(),
        argumentOIs[0]);
    if (retVal == null ){
      retVal = returnOIResolver.convertIfNecessary(arguments[1].get(),
          argumentOIs[1]);
    }
    return retVal;
  }
  ...
```

The final method to override is getDisplayString(), which is used inside the Hadoop tasks to display debugging information when the function is being used:

```
...
@Override
public String getDisplayString(String[] children) {
  StringBuilder sb = new StringBuilder();
  sb.append("if ");
  sb.append(children[0]);
  sb.append(" is null ");
  sb.append("returns");
  sb.append(children[1]);
  return sb.toString() ;
}
}
```

To test the generic nature of the UDF, it is called several times, each time passing values of different types, as shown the following example:

```
hive> ADD JAR /path/to/jar.jar;

hive> CREATE TEMPORARY FUNCTION nvl
    > AS 'org.apache.hadoop.hive.ql.udf.generic.GenericUDFNvl';

hive> SELECT nvl( 1 , 2 ) AS COL1,
    >        nvl( NULL, 5 ) AS COL2,
    >        nvl( NULL, "STUFF" ) AS COL3
    > FROM src LIMIT 1;
1       5       STUFF
```

Permanent Functions

Until this point we have bundled our code into JAR files, then used `ADD JAR` and `CREATE TEMPORARY FUNCTION` to make use of them.

Your function may also be added permanently to Hive, however this requires a small modification to a Hive Java file and then rebuilding Hive.

Inside the Hive source code, a one-line change is required to the `FunctionRegistry` class found at *ql/src/java/org/apache/hadoop/hive/ql/exec/FunctionRegistry.java*. Then you rebuild Hive following the instructions that come with the source distribution.

While it is recommended that you redeploy the entire new build, only the *hive-exec-*.jar*, where * is the version number, needs to be replaced.

Here is an example change to `FunctionRegistry` where the new `nvl()` function is added to Hive's list of built-in functions:

```
...
registerUDF("parse_url", UDFParseUrl.class, false);
registerGenericUDF("nvl", GenericUDFNvl.class);
registerGenericUDF("split", GenericUDFSplit.class);
...
```

User-Defined Aggregate Functions

Users are able to define aggregate functions, too. However, the interface is more complex to implement. Aggregate functions are processed in several phases. Depending on the transformation the UDAF performs, the types returned by each phase could be different. For example, a sum() UDAF could accept primitive integer input, create integer PARTIAL data, and produce a final integer result. However, an aggregate like median() could take primitive integer input, have an intermediate list of integers as PARTIAL data, and then produce a final integer as the result.

For an example of a generic user-defined *aggregate* function, see the source code for GenericUDAFAverage available at *http://svn.apache.org/repos/asf/hive/branches/branch-0.8/ql/src/java/org/apache/hadoop/hive/ql/udf/generic/GenericUDAFAverage.java*.

> Aggregations execute inside the context of a map or reduce task, which is a Java process with memory limitations. Therefore, storing large structures inside an aggregate may exceed available heap space. The min() UDAF only requires a single element be stored in memory for comparison. The collectset() UDAF uses a set internally to deduplicate data in order to limit memory usage. percentile_approx() uses approximations to achieve a near correct result while limiting memory usage. It is important to keep memory usage in mind when writing a UDAF. You can increase your available memory to some extent by adjusting mapred.child.java.opts, but that solution does not scale:
>
> ```
> <property>
>   <name>mapred.child.java.opts</name>
>   <value>-Xmx200m</value>
> </property>
> ```

Creating a COLLECT UDAF to Emulate GROUP_CONCAT

MySQL has a useful function known as GROUP_CONCAT (*http://dev.mysql.com/doc/refman/5.0/en/group-by-functions.html#function_group-concat*), which combines all the elements of a group into a single string using a user-specified delimiter. Below is an example MySQL query that shows how to use its version of this function:

```
mysql > CREATE TABLE people (
  name STRING,
  friendname STRING );

mysql > SELECT * FROM people;
bob      sara
bob      john
bob      ted
john     sara
ted      bob
ted      sara

mysql > SELECT name, GROUP_CONCAT(friendname SEPARATOR ',')
```

```
      FROM people
      GROUP BY name;
  bob      sara,john,ted
  john     sara
  ted      bob,sara
```

We can do the same transformation in Hive without the need for additional grammar in the language. First, we need an aggregate function that builds a list of all input to the aggregate. Hive already has a UDAF called `collect_set` that adds all input into a `java.util.Set` collection. Sets automatically de-duplicate entries on insertion, which is undesirable for `GROUP CONCAT`. To build `collect`, we will take the code in `col lect_set` and replace instances of `Set` with instances of `ArrayList`. This will stop the de-duplication. The result of the aggregate will be a single array of all values.

It is important to remember that the computation of your aggregation must be arbitrarily divisible over the data. Think of it as writing a divide-and-conquer algorithm where the partitioning of the data is completely out of your control and handled by Hive. More formally, given any subset of the input rows, you should be able to compute a partial result, and also be able to merge any pair of partial results into another partial result.

The following code is available on Github (*https://github.com/edwardcapriolo/hive-col lect*). All the input to the aggregation must be primitive types. Rather than returning an `ObjectInspector`, like `GenericUDFs`, aggregates return a subclass of `GenericUDAFEva luator`:

```
@Description(name = "collect", value = "_FUNC_(x) - Returns a list of objects. "+
"CAUTION will easily OOM on large data sets" )
public class GenericUDAFCollect extends AbstractGenericUDAFResolver {
  static final Log LOG = LogFactory.getLog(GenericUDAFCollect.class.getName());

  public GenericUDAFCollect() {
  }

  @Override
  public GenericUDAFEvaluator getEvaluator(TypeInfo[] parameters)
      throws SemanticException {
    if (parameters.length != 1) {
      throw new UDFArgumentTypeException(parameters.length - 1,
          "Exactly one argument is expected.");
    }
    if (parameters[0].getCategory() != ObjectInspector.Category.PRIMITIVE) {
      throw new UDFArgumentTypeException(0,
          "Only primitive type arguments are accepted but "
          + parameters[0].getTypeName() + " was passed as parameter 1.");
    }
    return new GenericUDAFMkListEvaluator();
  }
}
```

Table 13-1 describes the methods that are part of the base class.

Table 13-1. Methods in AbstractGenericUDAFResolver

Method	Description
init	Called by Hive to initialize an instance of the UDAF evaluator class.
getNewAggregationBuffer	Return an object that will be used to store temporary aggregation results.
iterate	Process a new row of data into the aggregation buffer.
terminatePartial	Return the contents of the current aggregation in a persistable way. Here, persistable means the return value can only be built up in terms of Java primitives, arrays, primitive wrappers (e.g., Double), Hadoop Writables, Lists, and Maps. Do NOT use your own classes (even if they implement java.io .Serializable).
merge	Merge a partial aggregation returned by terminatePartial into the current aggregation.
terminate	Return the final result of the aggregation to Hive.

In the init method, the object inspectors for the result type are set, after determining what mode the evaluator is in.

The iterate() and terminatePartial() methods are used on the map side, while ter minate() and merge() are used on the reduce side to produce the final result. In all cases the merges are building larger lists:

```
public static class GenericUDAFMkListEvaluator extends GenericUDAFEvaluator {
    private PrimitiveObjectInspector inputOI;
    private StandardListObjectInspector loi;
    private StandardListObjectInspector internalMergeOI;

    @Override
    public ObjectInspector init(Mode m, ObjectInspector[] parameters)
            throws HiveException {
        super.init(m, parameters);
        if (m == Mode.PARTIAL1) {
            inputOI = (PrimitiveObjectInspector) parameters[0];
            return ObjectInspectorFactory
                .getStandardListObjectInspector(
                    (PrimitiveObjectInspector) ObjectInspectorUtils
                .getStandardObjectInspector(inputOI));
        } else {
            if (!(parameters[0] instanceof StandardListObjectInspector)) {
                inputOI = (PrimitiveObjectInspector)  ObjectInspectorUtils
                    .getStandardObjectInspector(parameters[0]);
                return (StandardListObjectInspector) ObjectInspectorFactory
                    .getStandardListObjectInspector(inputOI);
            } else {
                internalMergeOI = (StandardListObjectInspector) parameters[0];
                inputOI = (PrimitiveObjectInspector)
                    internalMergeOI.getListElementObjectInspector();
```

```
        loi = (StandardListObjectInspector) ObjectInspectorUtils
              .getStandardObjectInspector(internalMergeOI);
      return loi;
    }
  }
}
...
```

The remaining methods and class definition define `MkArrayAggregationBuffer` as well as top-level methods that modify the contents of the buffer:

 You may have noticed that Hive tends to avoid allocating objects with new whenever possible. Hadoop and Hive use this pattern to create fewer temporary objects and thus less work for the JVM's `Garbage Collec` `tion` algorithms. Keep this in mind when writing UDFs, because references are typically reused. Assuming immutable objects will lead to bugs!

```
...
static class MkArrayAggregationBuffer implements AggregationBuffer {
  List<Object> container;
}

@Override
public void reset(AggregationBuffer agg) throws HiveException {
  ((MkArrayAggregationBuffer) agg).container =
    new ArrayList<Object>();
}

@Override
public AggregationBuffer getNewAggregationBuffer()
    throws HiveException {
  MkArrayAggregationBuffer ret = new MkArrayAggregationBuffer();
  reset(ret);
  return ret;
}

// Mapside
@Override
public void iterate(AggregationBuffer agg, Object[] parameters)
    throws HiveException {
  assert (parameters.length == 1);
  Object p = parameters[0];

  if (p != null) {
    MkArrayAggregationBuffer myagg = (MkArrayAggregationBuffer) agg;
    putIntoList(p, myagg);
  }
}

// Mapside
@Override
public Object terminatePartial(AggregationBuffer agg)
```

```
    throws HiveException {
  MkArrayAggregationBuffer myagg = (MkArrayAggregationBuffer) agg;
  ArrayList<Object> ret = new ArrayList<Object>(myagg.container.size());
  ret.addAll(myagg.container);
  return ret;
}

@Override
public void merge(AggregationBuffer agg, Object partial)
    throws HiveException {
  MkArrayAggregationBuffer myagg = (MkArrayAggregationBuffer) agg;
  ArrayList<Object> partialResult =
    (ArrayList<Object>) internalMergeOI.getList(partial);
  for(Object i : partialResult) {
    putIntoList(i, myagg);
  }
}

@Override
public Object terminate(AggregationBuffer agg) throws HiveException {
  MkArrayAggregationBuffer myagg = (MkArrayAggregationBuffer) agg;
  ArrayList<Object> ret = new ArrayList<Object>(myagg.container.size());
  ret.addAll(myagg.container);
  return ret;
}

private void putIntoList(Object p, MkArrayAggregationBuffer myagg) {
  Object pCopy =
    ObjectInspectorUtils.copyToStandardObject(p,this.inputOI);
  myagg.container.add(pCopy);
}
}
```

Using collect will return a single row with a single array of all of the aggregated values:

```
hive> dfs -cat $HOME/afile.txt;
twelve  12
twelve  1
eleven  11
eleven  10

hive> CREATE TABLE collecttest (str STRING, countVal INT)
    > ROW FORMAT DELIMITED FIELDS TERMINATED BY '09' LINES TERMINATED BY '10';

hive> LOAD DATA LOCAL INPATH '${env:HOME}/afile.txt' INTO TABLE collecttest;

hive> SELECT collect(str) FROM collecttest;
[twelve,twelve,eleven,eleven]
```

The concat_ws() takes a delimiter as its first argument. The remaining arguments can be string types or arrays of strings. The returned result contains the argument joined together by the delimiter. Hence, we have converted the array into a single comma-separated string:

```
hive> SELECT concat_ws( ',' , collect(str)) FROM collecttest;
twelve,twleve,eleven,eleven
```

`GROUP_CONCAT` can be done by combining `GROUP BY`, `COLLECT` and `concat_ws()` as shown here:

```
hive> SELECT str, concat_ws( ',' , collect(cast(countVal AS STRING)))
    > FROM collecttest GROUP BY str;
eleven  11,10
twelve  12,1
```

User-Defined Table Generating Functions

While UDFs can be used be return arrays or structures, they cannot return multiple columns or multiple rows. *User-Defined Table Generating Functions*, or UDTFs, address this need by providing a programmatic interface to return multiple columns and even multiple rows.

UDTFs that Produce Multiple Rows

We have already used the `explode` method in several examples. `Explode` takes an array as input and outputs one row for each element in the array. An alternative way to do this would have the UDTF generate the rows based on some input. We will demonstrate this with a UDTF that works like a `for` loop. The function receives user inputs of the start and stop values and then outputs N rows:

```
hive> SELECT forx(1,5) AS i FROM collecttest;
1
2
3
4
5
```

Our class extends the `GenericUDTF` interface. We declare three integer variables for the start, end, and increment. The `forwardObj` array will be used to return result rows:

```
package com.jointhegrid.udf.collect;

import java.util.ArrayList;
import org.apache.hadoop.hive.ql.exec.UDFArgumentException;
import org.apache.hadoop.hive.ql.metadata.HiveException;
import org.apache.hadoop.hive.ql.udf.generic.GenericUDFUtils.*;
import org.apache.hadoop.hive.ql.udf.generic.GenericUDTF;
import org.apache.hadoop.hive.serde2.objectinspector.*;
import org.apache.hadoop.hive.serde2.objectinspector.primitive.*;
import org.apache.hadoop.io.IntWritable;

public class GenericUDTFFor extends GenericUDTF {

  IntWritable start;
  IntWritable end;
  IntWritable inc;

  Object[] forwardObj = null;
  ...
```

Because the arguments to this function are constant, the value can be determined in the initialize method. Nonconstant values are typically not available until the evaluate method. The third argument for increment is optional, as it defaults to 1:

```
...
@Override
public StructObjectInspector initialize(ObjectInspector[] args)
        throws UDFArgumentException {
  start=((WritableConstantIntObjectInspector) args[0])
     .getWritableConstantValue();
  end=((WritableConstantIntObjectInspector) args[1])
     .getWritableConstantValue();
  if (args.length == 3) {
    inc =((WritableConstantIntObjectInspector) args[2])
     .getWritableConstantValue();
  } else {
    inc = new IntWritable(1);
  }
  ...
```

This function returns only a single column and its type is always an integer. We need to give it a name, but the user can always override this later:

```
...
this.forwardObj = new Object[1];
ArrayList<String> fieldNames = new ArrayList<String>();
ArrayList<ObjectInspector> fieldOIs = new ArrayList<ObjectInspector>();

fieldNames.add("col0");
fieldOIs.add(
  PrimitiveObjectInspectorFactory.getPrimitiveJavaObjectInspector(
    PrimitiveCategory.INT));

return ObjectInspectorFactory.getStandardStructObjectInspector(
    fieldNames, fieldOIs);

}
...
```

The process method is where the interesting work happens. Notice that the return type is void. This is because UDTF can forward zero or more rows, unlike a UDF, which has a single return. In this case the call to the **forward** method is nested inside a **for** loop, which causes it to forward a row for each iteration:

```
...
@Override
public void process(Object[] args)
        throws HiveException, UDFArgumentException {
  for (int i = start.get(); i < end.get(); i = i + inc.get()) {
    this.forwardObj[0] = new Integer(i);
    forward(forwardObj);
  }
}

@Override
```

```
    public void close() throws HiveException {
    }
}
```

UDTFs that Produce a Single Row with Multiple Columns

An example of a UDTF that returns multiple columns but only one row is the
parse_url_tuple function, which is a built-in Hive function. It takes as input a parameter that is a URL and one or more constants that specify the parts of the URL the user
wants returned:

```
hive> SELECT parse_url_tuple(weblogs.url, 'HOST', 'PATH')
    > AS (host, path) FROM weblogs;
google.com      /index.html
hotmail.com     /a/links.html
```

The benefit of this type of UDFT is the URL only needs to be parsed once, then returns
multiple columns—a clear performance win. The alternative, using UDFs, involves
writing several UDFs to extract specific parts of the URL. Using UDFs requires writing
more code as well as more processing time because the URL is parsed multiple times.
For example, something like the following:

```
SELECT PARSE_HOST(a.url) as host, PARSE_PORT(url) FROM weblogs;
```

UDTFs that Simulate Complex Types

A UDTF can be used as a technique for adding more complex types to Hive. For example, a complex type can be serialized as an encoded string and a UDTF will deserialize the complex type when needed. Suppose we have a Java class named Book. Hive
cannot work with this datatype directly, however a Book could be encoded to and
decoded from a string format:

```
public class Book {
  public Book () { }
  public String isbn;
  public String title;
  public String [] authors;

  /* note: this system will not work if your table is
     using '|' or ',' as the field delimiter! */
  public void fromString(String parts){
    String [] part = part.split("\|");
    isbn = Integer.parseInt( part[0] );
    title = part[1] ;
    authors = part[2].split(",");
  }

  public String toString(){
    return isbn+"\t"+title+"\t"+StringUtils.join(authors, ",");
  }
}
```

Imagine we have a flat text file with books in this format. For now lets assume we could not use a delimited SerDe to split on | and ,:

```
hive> SELECT * FROM books;
5555555|Programming Hive|Edward,Dean,Jason
```

In the pipe-delimited raw form it is possible to do some parsing of the data:

```
hive> SELECT cast(split(book_info,"\|")[0] AS INTEGER) AS isbn FROM books
    > WHERE split(book_info,"\|")[1] = "Programming Hive";
5555555
```

This HiveQL works correctly, however it could be made easier for the end user. For example, writing this type of query may require consulting documentation regarding which fields and types are used, remembering casting conversion rules, and so forth. By contrast, a UDTF makes this HiveQL simpler and more readable. In the following example, the parse_book() UDTF is introduced:

```
hive> FROM (
    >   parse_book(book_info) AS (isbn, title, authors) FROM Book ) a
    > SELECT a.isbn
    > WHERE a.title="Programming Hive"
    > AND array_contains (authors, 'Edward'));
5555555
```

The function parse_book() allows Hive to return multiple columns of different types representing the fields of a book:

```
package com.jointhegrid.udf.collect;

import java.util.ArrayList;
import org.apache.hadoop.hive.ql.exec.UDFArgumentException;
import org.apache.hadoop.hive.ql.metadata.HiveException;
import org.apache.hadoop.hive.ql.udf.generic.GenericUDTF;
import org.apache.hadoop.hive.serde2.objectinspector.ObjectInspector;
import org.apache.hadoop.hive.serde2.objectinspector.ObjectInspectorFactory;
import org.apache.hadoop.hive.serde2.objectinspector.PrimitiveObjectInspector
  .PrimitiveCategory;
import org.apache.hadoop.hive.serde2.objectinspector.StructObjectInspector;
import org.apache.hadoop.hive.serde2.objectinspector.primitive
  .PrimitiveObjectInspectorFactory;
import org.apache.hadoop.hive.serde2.objectinspector.primitive
  .WritableConstantStringObjectInspector;
import org.apache.hadoop.hive.serde2.objectinspector.primitive
  .WritableStringObjectInspector;
import org.apache.hadoop.io.Text;


public class UDTFBook extends GenericUDTF{

  private Text sent;
  Object[] forwardObj = null;
  ...
```

The function will return three properties and ISBN as an integer, a title as a string, and authors as an array of strings. Notice that we can return nested types with all UDFs, for example we can return an array of array of strings:

```
...
@Override
public StructObjectInspector initialize(ObjectInspector[] args)
        throws UDFArgumentException {

    ArrayList<String> fieldNames = new ArrayList<String>();
    ArrayList<ObjectInspector> fieldOIs = new ArrayList<ObjectInspector>();

    fieldNames.add("isbn");
    fieldOIs.add(PrimitiveObjectInspectorFactory.getPrimitiveJavaObjectInspector(
        PrimitiveCategory.INT));

    fieldNames.add("title");
    fieldOIs.add(PrimitiveObjectInspectorFactory.getPrimitiveJavaObjectInspector(
        PrimitiveCategory.STRING));

    fieldNames.add("authors");
    fieldOIs.add( ObjectInspectorFactory.getStandardListObjectInspector(
        PrimitiveObjectInspectorFactory.getPrimitiveJavaObjectInspector(
            PrimitiveCategory.STRING)
        )
    );

    forwardObj= new Object[3];
    return ObjectInspectorFactory.getStandardStructObjectInspector(
            fieldNames, fieldOIs);

}
...
```

The process method only returns a single row. However, each element in the object array will be bound to a specific variable:

```
...
@Override
public void process(Object[] os) throws HiveException {
    sent = new Text(((StringObjectInspector)args[0])
        .getPrimitiveJavaObject(os[0]));
    String parts = new String(this.sent.getBytes());
    String [] part = parts.split("\\|");
    forwardObj[0]=Integer.parseInt( part[0] );
    forwardObj[1]=part[1] ;
    forwardObj[2]=part[2].split(",");
    this.forward(forwardObj);
}

@Override
public void close() throws HiveException {
}
}
```

We have followed the call to the book UDTF with AS, which allows the result columns to be named by the user. They can then be used in other parts of the query without having to parse information from the book again:

```
client.execute(
    "create temporary function book as 'com.jointhegrid.udf.collect.UDTFBook'");
client.execute("create table  booktest (str string) ");
client.execute(
    "load data local inpath '" + p.toString() + "' into table booktest");
client.execute("select book(str) AS (book, title, authors) from booktest");
[555 Programming Hive "Dean","Jason","Edward"]
```

Accessing the Distributed Cache from a UDF

UDFs may access files inside the distributed cache, the local filesystem, or even the distributed filesystem. This access should be used cautiously as the overhead is significant.

A common usage of Hive is the analyzing of web logs. A popular operation is determining the geolocation of web traffic based on the IP address. Maxmind (*http://www .maxmind.com/app/api*) makes a GeoIP database available and a Java API to search this database. By wrapping a UDF around this API, location information may be looked up about an IP address from within a Hive query.

The GeoIP API uses a small data file. This is ideal for showing the functionality of accessing a distributed cache file from a UDF. The complete code for this example is found at *https://github.com/edwardcapriolo/hive-geoip/*.

ADD FILE is used to cache the necessary data files with Hive. ADD JAR is used to add the required Java JAR files to the cache and the classpath. Finally, the temporary function must be defined as the final step before performing queries:

```
hive> ADD FILE GeoIP.dat;
hive> ADD JAR geo-ip-java.jar;
hive> ADD JAR hive-udf-geo-ip-jtg.jar;
hive> CREATE TEMPORARY FUNCTION geoip
    > AS 'com.jointhegrid.hive.udf.GenericUDFGeoIP';

hive> SELECT ip, geoip(source_ip, 'COUNTRY_NAME', './GeoIP.dat') FROM weblogs;
209.191.139.200        United States
10.10.0.1      Unknown
```

The two examples returned include an IP address in the United States and a private IP address that has no fixed address.

The geoip() function takes three arguments: the IP address in either string or long format, a string that must match one of the constants COUNTRY_NAME or DMA_CODE, and a final argument that is the name of the data file that has already been placed in the distributed cache.

The first call to the UDF (which triggers the first call to the evaluate Java function in the implementation) will instantiate a LookupService object that uses the file located in the distributed cache. The lookup service is saved in a reference so it only needs to be initialized once in the lifetime of a map or reduce task that initializes it. Note that the LookupService has its own internal caching, LookupService.GEOIP_MEMORY_CACHE, so that optimization should avoid frequent disk access when looking up IPs.

Here is the source code for evaluate():

```
@Override
public Object evaluate(DeferredObject[] arguments) throws HiveException {
  if (argumentOIs[0] instanceof LongObjectInspector) {
    this.ipLong = ((LongObjectInspector)argumentOIs[0]).get(arguments[0].get());
  } else {
    this.ipString = ((StringObjectInspector)argumentOIs[0])
      .getPrimitiveJavaObject(arguments[0].get());
  }
  this.property = ((StringObjectInspector)argumentOIs[1])
      .getPrimitiveJavaObject(arguments[1].get());
  if (this.property != null) {
    this.property = this.property.toUpperCase();
  }
  if (ls ==null){
    if (argumentOIs.length == 3){
      this.database = ((StringObjectInspector)argumentOIs[1])
            .getPrimitiveJavaObject(arguments[2].get());
      File f = new File(database);
      if (!f.exists())
        throw new HiveException(database+" does not exist");
      try {
        ls = new LookupService ( f , LookupService.GEOIP_MEMORY_CACHE );
      } catch (IOException ex){
        throw new HiveException (ex);
      }
    }
  }
}
...
```

An if statement in evaluate determines which data the method should return. In our example, the country name is requested:

```
...
if (COUNTRY_PROPERTIES.contains(this.property)) {
  Country country = ipString != null ?
      ls.getCountry(ipString) : ls.getCountry(ipLong);
  if (country == null) {
    return null;
  } else if (this.property.equals(COUNTRY_NAME)) {
    return country.getName();
  } else if (this.property.equals(COUNTRY_CODE)) {
    return country.getCode();
  }
  assert(false);
} else if (LOCATION_PROPERTIES.contains(this.property)) {
  ...
```

```
    }
  }
```

Annotations for Use with Functions

In this chapter we mentioned the Description annotation and how it is used to provide documentation for Hive methods at runtime. Other annotations exist for UDFs that can make functions easier to use and even increase the performance of some Hive queries:

```
public @interface UDFType {
  boolean deterministic() default true;
  boolean stateful() default false;
  boolean distinctLike() default false;
}
```

Deterministic

By default, deterministic is automatically turned on for most queries because they are inherently deterministic by nature. An exception is the function rand().

If a UDF is not deterministic, it is not included in the partition pruner.

An example of a nondeterministic query using rand() is the following:

```
SELECT * FROM t WHERE rand() < 0.01;
```

If rand() were deterministic, the result would only be calculated a single time in the computation state. Because a query with rand() is nondeterministic, the result of rand() is recomputed for each row.

Stateful

Almost all the UDFs are stateful by default; a UDF that is not stateful is rand() because it returns a different value for each invocation. The Stateful annotation may be used under the following conditions:

- A stateful UDF can only be used in the SELECT list, not in other clauses such as WHERE/ON/ORDER/GROUP.
- When a stateful UDF is present in a query, the implication is the SELECT will be treated similarly to TRANSFORM (i.e., a DISTRIBUTE/CLUSTER/SORT clause), then run inside the corresponding reducer to ensure the results are as expected.
- If stateful is set to true, the UDF should also be treated as nondeterministic (even if the deterministic annotation explicitly returns true).

See *https://issues.apache.org/jira/browse/HIVE-1994* for more details.

DistinctLike

Used for cases where the function behaves like `DISTINCT` even when applied to a non-distinct column of values. Examples include `min` and `max` functions that return a distinct value even though the underlying numeric data can have repeating values.

Macros

Macros provide the ability to define functions in HiveQL that call other functions and operators. When appropriate for the particular situation, macros are a convenient alternative to writing UDFs in Java or using Hive streaming, because they require no external code or scripts.

To define a macro, use the `CREATE TEMPORARY MACRO` syntax. Here is an example that creates a `SIGMOID` function calculator:

```
hive> CREATE TEMPORARY MACRO SIGMOID (x DOUBLE) 1.0 / (1.0 + EXP(-x));
hive> SELECT SIGMOID(2) FROM src LIMIT 1;
```

CHAPTER 14

Streaming

Hive works by leveraging and extending the components of Hadoop, common abstractions such as `InputFormat`, `OutputFormat`, `Mapper`, and `Reducer`, plus its own abstractions, like `SerializerDeserializer` (SerDe), User-Defined Functions (UDFs), and `StorageHandlers`.

These components are all Java components, but Hive hides the complexity of implementing and using these components by letting the user work with SQL abstractions, rather than Java code.

Streaming offers an alternative way to transform data. During a streaming job, the Hadoop Streaming API opens an I/O pipe to an external process. Data is then passed to the process, which operates on the data it reads from the *standard input* and writes the results out through the *standard output*, and back to the Streaming API job. While Hive does not leverage the Hadoop streaming API directly, it works in a very similar way.

This pipeline computing model is familiar to users of Unix operating systems and their descendants, like Linux and Mac OS X.

 Streaming is usually less efficient than coding the comparable UDFs or `InputFormat` objects. Serializing and deserializing data to pass it in and out of the pipe is relatively inefficient. It is also harder to debug the whole program in a unified manner. However, it is useful for fast prototyping and for leveraging existing code that is not written in Java. For Hive users who don't want to write Java code, it can be a very effective approach.

Hive provides several clauses to use streaming: `MAP()`, `REDUCE()`, and `TRANSFORM()`. An important point to note is that `MAP()` does not actually force streaming during the map phase nor does reduce force streaming to happen in the reduce phase. For this reason, the functionally equivalent yet more generic `TRANSFORM()` clause is suggested to avoid misleading the reader of the query.

For our streaming examples we will use a small table named a, with columns named col1 and col2, both of type INT, and two rows:

```
hive> CREATE TABLE a (col1 INT, col2 INT)
    > ROW FORMAT DELIMITED FIELDS TERMINATED BY '\t';

hive> SELECT * FROM a;
4       5
3       2

hive> DESCRIBE a;
a       int
b       int
```

Identity Transformation

The most basic streaming job is an identity operation. The /bin/cat command echoes the data sent to it and meets the requirements. In this example, /bin/cat is assumed to be installed on all TaskTracker nodes. Any Linux system should have it! Later, we will show how Hive can "ship" applications with the job when they aren't already installed around the cluster:

```
hive> SELECT TRANSFORM (a, b)
    > USING '/bin/cat' AS newA, newB
    > FROM default.a;
4       5
3       2
```

Changing Types

The return columns from TRANSFORM are typed as strings, by default. There is an alternative syntax that casts the results to different types.

```
hive> SELECT TRANSFORM (col1, col2)
    > USING '/bin/cat' AS (newA INT , newB DOUBLE) FROM a;
4       5.0
3       2.0
```

Projecting Transformation

The cut command can be used with streaming to extract or project specific fields. In other words, this behaves like the SELECT statement:

```
hive> SELECT TRANSFORM (a, b)
    > USING '/bin/cut -f1'
    > AS newA, newB FROM a;
4       NULL
3       NULL
```

Note that the query attempts to read more columns than are actually returned from the external process, so newB is always NULL. By default, TRANSFORM assumes two columns but there can be any number of them:

```
hive> SELECT TRANSFORM (a, b)
    > USING '/bin/cut -f1'
    > AS newA FROM a;
4
3
```

Manipulative Transformations

The /bin/sed program (or /usr/bin/sed on Mac OS X systems) is a stream editor. It takes the input stream, edits it according to the user's specification, and then writes the results to the output stream. The example below replaces the string 4 with the string 10:

```
hive> SELECT TRANSFORM (a, b)
    > USING '/bin/sed s/4/10/'
    > AS newA, newB FROM a;
10  5
3       2
```

Using the Distributed Cache

All of the streaming examples thus far have used applications such as cat and sed that are core parts of Unix operating systems and their derivatives. When a query requires files that are not already installed on every *TaskTracker*, users can use the *distributed cache* to transmit data or program files across the cluster that will be cleaned up when the job is complete.

This is helpful, because installing (and sometimes removing) lots of little components across large clusters can be a burden. Also, the cache keeps one job's cached files separate from those files belonging to other jobs.

The following example is a bash shell script that converts degrees in Celsius to degrees in Fahrenheit:

```
while read LINE
do
  res=$(echo "scale=2;((9/5) * $LINE) + 32" | bc)
  echo $res
done
```

To test this script, launch it locally. It will not prompt for input. Type 100 and then strike Enter. The process prints 212.00 to the standard output. Then enter another number and the program returns another result. You can continue entering numbers or use Control-D to end the input.

```
#!/bin/bash
$ sh ctof.sh
100
212.00
0
32.00
^D
```

Hive's `ADD FILE` feature adds files to the distributed cache. The added file is put in the current working directory of each task. This allows the transform task to use the script without needing to know where to find it:

```
hive> ADD FILE ${env:HOME}/prog_hive/ctof.sh;
Added resource: /home/edward/prog_hive/ctof.sh

hive> SELECT TRANSFORM(col1) USING 'ctof.sh' AS convert FROM a;
39.20
37.40
```

Producing Multiple Rows from a Single Row

The examples shown thus far have taken one row of input and produced one row of output. Streaming can be used to produce multiple rows of output for each input row. This functionality produces output similar to the `EXPLODE()` UDF and the `LATERAL VIEW` syntax[1].

Given an input file *$HOME/kv_data.txt* that looks like:

```
k1=v1,k2=v2
k4=v4,k5=v5,k6=v6
k7=v7,k7=v7,k3=v7
```

We would like the data in a tabular form. This will allow the rows to be processed by familiar HiveQL operators:

```
k1      v1
k2      v2
k4      k4
```

Create this Perl script and save it as `$HOME/split_kv.pl`:

```
#!/usr/bin/perl
while (<STDIN>) {
    my $line = $_;
    chomp($line);
    my @kvs = split(/,/, $line);
    foreach my $p (@kvs) {
        my @kv = split(/=/, $p);
        print $kv[0] . "\t" . $kv[1] . "\n";
    }
```

---

1. The source code (*http://com-bizo-public.s3.amazonaws.com/hive/mapper/split_kv.pl*) and concept for this example comes from Larry Ogrodnek, "Custom Map Scripts and Hive" (*http://dev.bizo.com/2009/07/custom-map-scripts-and-hive.html*), Bizo development (blog), July 14, 2009.

```
    }
  }
```

Create a kv_data table. The entire table is defined as a single string column. The row format does not need to be configured because the streaming script will do all the tokenization of the fields:

```
hive> CREATE TABLE kv_data ( line STRING );

hive> LOAD DATA LOCAL INPATH '${env:HOME}/kv_data.txt' INTO TABLE kv_data;
```

Use the transform script on the source table. The ragged, multiple-entry-per-row format is converted into a two-column result set of key-value pairs:

```
hive> SELECT TRANSFORM (line)
    > USING 'perl split_kv.pl'
    > AS (key, value) FROM kv_data;
k1      v1
k2      v2
k4      v4
k5      v5
k6      v6
k7      v7
k7      v7
k3      v7
```

Calculating Aggregates with Streaming

Streaming can also be used to do aggregating operations like Hive's built-in SUM function. This is possible because streaming processes can return zero or more rows of output for every given input.

To accomplish aggregation in an external application, declare an accumulator before the loop that reads from the input stream and output the sum after the completion of the input:

```
#!/usr/bin/perl
my $sum=0;
while (<STDIN>) {
  my $line = $_;
  chomp($line);
  $sum=${sum}+${line};
}
print $sum;
```

Create a table and populate it with integer data, one integer per line, for testing:

```
hive> CREATE TABLE sum (number INT);

hive> LOAD DATA LOCAL INPATH '${env:HOME}/data_to_sum.txt' INTO TABLE sum;
```

```
hive> SELECT * FROM sum;
5
5
4
```

Add the streaming program to the distributed cache and use it in a `TRANSFORM` query. The process returns a single row, which is the sum of the input:

```
hive> ADD FILE ${env:HOME}/aggregate.pl;
Added resource: /home/edward/aggregate.pl

hive> SELECT TRANSFORM (number)
    > USING 'perl aggregate.pl' AS total FROM sum;
14
```

Unfortunately, it is not possible to do multiple `TRANSFORM`s in a single query like the UDAF `SUM()` can do. For example:

```
hive> SELECT sum(number) AS one, sum(number) AS two FROM sum;
14      14
```

Also, without using `CLUSTER BY` or `DISTRIBUTE BY` for the intermediate data, this job may run single, very long map and reduce tasks. While not all operations can be done in parallel, many can. The next section discusses how to do streaming in parallel, when possible.

CLUSTER BY, DISTRIBUTE BY, SORT BY

Hive offers syntax to control how data is distributed and sorted. These features can be used on most queries, but are particularly useful when doing streaming processes. For example, data for the same key may need to be sent to the same processing node, or data may need to be sorted by a specific column, or by a function. Hive provides several ways to control this behavior.

The first way to control this behavior is the `CLUSTER BY` clause, which ensures like data is routed to the same reduce task and sorted.

To demonstrate the use of `CLUSTER BY`, let's see a nontrivial example: another way to perform the *Word Count* algorithm that we introduced in Chapter 1. Now, we will use the `TRANSFORM` feature and two Python scripts, one to tokenize lines of text into words, and the second to accept a stream of word occurrences and an intermediate count of the words (mostly the number "1") and then sum up the counts for each word.

Here is the first Python script that tokenizes lines of text on whitespace (which doesn't properly handle punctuation, etc.):

```
import sys

for line in sys.stdin:
    words = line.strip().split()
    for word in words:
        print "%s\t1" % (word.lower())
```

Without explaining all the Python syntax, this script imports common functions from a sys module, then it loops over each line on the "standard input," stdin, splits each line on whitespace into a collection of words, then iterates over the word and writes each word, followed by a tab, \t, and the "count" of one.[2]

Before we show the second Python script, let's discuss the data that's passed to it. We'll use CLUSTER BY for the words output from the first Python script in our TRANSFORM Hive query. This will have the effect of causing all occurrences of the word\t1 "pairs" for a give, word to be grouped together, one pair per line:

```
word1   1
word1   1
word1   1
word2   1
word3   1
word3   1
...
```

Hence, the second Python script will be more complex, because it needs to cache the word it's currently processing and the count of occurrences seen so far. When the word changes, the script must output the count for the previous word and reset its caches. So, here it is:

```
import sys

(last_key, last_count) = (None, 0)
for line in sys.stdin:
    (key, count) = line.strip().split("\t")
    if last_key and last_key != key:
        print "%s\t%d" % (last_key, last_count)
        (last_key, last_count) = (key, int(count))
    else:
        last_key = key
        last_count += int(count)

if last_key:
    print "%s\t%d" % (last_key, last_count)
```

We'll assume that both Python scripts are in your home directory.

Finally, here is the Hive query that glues it all together. We'll start by repeating a CREATE TABLE statement for an input table of lines of text, one that we used in Chapter 1. Any text file could serve as the data for this table. Next we'll show the TABLE for the output

---

2. This is the most naive approach. We could cache the counts of words seen and then write the final count. That would be faster, by minimizing I/O overhead, but it would also be more complex to implement.

of word count. It will have two columns, the word and count, and data will be tab-delimited. Finally, we show the TRANSFORM query that glues it all together:

```
hive> CREATE TABLE docs (line STRING);

hive> CREATE TABLE word_count (word STRING, count INT)
    > ROW FORMAT DELIMITED FIELDS TERMINATED BY '\t';

hive> FROM (
    >   FROM docs
    >   SELECT TRANSFORM (line) USING '${env:HOME}/mapper.py'
    >   AS word, count
    >   CLUSTER BY word) wc
    > INSERT OVERWRITE TABLE word_count
    > SELECT TRANSFORM (wc.word, wc.count) USING '${env:HOME}/reducer.py'
    > AS word, count;
```

The USING clauses specify an absolute path to the Python scripts.

A more flexible alternative to CLUSTER BY is to use DISTRIBUTE BY and SORT BY. This is used in the general case when you wish to partition the data by one column and sort it by another. In fact, CLUSTER BY word is equivalent to DISTRIBUTE BY word SORT BY word ASC.

The following version of the TRANSFORM query outputs the word count results in reverse order:

```
FROM (
  FROM docs
  SELECT TRANSFORM (line) USING '/.../mapper.py'
  AS word, count
  DISTRIBUTE BY word SORT BY word DESC) wc
INSERT OVERWRITE TABLE word_count
SELECT TRANSFORM (wc.word, wc.count) USING '/.../reducer.py'
AS word, count;
```

Using either CLUSTER BY or DISTRIBUTE BY with SORT BY is important. Without these directives, Hive may not be able to parallelize the job properly. All the data might be sent to a single reducer, which would extend the job processing time.

GenericMR Tools for Streaming to Java

Typically, streaming is used to integrate non-Java code into Hive. Streaming works with applications written in essentially any language, as we saw. It is possible to use Java for streaming, and Hive includes a GenericMR API that attempts to give the feel of the Hadoop MapReduce API to streaming:

```
FROM (
  FROM src
  MAP value, key
  USING 'java -cp hive-contrib-0.9.0.jar
    org.apache.hadoop.hive.contrib.mr.example.IdentityMapper'
  AS k, v
```

```
  CLUSTER BY k) map_output
REDUCE k, v
USING 'java -cp hive-contrib-0.9.0.jar
  org.apache.hadoop.hive.contrib.mr.example.WordCountReduce'
AS k, v;
```

To understand how the `IdentityMapper` is written, we can take a look at the interfaces GenericMR provides. The `Mapper` interface is implemented to build custom Mapper implementations. It provides a map method where the column data is sent as a string array, `String []`:

```
package org.apache.hadoop.hive.contrib.mr;

public interface Mapper {
  void map(String[] record, Output output) throws Exception;
}
```

The `IdentityMapper` makes no changes to the input data and passes it to the collector. This is functionally equivalent to the identity streaming done with `/bin/cat` earlier in the chapter:

```
package org.apache.hadoop.hive.contrib.mr.example;

import org.apache.hadoop.hive.contrib.mr.GenericMR;
import org.apache.hadoop.hive.contrib.mr.Mapper;
import org.apache.hadoop.hive.contrib.mr.Output;

public final class IdentityMapper {
  public static void main(final String[] args) throws Exception {
    new GenericMR().map(System.in, System.out, new Mapper() {
      @Override
      public void map(final String[] record, final Output output) throws Exception {
        output.collect(record);
      }
    });
  }

  private IdentityMapper() {
  }
}
```

The `Reducer` interface provides the first column as a `String`, and the remaining columns are available through the record `Iterator`. Each iteration returns a pair of `Strings`, where the 0th element is the key repeated and the next element is the value. The output object is the same one used to emit results:

```
package org.apache.hadoop.hive.contrib.mr;

import java.util.Iterator;

public interface Reducer {
  void reduce(String key, Iterator<String[]> records, Output output)
      throws Exception;
}
```

`WordCountReduce` has an accumulator that is added by each element taken from the records `Iterator`. When all the records have been counted, a single two-element array of the key and the count is emitted:

```
package org.apache.hadoop.hive.contrib.mr.example;

import java.util.Iterator;
import org.apache.hadoop.hive.contrib.mr.GenericMR;
import org.apache.hadoop.hive.contrib.mr.Output;
import org.apache.hadoop.hive.contrib.mr.Reducer;

public final class WordCountReduce {

  private WordCountReduce() {
  }

  public static void main(final String[] args) throws Exception {
    new GenericMR().reduce(System.in, System.out, new Reducer() {
      public void reduce(String key, Iterator<String[]> records, Output output)
          throws Exception {
        int count = 0;
        while (records.hasNext()) {
          // note we use col[1] -- the key is provided again as col[0]
          count += Integer.parseInt(records.next()[1]);
        }
        output.collect(new String[] {key, String.valueOf(count)});
      }
    });
  }
}
```

Calculating Cogroups

It's common in MapReduce applications to join together records from multiple data sets and then stream them through a final `TRANSFORM` step. Using `UNION ALL` and `CLUSTER BY`, we can perform this generalization of a `GROUP BY` operation

 Pig provides a native `COGROUP BY` operation.

Suppose we have several sources of logfiles, with similar schema, that we wish to bring together and analyze with a `reduce_script`:

```
FROM (
  FROM (
    FROM order_log ol
    -- User Id, order Id, and timestamp:
    SELECT ol.userid AS uid, ol.orderid AS id, av.ts AS ts

    UNION ALL

    FROM clicks_log cl
    SELECT cl.userid AS uid, cl.id AS id, ac.ts AS ts
  ) union_msgs
  SELECT union_msgs.uid, union_msgs.id, union_msgs.ts
  CLUSTER BY union_msgs.uid, union_msgs.ts) map
INSERT OVERWRITE TABLE log_analysis
SELECT TRANSFORM(map.uid, map.id, map.ts) USING 'reduce_script'
AS (uid, id, ...);
```

CHAPTER 15

Customizing Hive File and Record Formats

Hive functionality can be customized in several ways. First, there are the variables and properties that we discussed in "Variables and Properties" on page 31. Second, you may extend Hive using custom *UDFs*, or user-defined functions, which was discussed in Chapter 13. Finally, you can customize the file and record formats, which we discuss now.

File Versus Record Formats

Hive draws a clear distinction between the file format, how records are encoded in a file, the record format, and how the stream of bytes for a given record are encoded in the record.

In this book we have been using text files, with the default STORED AS TEXTFILE in CREATE TABLE statements (see "Text File Encoding of Data Values" on page 45), where each line in the file is a record. Most of the time those records have used the default separators, with occasional examples of data that use commas or tabs as field separators. However, a text file could contain JSON or XML "documents."

For Hive, the file format choice is orthogonal to the record format. We'll first discuss options for file formats, then we'll discuss different record formats and how to use them in Hive.

Demystifying CREATE TABLE Statements

Throughout the book we have shown examples of creating tables. You may have noticed that CREATE TABLE has a variety of syntax. Examples of this syntax are STORED AS SEQUENCEFILE, ROW FORMAT DELIMITED , SERDE, INPUTFORMAT, OUTPUTFORMAT. This chapter will cover much of this syntax and give examples, but as a preface note that some syntax is *sugar* for other syntax, that is, syntax used to make concepts easier (sweeter) to understand. For example, specifying `STORED AS SEQUENCEFILE` is an alternative to specifying an `INPUTFORMAT` of `org.apache.hadoop.mapred.SequenceFileInputFormat` and an `OUTPUTFORMAT` of `org.apache.hadoop.hive.ql.io.HiveSequenceFileOutputFormat`.

Let's create some tables and use `DESCRIBE TABLE EXTENDED` to peel away the *sugar* and expose the internals. First, we will create and then describe a simple table (we have formatted the output here, as Hive otherwise would not have indented the output):

```
hive> create table text (x int) ;
hive> describe extended text;
OK
x       int

Detailed Table Information
Table(tableName:text, dbName:default, owner:edward, createTime:1337814583,
lastAccessTime:0, retention:0,
sd:StorageDescriptor(
  cols:[FieldSchema(name:x, type:int, comment:null)],
  location:file:/user/hive/warehouse/text,
  inputFormat:org.apache.hadoop.mapred.TextInputFormat,
  outputFormat:org.apache.hadoop.hive.ql.io.HiveIgnoreKeyTextOutputFormat,
  compressed:false,
  numBuckets:-1,
  serdeInfo:SerDeInfo(
    name:null,
    serializationLib:org.apache.hadoop.hive.serde2.lazy.LazySimpleSerDe,
    parameters:{serialization.format=1}
  ),
  bucketCols:[], sortCols:[], parameters:{}), partitionKeys:[],
  parameters:{transient_lastDdlTime=1337814583},
  viewOriginalText:null, viewExpandedText:null, tableType:MANAGED_TABLE
)
```

Now let's create a table using `STORED AS SEQUENCEFILE` for comparison:

```
hive> CREATE TABLE seq (x int) STORED AS SEQUENCEFILE;
hive> DESCRIBE EXTENDED seq;
OK
x       int

Detailed Table Information
Table(tableName:seq, dbName:default, owner:edward, createTime:1337814571,
lastAccessTime:0, retention:0,
sd:StorageDescriptor(
  cols:[FieldSchema(name:x, type:int, comment:null)],
  location:file:/user/hive/warehouse/seq,
  inputFormat:org.apache.hadoop.mapred.SequenceFileInputFormat,
  outputFormat:org.apache.hadoop.hive.ql.io.HiveSequenceFileOutputFormat,
  compressed:false, numBuckets:-1,
  serdeInfo:SerDeInfo(
    name:null,
    serializationLib:org.apache.hadoop.hive.serde2.lazy.LazySimpleSerDe,
    parameters:{serialization.format=1}
  ),
```

```
    bucketCols:[], sortCols:[], parameters:{}), partitionKeys:[],
    parameters:{transient_lastDdlTime=1337814571},
    viewOriginalText:null, viewExpandedText:null, tableType:MANAGED_TABLE
)
Time taken: 0.107 seconds
```

Unless you have been blinded by Hive's awesomeness, you would have picked up on the difference between these two tables. That `STORED AS SEQUENCEFILE` has changed the `InputFormat` and the `OutputFormat`:

```
inputFormat:org.apache.hadoop.mapred.TextInputFormat,
outputFormat:org.apache.hadoop.hive.ql.io.HiveIgnoreKeyTextOutputFormat,

inputFormat:org.apache.hadoop.mapred.SequenceFileInputFormat,
outputFormat:org.apache.hadoop.hive.ql.io.HiveSequenceFileOutputFormat,
```

Hive uses the `InputFormat` when reading data from the table, and it uses the `OutputFormat` when writing data to the table.

> `InputFormat` reads key-value pairs from files; Hive currently ignores the key and works only with the data found in the value by default. The reason for this is that the key, which comes from `TextInputFormat`, is a long integer that represents the byte offset in the block (which is not user data).

The rest of the chapter describes other aspects of the table metadata.

File Formats

We discussed in "Text File Encoding of Data Values" on page 45 that the simplest data format to use is the text format, with whatever delimiters you prefer. It is also the default format, equivalent to creating a table with the clause `STORED AS TEXTFILE`.

The text file format is convenient for sharing data with other tools, such as *Pig*, Unix text tools like `grep`, `sed`, and `awk`, etc. It's also convenient for viewing or editing files manually. However, the text format is not space efficient compared to binary formats. We can use compression, as we discussed in Chapter 11, but we can also gain more efficient usage of disk space and better disk I/O performance by using binary file formats.

SequenceFile

The first alternative is the *SequenceFile* format (*http://wiki.apache.org/hadoop/Sequen ceFile*), which we can specify using the `STORED AS SEQUENCEFILE` clause during table creation.

Sequence files are flat files consisting of binary key-value pairs. When Hive converts queries to MapReduce jobs, it decides on the appropriate key-value pairs to use for a given record.

The sequence file is a standard format supported by Hadoop itself, so it is an acceptable choice when sharing files between Hive and other Hadoop-related tools. It's less suitable for use with tools outside the Hadoop ecosystem. As we discussed in Chapter 11, sequence files can be compressed at the block and record level, which is very useful for optimizing disk space utilization and I/O, while still supporting the ability to split files on block boundaries for parallel processing.

Another efficient binary format that is supported natively by Hive is RCFile.

RCFile

Most Hadoop and Hive storage is row oriented, which is efficient in most cases. The efficiency can be attributed to several factors: most tables have a smaller number (1–20) of columns. Compression on blocks of a file is efficient for dealing with repeating data, and many processing and debugging tools (more, head, awk) work well with row-oriented data.

Not all tools and data stores take a row-oriented approach; column-oriented organization is a good storage option for certain types of data and applications. For example, if a given table has hundreds of columns but most queries use only a few of the columns, it is wasteful to scan entire rows then discard most of the data. However, if the data is stored by *column* instead of by row, then only the data for the desired columns has to be read, improving performance.

It also turns out that compression on columns is typically very efficient, especially when the column has low cardinality (only a few distinct entries). Also, some column-oriented stores do not physically need to store null columns.

Hive's RCFile is designed for these scenarios.

While books like *Programming Hive* are invaluable sources of information, sometimes the best place to find information is inside the source code itself. A good description of how Hive's column storage known as RCFile works is found in the source code:

```
cd hive-trunk
find . -name "RCFile*"
vi ./ql/src/java/org/apache/hadoop/hive/ql/io/RCFile.java
 * <p>
 * RCFile stores columns of a table in a record columnar way. It first
 * partitions rows horizontally into row splits. and then it vertically
 * partitions each row split in a columnar way. RCFile first stores the meta
 * data of a row split, as the key part of a record, and all the data of a row
 * split as the value part.
 * </p>
```

A powerful aspect of Hive is that converting data between different formats is simple. Storage information is stored in the tables metadata. When a query SELECTs from one table and INSERTs into another, Hive uses the metadata about the tables and handles the conversion automatically. This makes for easy evaluation of the different options without writing one-off programs to convert data between the different formats.

Creating a table using the ColumnarSerDe, RCFileInputFormat, and RCFileOutputFormat:

```
hive> select * from a;
OK
4       5
3       2
Time taken: 0.336 seconds
hive> create table columnTable (key int , value int)
    > ROW FORMAT SERDE
    >   'org.apache.hadoop.hive.serde2.columnar.ColumnarSerDe'
    > STORED AS
    >   INPUTFORMAT  'org.apache.hadoop.hive.ql.io.RCFileInputFormat'
    >   OUTPUTFORMAT 'org.apache.hadoop.hive.ql.io.RCFileOutputFormat';

hive> FROM a INSERT OVERWRITE TABLE columnTable SELECT a.col1, a.col2;
```

RCFile's cannot be opened with the tools that open typical sequence files. However, Hive provides an rcfilecat tool to display the contents of RCFiles:

```
$ bin/hadoop dfs -text /user/hive/warehouse/columntable/000000_0
text: java.io.IOException: WritableName can't load class:
org.apache.hadoop.hive.ql.io.RCFile$KeyBuffer
$ bin/hive --service rcfilecat /user/hive/warehouse/columntable/000000_0
4       5
3       2
```

Example of a Custom Input Format: DualInputFormat

Many databases allow users to SELECT without FROM. This can be used to perform simple calculations, such as SELECT 1+2. If Hive did not allow this type of query, then a user would instead select from an existing table and limit the results to a single row. Or the user may create a table with a single row. Some databases provide a table named *dual*, which is a single row table to be used in this manner.

By default, a standard Hive table uses the TextInputFormat. The TextInputFormat calculates zero or more *splits* for the input. Splits are opened by the framework and a RecordReader is used to read the data. Each row of text becomes an input record. To create an input format that works with a dual table, we need to create an input format that returns one split with one row, regardless of the input path specified.[1]

In the example below, DualInputFormat returns a single split:

---

1. The source code for the DualInputFormat is available at: *https://github.com/edwardcapriolo/ DualInputFormat*.

```
public class DualInputFormat implements InputFormat{
  public InputSplit[] getSplits(JobConf jc, int i) throws IOException {
    InputSplit [] splits = new DualInputSplit[1];
    splits[0]= new DualInputSplit();
    return splits;
  }
  public RecordReader<Text,Text> getRecordReader(InputSplit split, JobConf jc,
          Reporter rprtr) throws IOException {
    return new DualRecordReader(jc, split);
  }
}
```

In the example below the split is a single row. There is nothing to serialize or deserialize:

```
public class DualInputSplit implements InputSplit {
  public long getLength() throws IOException {
    return 1;
  }
  public String[] getLocations() throws IOException {
    return new String [] { "localhost" };
  }
  public void write(DataOutput d) throws IOException {
  }
  public void readFields(DataInput di) throws IOException {
  }
}
```

The DualRecordReader has a Boolean variable hasNext. After the first invocation of next(), its value is set to false. Thus, this record reader returns a single row and then is finished with virtual input:

```
public class DualRecordReader implements RecordReader<Text,Text>{
  boolean hasNext=true;
  public DualRecordReader(JobConf jc, InputSplit s) {
  }
  public DualRecordReader(){
  }
  public long getPos() throws IOException {
    return 0;
  }
  public void close() throws IOException {
  }
  public float getProgress() throws IOException {
    if (hasNext)
      return 0.0f;
    else
      return 1.0f;
  }
  public Text createKey() {
    return new Text("");
  }
  public Text createValue() {
    return new Text("");
  }
  public boolean next(Text k, Text v) throws IOException {
    if (hasNext){
```

```
        hasNext=false;
        return true;
      } else {
        return hasNext;
      }
    }
  }
}
```

We can create a table using our `DualInputFormat` and the default `HiveIgnoreKeyTextOut` `putFormat`. Selecting from the table confirms that it returns a single empty row. `Input` `Formats` should be placed inside the Hadoop *lib* directory or preferably inside the Hive *auxlib* directory.

```
client.execute("add jar dual.jar");
client.execute("create table dual (fake string) "+
  "STORED AS INPUTFORMAT 'com.m6d.dualinputformat.DualInputFormat'"+
  "OUTPUTFORMAT 'org.apache.hadoop.hive.ql.io.HiveIgnoreKeyTextOutputFormat'");
client.execute("select count(1) as cnt from dual");
String row = client.fetchOne();
assertEquals("1", row);
client.execute("select * from dual");
row = client.fetchOne();
assertEquals( "", row);
```

Record Formats: SerDes

SerDe is short for serializer/deserializer. A SerDe encapsulates the logic for converting the unstructured bytes in a *record*, which is stored as part of a file, into a record that Hive can use. SerDes are implemented using Java. Hive comes with several built-in SerDes and many other third-party SerDes are available.

Internally, the Hive engine uses the defined `InputFormat` to read a record of data. That record is then passed to the `SerDe.deserialize()` method.

A lazy SerDe does not fully materialize an object until individual attributes are necessary.

The following example uses a `RegexSerDe` to parse a standard formatted Apache web log. The `RegexSerDe` is included as a standard feature as a part of the Hive distribution:

```
CREATE TABLE serde_regex(
  host STRING,
  identity STRING,
  user STRING,
  time STRING,
  request STRING,
  status STRING,
  size STRING,
  referer STRING,
  agent STRING)
ROW FORMAT SERDE 'org.apache.hadoop.hive.contrib.serde2.RegexSerDe'
WITH SERDEPROPERTIES (
  "input.regex" = "([^ ]*) ([^ ]*) ([^ ]*) (-|\\[[^\\]]*\\])
```

```
        ([^ \"]*|\"[^\"]*\") (-|[0-9]*) (-|[0-9]*)(?: ([^ \"]*|\"[^\"]*\")
        ([^ \"]*|\"[^\"]*\"))?",
    "output.format.string" = "%1$s %2$s %3$s %4$s %5$s %6$s %7$s %8$s %9$s"
)
STORED AS TEXTFILE;
```

Now we can load data and write queries:

```
hive> LOAD DATA LOCAL INPATH "../data/files/apache.access.log" INTO TABLE serde_regex;
hive> LOAD DATA LOCAL INPATH "../data/files/apache.access.2.log" INTO TABLE serde_regex;

hive> SELECT * FROM serde_regex ORDER BY time;
```

(The long regular expression was wrapped to fit.)

CSV and TSV SerDes

What about CSV (comma-separated values) and TSV (tab-separated values) files? Of course, for simple data such as numerical data, you can just use the default test file format and specify the field delimiter, as we saw previously. However, this simplistic approach doesn't handle strings with embedded commas or tabs, nor does it handle other common conventions, like whether or not to quote all or no strings, or the optional presence of a "column header" row as the first line in each file.

First, it's generally safer to remove the column header row, if present. Then one of several third-party SerDes are available for properly parsing CSV or TSV files. For CSV files, consider CSVSerde (*https://github.com/ogrodnek/csv-serde*):

```
ADD JAR /path/to/csv-serde.jar;

CREATE TABLE stocks(ymd STRING, ...)
ROW FORMAT SERDE 'com.bizo.hive.serde.csv.CSVSerde'
STORED AS TEXTFILE
...;
```

While TSV support should be similar, there are no comparable third-party TSV SerDes available at the time of this writing.

ObjectInspector

Underneath the covers, Hive uses what is known as an `ObjectInspector` to transform raw records into objects that Hive can access.

Think Big Hive Reflection ObjectInspector

Think Big Analytics has created an `ObjectInspector` based on Java reflection called BeansStructObjectInspector   (*https://github.com/ThinkBigAnalytics/Hive-Extensions -from-Think-Big-Analytics*). Using the *JavaBeans* model for introspection, any "property" on objects that are exposed through **get** methods or as public member variables may be referenced in queries.

An example of how to use the `BeansStructObjectInspector` is as follows:

```
public class SampleDeserializer implements Deserializer {
  @Override
  public ObjectInspector getObjectInspector() throws SerDeException {
    return BeansStructObjectInspector.getBeansObjectInspector(YourObject.class);
  }
}
```

XML UDF

XML is inherently unstructured, which makes Hive a powerful database platform for XML. One of the reasons Hadoop is ideal as an XML database platform is the complexity and resource consumption to parse and process potentially large XML documents. Because Hadoop parallelizes processing of XML documents, Hive becomes a perfect tool for accelerating XML-related data solutions. Additionally, HiveQL natively enables access to XML's nested elements and values, then goes further by allowing joins on any of the nested fields, values, and attributes.

XPath (XML Path Language) is a global standard created by the W3C for addressing parts of an XML document. Using XPath as an expressive XML query language, Hive becomes extremely useful for extracting data from XML documents and into the Hive subsystem.

XPath models an XML document as a tree of nodes. Basic facilities are provided for access to primitive types, such as string, numeric, and Boolean types.

While commercial solutions such as Oracle XML DB and MarkLogic provide native XML database solutions, open source Hive leverages the advantages provided by the parallel petabyte processing of the Hadoop infrastructure to enable widely effective XML database vivification.

XPath-Related Functions

Hive contains a number of XPath-related UDFs since the 0.6.0 release (Table 15-1).

Table 15-1. XPath UDFs

Name	Description
xpath	Returns a Hive array of strings
xpath_string	Returns a string
xpath_boolean	Returns a Boolean
xpath_short	Returns a short integer
xpath_int	Returns an integer

Name	Description
xpath_long	Returns a long integer
xpath_float	Returns a floating-point number
xpath_double, xpath_number	Returns a double-precision floating-point number

Here are some examples where these functions are run on string literals:

```
hive> SELECT xpath(\'<a><b id="foo">b1</b><b id="bar">b2</b></a>\',\'//@id\')
    > FROM src LIMIT 1;
[foo","bar]
```

```
hive> SELECT xpath (\'<a><b class="bb">b1</b><b>b2</b><b>b3</b><c class="bb">c1</c>
<c>c2</c></a>\', \'a/*[@class="bb"]/text()\')
    > FROM src LIMIT 1;
[b1","c1]
```

(The long XML string was wrapped for space.)

```
hive> SELECT xpath_double (\'<a><b>2</b><c>4</c></a>\', \'a/b + a/c\')
    > FROM src LIMIT 1;
6.0
```

JSON SerDe

What if you want to query JSON (JavaScript Object Notation) data with Hive? If each JSON "document" is on a separate line, you can use TEXTFILE as the input and output format, then use a JSON SerDe to parse each JSON document as a record.

There is a third-party JSON SerDe that started as a Google "Summer of Code" project (*http://code.google.com/p/hive-json-serde/*) and was subsequently cloned and forked by other contributors. *Think Big Analytics (http://thinkbiganalytics.com)* created its own fork (*https://github.com/thinkbiganalytics/hive-json-serde*) and added an enhancement we'll go over in the discussion that follows.

In the following example, this SerDe is used to extract a few fields from JSON data for a fictitious messaging system. Not all the available fields are exposed. Those that are exposed become available as columns in the table:

```
CREATE EXTERNAL TABLE messages (
  msg_id     BIGINT,
  tstamp     STRING,
  text       STRING,
  user_id    BIGINT,
  user_name  STRING
)
ROW FORMAT SERDE "org.apache.hadoop.hive.contrib.serde2.JsonSerde"
WITH SERDEPROPERTIES (
  "msg_id"="$.id",
  "tstamp"="$.created_at",
  "text"="$.text",
  "user_id"="$.user.id",
```

```
    "user_name"="$.user.name"
)
LOCATION '/data/messages';
```

The `WITH SERDEPROPERTIES` is a Hive feature that allows the user to define properties that will be passed to the SerDe. The SerDe interprets those properties as it sees fit. Hive doesn't know or care what they mean.

In this case, the properties are used to map fields in the JSON documents to columns in the table. A string like `$.user.id` means to take each record, represented by `$`, find the `user` key, which is assumed to be a JSON map in this case, and finally extract the value for the `id` key inside the `user`. This value for the `id` is used as the value for the `user_id` column.

Once defined, the user runs queries as always, blissfully unaware that the queries are actually getting data from JSON!

Avro Hive SerDe

Avro is a serialization system—it's main feature is an evolvable schema-driven binary data format. Initially, Avro's goals appeared to be in conflict with Hive since both wish to provide schema or metadata information. However Hive and the Hive metastore have pluggable design and can defer to the Avro support to infer the schema.

The Hive Avro SerDe system was created by LinkedIn and has the following features:

- Infers the schema of the Hive table from the Avro schema
- Reads all Avro files within a table against a specified schema, taking advantage of Avro's backwards compatibility
- Supports arbitrarily nested schemas
- Translates all Avro data types into equivalent Hive types. Most types map exactly, but some Avro types do not exist in Hive and are automatically converted by Hive with Avro
- Understands compressed Avro files
- Transparently converts the Avro idiom of handling nullable types as `Union[T, null]` into just `T` and returns `null` when appropriate
- Writes any Hive table to Avro files

Defining Avro Schema Using Table Properties

Create an Avro table by specifying the `AvroSerDe`, `AvroContainerInputFormat`, and `Avro ContainerOutputFormat`. Avro has its own schema definition language. This schema definition language can be stored in the table properties as a string literal using the property `avro.schema.literal`. The schema specifies three columns: `number` as `int`, `firstname` as `string`, and `lastname` as `string`.

```
CREATE TABLE doctors
ROW FORMAT
SERDE 'org.apache.hadoop.hive.serde2.avro.AvroSerDe'
STORED AS
INPUTFORMAT 'org.apache.hadoop.hive.ql.io.avro.AvroContainerInputFormat'
OUTPUTFORMAT 'org.apache.hadoop.hive.ql.io.avro.AvroContainerOutputFormat'
TBLPROPERTIES ('avro.schema.literal'='{
  "namespace": "testing.hive.avro.serde",
  "name": "doctors",
  "type": "record",
  "fields": [
    {
      "name":"number",
      "type":"int",
      "doc":"Order of playing the role"
    },
    {
      "name":"first_name",
      "type":"string",
      "doc":"first name of actor playing role"
    },
    {
      "name":"last_name",
      "type":"string",
      "doc":"last name of actor playing role"
    }
  ]
}');
```

When the DESCRIBE command is run, Hive shows the name and types of the columns. In the output below you will notice that the third column of output states from deser ializer. This shows that the SerDe itself returned the information from the column rather than static values stored in the metastore:

```
hive> DESCRIBE doctors;
number          int     from deserializer
first_name      string  from deserializer
last_name       string  from deserializer
```

Defining a Schema from a URI

It is also possible to provide the schema as a URI. This can be a path to a file in HDFS or a URL to an HTTP server. To do this, specify avro.schema.url in table properties and do not specify avro.schema.literal.

The schema can be a file in HDFS:

```
TBLPROPERTIES ('avro.schema.url'='hdfs://hadoop:9020/path/to.schema')
```

The schema can also be stored on an HTTP server:

```
TBLPROPERTIES ('avro.schema.url'='http://site.com/path/to.schema')
```

Evolving Schema

Over time fields may be added or deprecated from data sets. Avro is designed with this in mind. An evolving schema is one that changes over time. Avro allows fields to be null. It also allows for default values to be returned if the column is not defined in the data file.

For example, if the Avro schema is changed and a field added, the `default` field supplies a value if the column is not found:

```
{
  "name":"extra_field",
  "type":"string",
  "doc:":"an extra field not in the original file",
  "default":"fishfingers and custard"
}
```

Binary Output

There are several kinds of binary output. We have already seen compression of files, sequence files (compressed or not), and related file types.

Sometimes, it's also useful to read and write streams of bytes. For example, you may have tools that expect a stream of bytes, without field separators of any kind, and you either use Hive to generate suitable files for those tools or you want to query such files with Hive. You may also want the benefits of storing numbers in compact binary forms instead of strings like "5034223," which consume more space. A common example is to query the output of the `tcpdump` command to analyze network behavior.

The following table expects its own files to be in text format, but it writes query results as binary streams:

```
CREATE TABLE binary_table (num1 INT, num2 INT)
ROW FORMAT SERDE 'org.apache.hadoop.hive.serde2.lazy.LazySimpleSerDe'
WITH SERDEPROPERTIES ('serialization.last.column.takes.rest'='true')
STORED AS
INPUTFORMAT 'org.apache.hadoop.mapred.TextInputFormat'
OUTPUTFORMAT 'org.apache.hadoop.hive.ql.io.HiveBinaryOutputFormat';
```

Here's a `SELECT TRANSFORM` query that reads binary data from a `src` table, streams it through the shell `cat` command and overwrites the contents of a `destination1` table:

```
INSERT OVERWRITE TABLE destination1
SELECT TRANSFORM(*)
USING 'cat' AS mydata STRING
ROW FORMAT SERDE 'org.apache.hadoop.hive.serde2.lazy.LazySimpleSerDe'
WITH SERDEPROPERTIES ('serialization.last.column.takes.rest'='true')
RECORDREADER 'org.apache.hadoop.hive.ql.exec.BinaryRecordReader'
FROM src;
```

CHAPTER 16

Hive Thrift Service

Hive has an optional component known as HiveServer or HiveThrift that allows access to Hive over a single port. Thrift is a software framework for scalable cross-language services development. See *http://thrift.apache.org/* for more details. Thrift allows clients using languages including Java, C++, Ruby, and many others, to programmatically access Hive remotely.

The CLI is the most common way to access Hive. However, the design of the CLI can make it difficult to use programmatically. The CLI is a fat client; it requires a local copy of all the Hive components and configuration as well as a copy of a Hadoop client and its configuration. Additionally, it works as an HDFS client, a MapReduce client, and a JDBC client (to access the metastore). Even with the proper client installation, having all of the correct network access can be difficult, especially across subnets or datacenters.

Starting the Thrift Server

To Get started with the HiveServer, start it in the background using the `service` knob for `hive`:

```
$ cd $HIVE_HOME
$ bin/hive --service hiveserver &
Starting Hive Thrift Server
```

A quick way to ensure the HiveServer is running is to use the `netstat` command to determine if port 10,000 is open and listening for connections:

```
$ netstat -nl | grep 10000
tcp  0  0 :::10000          :::*            LISTEN
```

(Some whitespace removed.) As mentioned, the HiveService uses Thrift. Thrift provides an interface language. With the interface, the Thrift compiler generates code that creates network RPC clients for many languages. Because Hive is written in Java, and Java bytecode is cross-platform, the clients for the Thrift server are included in the Hive release. One way to use these clients is by starting a Java project with an IDE and including these libraries or fetching them through Maven.

Setting Up Groovy to Connect to HiveService

For this example we will use Groovy (*http://groovy.codehaus.org/*). Groovy is an agile and dynamic language for the Java Virtual Machine. Groovy is ideal for prototyping because it integrates with Java and provides a read-eval-print-loop (REPL) for writing code on the fly:

```
$ curl -o http://dist.groovy.codehaus.org/distributions/groovy-binary-1.8.6.zip
$ unzip groovy-binary-1.8.6.zip
```

Next, add all Hive JARs to Groovy's `classpath` by editing the `groovy-starter.conf`. This will allow Groovy to communicate with Hive without having to manually load JAR files each session:

```
# load required libraries
load !{groovy.home}/lib/*.jar

# load user specific libraries
load !{user.home}/.groovy/lib/*.jar

# tools.jar for ant tasks
load ${tools.jar}

load /home/edward/hadoop/hadoop-0.20.2_local/*.jar
load /home/edward/hadoop/hadoop-0.20.2_local/lib/*.jar
load /home/edward/hive-0.9.0/lib/*.jar
```

 Groovy has an `@grab` annotation that can fetch JAR files from Maven web repositories, but currently some packaging issues with Hive prevent this from working correctly.

Groovy provides a shell found inside the distribution at *bin/groovysh*. Groovysh provides a REPL for interactive programming. Groovy code is similar to Java code, although it does have other forms including closures. For the most part, you can write Groovy as you would write Java.

Connecting to HiveServer

From the REPL, import Hive- and Thrift-related classes. These classes are used to connect to Hive and create an instance of HiveClient. HiveClient has the methods users will typically use to interact with Hive:

```
$ $HOME/groovy/groovy-1.8.0/bin/groovysh
Groovy Shell (1.8.0, JVM: 1.6.0_23)
Type 'help' or '\h' for help.
```

```
groovy:000> import org.apache.hadoop.hive.service.*;
groovy:000> import org.apache.thrift.protocol.*;
groovy:000> import org.apache.thrift.transport.*;
groovy:000> transport = new TSocket("localhost" , 10000);
groovy:000> protocol = new TBinaryProtocol(transport);
groovy:000> client = new HiveClient(protocol);
groovy:000> transport.open();
groovy:000> client.execute("show tables");
```

Getting Cluster Status

The getClusterStatus method retrieves information from the Hadoop JobTracker. This can be used to collect performance metrics and can also be used to wait for a lull to launch a job:

```
groovy:000> client.getClusterStatus()
===> HiveClusterStatus(taskTrackers:50, mapTasks:52, reduceTasks:40,
maxMapTasks:480, maxReduceTasks:240, state:RUNNING)
```

Result Set Schema

After executing a query, you can get the schema of the result set using the get Schema() method. If you call this method before a query, it may return a null schema:

```
groovy:000> client.getSchema()
===> Schema(fieldSchemas:null, properties:null)
groovy:000> client.execute("show tables");
===> null
groovy:000> client.getSchema()
===> Schema(fieldSchemas:[FieldSchema(name:tab_name, type:string,
comment:from deserializer)], properties:null)
```

Fetching Results

After a query is run, you can fetch results with the fetchOne() method. Retrieving large result sets with the Thrift interface is not suggested. However, it does offer several methods to retrieve data using a one-way cursor. The fetchOne() method retrieves an entire row:

```
groovy:000> client.fetchOne()
===> cookjar_small
```

Instead of retrieving rows one at a time, the entire result set can be retrieved as a string array using the fetchAll() method:

```
groovy:000> client.fetchAll()
===> [macetest, missing_final, one, time_to_serve, two]
```

Also available is fetchN, which fetches N rows at a time.

Retrieving Query Plan

After a query is started, the getQueryPlan() method is used to retrieve status information about the query. The information includes information on counters and the state of the job:

```
groovy:000> client.execute("SELECT * FROM time_to_serve");
===> null
groovy:000> client.getQueryPlan()
===> QueryPlan(queries:[Query(queryId:hadoop_20120218180808_...-aedf367ea2f3,
queryType:null, queryAttributes:{queryString=SELECT * FROM time_to_serve},
queryCounters:null, stageGraph:Graph(nodeType:STAGE, roots:null,
adjacencyList:null), stageList:null, done:true, started:true)],
done:false, started:false)
```

(A long number was elided.)

Metastore Methods

The Hive service also connects to the Hive metastore via Thrift. Generally, users should not call metastore methods that modify directly and should only interact with Hive via the HiveQL language. Users should utilize the read-only methods that provide meta-information about tables. For example, the get_partition_names (String, String, short) method can be used to determine which partitions are available to a query:

```
groovy:000> client.get_partition_names("default", "fracture_act", (short)0)
[ hit_date=20120218/mid=001839,hit_date=20120218/mid=001842,
hit_date=20120218/mid=001846 ]
```

It is important to remember that while the metastore API is relatively stable in terms of changes, the methods inside, including their signatures and purpose, can change between releases. Hive tries to maintain compatibility in the HiveQL language, which masks changes at these levels.

Example Table Checker

The ability to access the metastore programmatically provides the capacity to monitor and enforce conditions across your deployment. For example, a check can be written to ensure that all tables use compression, or that tables with names that start with zz should not exist longer than 10 days. These small "Hive-lets" can be written quickly and executed remotely, if necessary.

Finding tables not marked as external

By default, managed tables store their data inside the warehouse directory, which is /user/hive/warehouse by default. Usually, external tables do not use this directory, but there is nothing that prevents you from putting them there. Enforcing a rule that managed tables should only be inside the warehouse directory will keep the environment sane.

In the following application, the outer loop iterates through the list returned from get_all_databases(). The inner loop iterates through the list returned from get_all_tables(database). The Table object returned from get_table(data base,table) has all the information about the table in the metastore. We determine the location of the table and check that the type matches the string MANAGED_TABLE. External tables have a type EXTERNAL. A list of "bad" table names is returned:

```
public List<String> check(){
  List<String> bad = new ArrayList<String>();
  for (String database: client.get_all_databases() ){
    for (String table: client.get_all_tables(database) ){
      try {
        Table t = client.get_table(database,table);
        URI u = new URI(t.getSd().getLocation());
        if (t.getTableType().equals("MANAGED_TABLE") &&
          ! u.getPath().contains("/user/hive/warehouse") ){
          System.out.println(t.getTableName()
            + " is a non external table mounted inside /user/hive/warehouse" );
          bad.add(t.getTableName());
        }
      } catch (Exception ex){
        System.err.println("Had exception but will continue " +ex);
      }
    }
  }
  return bad;
}
```

Administrating HiveServer

The Hive CLI creates local artifacts like the *.hivehistory* file along with entries in */tmp* and hadoop.tmp.dir. Because the HiveService becomes the place where Hadoop jobs launch from, there are some considerations when deploying it.

Productionizing HiveService

HiveService is a good alternative to having the entire Hive client install local to the machine that launches the job. Using it in production does bring up some added issues that need to be addressed. The work that used to be done on the client machine, in planning and managing the tasks, now happens on the server. If you are launching many clients simultaneously, this could cause too much load for a single HiveService. A simple solution is to use a TCP load balancer or proxy to alternate connections between a pool of backend servers.

There are several ways to do TCP load balancing and you should consult your network administrator for the best solution. We suggest a simple solution that uses the hap roxy tool to balance connections between backend ThriftServers.

First, inventory your physical ThriftServers and document the virtual server that will be your proxy (Tables 16-1 and 16-2).

Table 16-1. Physical server inventory

Short name	Hostname and port
HiveService1	hiveservice1.example.pvt:10000
HiveService2	hiveservice2.example.pvt:10000

Table 16-2. Proxy Configuration

Hostname	IP
hiveprimary.example.pvt	10.10.10.100

Install ha-proxy (HAP). Depending on your operating system and distribution these steps may be different. Example assumes a RHEL/CENTOS distribution:

```
$sudo yum install haproxy
```

Use the inventory prepared above to build the configuration file:

```
$ more /etc/haproxy/haproxy.cfg
listen hiveprimary 10.10.10.100:10000
balance leastconn
mode tcp
server hivethrift1 hiveservice1.example.pvt:10000 check
server hivethrift2 hiveservice1.example.pvt:10000 check
```

Start HAP via the system init script. After you have confirmed it is working, add it to the default system start-up with chkconfig:

```
$ sudo /etc/init.d/haproxy start
$ sudo chkconfig haproxy on
```

Cleanup

Hive offers the configuration variable hive.start.cleanup.scratchdir, which is set to false. Setting it to true will cause the service to clean up its scratch directory on restart:

```
<property>
  <name>hive.start.cleanup.scratchdir</name>
  <value>true</value>
  <description>To clean up the Hive scratchdir while
  starting the Hive server</description>
</property>
```

Hive ThriftMetastore

Typically, a Hive session connects directly to a JDBC database, which it uses as a met-astore. Hive provides an optional component known as the ThriftMetastore. In this setup, the Hive client connects to the ThriftMetastore, which in turn communicates to the JDBC Metastore. Most deployments will not require this component. It is useful for deployments that have non-Java clients that need access to information in the met-astore. Using the metastore will require two separate configurations.

ThriftMetastore Configuration

The ThriftMetastore should be set up to communicate with the actual metastore using JDBC. Then start up the metastore in the following manner:

```
$ cd ~
$ bin/hive --service metastore &
[1] 17096
Starting Hive Metastore Server
```

Confirm the metastore is running using the `netstat` command:

```
$ netstat -an | grep 9083
tcp  0  0 :::9083     :::*          LISTEN
```

Client Configuration

Clients like the CLI should communicate with the metastore directory:

```
<property>
  <name>hive.metastore.local</name>
  <value>false</value>
  <description>controls whether to connect to remove metastore server
    or open a new metastore server in Hive Client JVM</description>
</property>

<property>
  <name>hive.metastore.uris</name>
  <value>thrift://metastore_server:9083</value>
  <description>controls whether to connect to remove metastore server
    or open a new metastore server in Hive Client JVM</description>
</property>
```

This change should be seamless from the user experience. Although, there are some nuances with Hadoop Security and the metastore having to do work as the user.

CHAPTER 17

Storage Handlers and NoSQL

Storage Handlers are a combination of `InputFormat`, `OutputFormat`, `SerDe`, and specific code that Hive uses to treat an external entity as a standard Hive table. This allows the user to issue queries seamlessly whether the table represents a text file stored in Hadoop or a column family stored in a NoSQL database such as *Apache HBase*, *Apache Cassandra*, and *Amazon DynamoDB*. Storage handlers are not only limited to NoSQL databases, a storage handler could be designed for many different kinds of data stores.

 A specific storage handler may only implement some of the capabilities. For example, a given storage handler may allow read-only access or impose some other restriction.

Storage handlers offer a streamlined system for ETL. For example, a Hive query could be run that selects a data table that is backed by sequence files, however it could output

Storage Handler Background

Hadoop has an abstraction known as `InputFormat` that allows data from different sources and formats to be used as input for a job. The `TextInputFormat` is a concrete implementation of `InputFormat`. It works by providing Hadoop with information on how to split a given path into multiple tasks, and it provides a `RecordReader` that provides methods for reading data from each split.

Hadoop also has an abstraction known as `OutputFormat`, which takes the output from a job and outputs it to an entity. The `TextOutputFormat` is a concrete implementation of `OutputFormat`. It works by persisting output to a file which could be stored on HDFS or locally.

Input and output that represent physical files are common in Hadoop, however `Input Format` and `OutputFormat` abstractions can be used to load and persist data from other sources including relational databases, NoSQL stores like Cassandra or HBase, or any-thing that `InputFormat` or `OutputFormat` can be designed around!

In the HiveQL chapter, we demonstrated the *Word Count* example written in Java Code, and then demonstrated an equivalent solution written in Hive. Hive's abstractions such as tables, types, row format, and other metadata are used by Hive to understand the source data. Once Hive understands the source data, the query engine can process the data using familiar HiveQL operators.

Many NoSQL databases have implemented Hive connectors using custom adapters.

HiveStorageHandler

`HiveStorageHandler` is the primary interface Hive uses to connect with NoSQL stores such as HBase, Cassandra, and others. An examination of the interface shows that a custom `InputFormat`, `OutputFormat`, and `SerDe` must be defined. The storage handler enables both reading from and writing to the underlying storage subsystem. This translates into writing `SELECT` queries against the data system, as well as writing into the data system for actions such as reports.

When executing Hive queries over NoSQL databases, the performance is less than normal Hive and MapReduce jobs on HDFS due to the overhead of the NoSQL system. Some of the reasons include the socket connection to the server and the merging of multiple underlying files, whereas typical access from HDFS is completely sequential I/O. Sequential I/O is very fast on modern hard drives.

A common technique for combining NoSQL databases with Hadoop in an overall system architecture is to use the NoSQL database cluster for real-time work, and utilize the Hadoop cluster for batch-oriented work. If the NoSQL system is the master data store, and that data needs to be queried on using batch jobs with Hadoop, bulk exporting is an efficient way to convert the NoSQL data into HDFS files. Once the HDFS files are created via an export, batch Hadoop jobs may be executed with a maximum efficiency.

HBase

The following creates a Hive table and an HBase table using HiveQL:

```
CREATE TABLE hbase_stocks(key INT, name STRING, price FLOAT)
STORED BY 'org.apache.hadoop.hive.hbase.HBaseStorageHandler'
WITH SERDEPROPERTIES ("hbase.columns.mapping" = ":key,stock:val")
TBLPROPERTIES ("hbase.table.name" = "stocks");
```

To create a Hive table that points to an existing HBase table, the `CREATE EXTERNAL TABLE` HiveQL statement must be used:

```
CREATE EXTERNAL TABLE hbase_stocks(key INT, name STRING, price FLOAT)
STORED BY 'org.apache.hadoop.hive.hbase.HBaseStorageHandler'
```

```
WITH SERDEPROPERTIES ("hbase.columns.mapping" = "cf1:val")
TBLPROPERTIES("hbase.table.name" = "stocks");
```

Instead of scanning the entire HBase table for a given Hive query, filter pushdowns will constrain the row data returned to Hive.

Examples of the types of predicates that are converted into pushdowns are:

- key < 20
- key = 20
- key < 20 and key > 10

Any other more complex types of predicates will be ignored and not utilize the pushdown feature.

The following is an example of creating a simple table and a query that will use the filter pushdown feature. Note the pushdown is always on the HBase key, and not the column values of a column family:

```
CREATE TABLE hbase_pushdown(key int, value string)
STORED BY 'org.apache.hadoop.hive.hbase.HBaseStorageHandler'
WITH SERDEPROPERTIES ("hbase.columns.mapping" = ":key,cf:string");

SELECT * FROM hbase_pushdown WHERE key = 90;
```

The following query will not result in a pushdown because it contains an OR on the predicate:

```
SELECT * FROM hbase_pushdown
WHERE key <= '80' OR key >= '100';
```

Hive with HBase supports joins on HBase tables to HBase tables, and HBase tables to non-HBase tables.

By default, pushdowns are turned on, however they may be turned off with the following:

```
set hive.optimize.ppd.storage=false;
```

It is important to note when inserting data into HBase from Hive that HBase requires unique keys, whereas Hive has no such constraint.

A few notes on column mapping Hive for HBase:

- There is no way to access the HBase row timestamp, and only the latest version of a row is returned
- The HBase key must be defined explicitly

Cassandra

Cassandra has implemented the `HiveStorageHandler` interface in a similar way to that of HBase. The implementation was originally performed by Datastax on the Brisk project.

The model is fairly straightforward, a Cassandra column family maps to a Hive table. In turn, Cassandra column names map directly to Hive column names.

Static Column Mapping

Static column mapping is useful when the user has specific columns inside Cassandra which they wish to map to Hive columns. The following is an example of creating an external Hive table that maps to an existing Cassandra keyspace and column family:

```
CREATE EXTERNAL TABLE Weblog(useragent string, ipaddress string, timestamp string)
STORED BY 'org.apache.hadoop.hive.cassandra.CassandraStorageHandler'
WITH SERDEPROPERTIES (
  "cassandra.columns.mapping" = ":key,user_agent,ip_address,time_stamp")
TBLPROPERTIES (
  "cassandra.range.size" = "200",
  "cassandra.slice.predicate.size" = "150" );
```

Transposed Column Mapping for Dynamic Columns

Some use cases of Cassandra use dynamic columns. This use case is where a given column family does not have fixed, named columns, but rather the columns of a row key represent some piece of data. This is often used in time series data where the column name represents a time and the column value represents the value at that time. This is also useful if the column names are not known or you wish to retrieve all of them:

```
CREATE EXTERNAL TABLE Weblog(useragent string, ipaddress string, timestamp string)
STORED BY 'org.apache.hadoop.hive.cassandra.CassandraStorageHandler'
WITH SERDEPROPERTIES (
  "cassandra.columns.mapping" = ":key,:column,:value");
```

Cassandra SerDe Properties

The following properties in Table 17-1 can be declared in a `WITH SERDEPROPERTIES` clause:

Table 17-1. Cassandra SerDe storage handler properties

Name	Description
cassandra.columns.mapping	Mapping of Hive to Cassandra columns
cassandra.cf.name	Column family name in Cassandra
cassandra.host	IP of a Cassandra node to connect to
cassandra.port	Cassandra RPC port: default 9160

Name	Description
cassandra.partitioner	Partitioner: default RandomPartitioner

The following properties in Table 17-2 can be declared in a TBLPROPERTIES clause:

Table 17-2. Cassandra table properties

Name	Description
cassandra.ks.name	Cassandra keyspace name
cassandra.ks.repfactor	Cassandra replication factor: default 1
cassandra.ks.strategy	Replication strategy: default SimpleStrategy
cassandra.input.split.size	MapReduce split size: default 64 * 1024
cassandra.range.size	MapReduce range batch size: default 1000
cassandra.slice.predicate.size	MapReduce slice predicate size: default 1000

DynamoDB

Amazon's *Dynamo* was one of the first NoSQL databases. Its design influenced many other databases, including Cassandra and HBase. Despite its influence, Dynamo was restricted to internal use by Amazon until recently. Amazon released another database influenced by the original Dynamo called DynamoDB.

DynamoDB is in the family of key-value databases. In DynamoDB, tables are a collection of items and they are required to have a primary key. An item consists of a key and an arbitrary number of attributes. The set of attributes can vary from item to item.

You can query a table with Hive and you can move data to and from S3. Here is another example of a Hive table for stocks that is backed by a DynamoDB table:

```
CREATE EXTERNAL TABLE dynamo_stocks(
  key INT, symbol STRING,
  ymd STRING, price FLOAT)
STORED BY
'org.apache.hadoop.hive.dynamodb.DynamoDBStorageHandler'
TBLPROPERTIES (
  "dynamodb.table.name" = "Stocks",
  "dynamodb.column.mapping" =
  "key:Key,symbol:Symbol,
    ymd:YMD,price_close:Close");
```

See *http://aws.amazon.com/dynamodb/* for more information about DynamoDB.

CHAPTER 18

Security

To understand Hive security, we have to backtrack and understand Hadoop security and the history of Hadoop. Hadoop started out as a subproject of Apache Nutch. At that time and through its early formative years, features were prioritized over security. Security is more complex in a distributed system because multiple components across different machines need to communicate with each other.

Unsecured Hadoop like the versions before the v0.20.205 release derived the username by forking a call to the *whoami* program. Users are free to change this parameter by setting the `hadoop.job.ugi` property for `FSShell` (filesystem) commands. Map and reduce tasks all run under the same system user (usually `hadoop` or `mapred`) on *TaskTracker* nodes. Also, Hadoop components are typically listening on ports with high numbers. They are also typically launched by nonprivileged users (i.e., users other than root).

The recent efforts to secure Hadoop involved several changes, primarily the incorporation of *Kerberos* (*http://web.mit.edu/kerberos*) authorization support, but also other changes to close vulnerabilities. Kerberos allows mutual authentication between client and server. A client's request for a ticket is passed along with a request. Tasks on the *TaskTracker* are run as the user who launched the job. Users are no longer able to impersonate other users by setting the `hadoop.job.ugi` property. For this to work, all Hadoop components must use Kerberos security from end to end.

Hive was created before any of this Kerberos support was added to Hadoop, and Hive is not yet fully compliant with the Hadoop security changes. For example, the connection to the Hive metastore may use a direct connection to a JDBC database or it may go through Thrift, which will have to take actions on behalf of the user. Components like the Thrift-based HiveService also have to impersonate other users. The file ownership model of Hadoop, where one owner and group own a file, is different than the model many databases have implemented where access is granted and revoked on a table in a row- or column-based manner.

This chapter attempts to highlight components of Hive that operate differently between secure and nonsecure Hadoop. For more information on Hadoop security, consult Hadoop: The Definitive Guide by Tom White (O'Reilly).

 Security support in Hadoop is still relatively new and evolving. Some parts of Hive are not yet compliant with Hadoop security support. The discussion in this section summarizes the current state of Hive security, but it is not meant to be definitive.

For more information on Hive security, consult the Security wiki page *https://cwiki .apache.org/confluence/display/Hive/Security*. Also, more than in any other chapter in this book, we'll occasionally refer you to Hive JIRA entries for more information.

Integration with Hadoop Security

Hive v0.7.0 added integration with Hadoop security,[1] meaning, for example, that when Hive sends MapReduce jobs to the *JobTracker* in a secure cluster, it will use the proper authentication procedures. User privileges can be granted and revoked, as we'll discuss below.

There are still several known security gaps involving Thrift and other components, as listed on the security wiki page.

Authentication with Hive

When files and directories are owned by different users, the permissions set on the files become important. The HDFS permissions system is very similar to the Unix model, where there are three entities: *user*, *group*, and *others*. Also, there are three permissions: *read*, *write*, and *execute*. Hive has a configuration variable `hive.files.umask.value` that defines a `umask` value used to set the default permissions of newly created files, by masking bits:

```
<property>
  <name>hive.files.umask.value</name>
  <value>0002</value>
  <description>The dfs.umask value for the hive created folders</description>
</property>
```

Also, when the property `hive.metastore.authorization.storage.checks` is `true`, Hive prevents a user from dropping a table when the user does not have permission to delete the underlying files that back the table. The default value for this property is `false`, but it should be set to `true`:

---

1. See *https://issues.apache.org/jira/browse/HIVE-1264*.

```
<property>
  <name>hive.metastore.authorization.storage.checks</name>
  <value>true</value>
  <description>Should the metastore do authorization checks against
        the underlying storage for operations like drop-partition (disallow
    the drop-partition if the user in question doesn't have permissions
    to delete the corresponding directory on the storage).</description>
</property>
```

When running in secure mode, the Hive metastore will make a best-effort attempt to set hive.metastore.execute.setugi to true:

```
<property>
  <name>hive.metastore.execute.setugi</name>
  <value>false</value>
  <description>In unsecure mode, setting this property to true will
    cause the metastore to execute DFS operations using the client's
    reported user and group permissions. Note that this property must
    be set on both the client and server sides. Further note that its
    best effort. If client sets it to true and server sets it to false,
    client setting will be ignored.</description>
</property>
```

More details can be found at *https://issues.apache.org/jira/browse/HIVE-842*, "Authentication Infrastructure for Hive."

Authorization in Hive

Hive v0.7.0 also added support for specifying authorization settings through HiveQL.[2]

By default, the authorization component is set to false. This needs to be set to true to enable authentication:

```
<property>
  <name>hive.security.authorization.enabled</name>
  <value>true</value>
  <description>Enable or disable the hive client authorization</description>
</property>
<property>
  <name>hive.security.authorization.createtable.owner.grants</name>
  <value>ALL</value>
  <description>The privileges automatically granted to the owner whenever
    a table gets created.An example like "select,drop" will grant select
        and drop privilege to the owner of the table</description>
</property>
```

By default, hive.security.authorization.createtable.owner.grants is set to null, disabling user access to her own tables. So, we also gave table creators subsequent access to their tables!

---

2. See *https://issues.apache.org/jira/browse/HIVE-78*, "Authorization infrastructure for Hive," and a draft description of this feature at *https://cwiki.apache.org/Hive/languagemanual-auth.html*.

Currently it is possible for users to use the set command to disable authentication by setting this property to false.

Users, Groups, and Roles

Privileges are granted or revoked to a user, a group, or a role. We will walk through granting privileges to each of these entities:

```
hive> set hive.security.authorization.enabled=true;

hive> CREATE TABLE authorization_test (key int, value string);
Authorization failed:No privilege 'Create' found for outputs { database:default}.
Use show grant to get more details.
```

Already we can see that our user does not have the privilege to create tables in the default database. Privileges can be assigned to several entities. The first entity is a user: the user in Hive is your system user. We can determine the user and then grant that user permission to create tables in the default database:

```
hive> set system:user.name;
system:user.name=edward

hive> GRANT CREATE ON DATABASE default TO USER edward;

hive> CREATE TABLE authorization_test (key INT, value STRING);
```

We can confirm our privileges using SHOW GRANT:

```
hive> SHOW GRANT USER edward ON DATABASE default;

database        default
principalName   edward
principalType   USER
privilege       Create
grantTime       Mon Mar 19 09:18:10 EDT 2012
grantor edward
```

Granting permissions on a per-user basis becomes an administrative burden quickly with many users and many tables. A better option is to grant permissions based on groups. A group in Hive is equivalent to the user's primary POSIX group:

```
hive> CREATE TABLE authorization_test_group(a int,b int);

hive> SELECT * FROM authorization_test_group;
Authorization failed:No privilege 'Select' found for inputs
{ database:default, table:authorization_test_group, columnName:a}.
Use show grant to get more details.

hive> GRANT SELECT on table authorization_test_group to group edward;

hive> SELECT * FROM authorization_test_group;
OK
Time taken: 0.119 seconds
```

When user and group permissions are not flexible enough, `roles` can be used. Users are placed into roles and then roles can be granted privileges. Roles are very flexible, because unlike groups that are controlled externally by the system, roles are controlled from inside Hive:

```
hive> CREATE TABLE authentication_test_role (a int , b int);

hive> SELECT * FROM authentication_test_role;
Authorization failed:No privilege 'Select' found for inputs
{ database:default, table:authentication_test_role, columnName:a}.
Use show grant to get more details.

hive> CREATE ROLE users_who_can_select_authentication_test_role;

hive> GRANT ROLE users_who_can_select_authentication_test_role TO USER edward;

hive> GRANT SELECT ON TABLE authentication_test_role
    > TO ROLE users_who_can_select_authentication_test_role;

hive> SELECT * FROM authentication_test_role;
OK
Time taken: 0.103 seconds
```

Privileges to Grant and Revoke

Table 18-1 lists the available privileges that can be configured.

Table 18-1. Privileges

Name	Description
ALL	All the privileges applied at once.
ALTER	The ability to alter tables.
CREATE	The ability to create tables.
DROP	The ability to remove tables or partitions inside of tables.
INDEX	The ability to create an index on a table (NOTE: not currently implemented).
LOCK	The ability to lock and unlock tables when concurrency is enabled.
SELECT	The ability to query a table or partition.
SHOW_DATABASE	The ability to view the available databases.
UPDATE	The ability to load or insert table into table or partition.

Here is an example session that illustrates the use of `CREATE` privileges:

```
hive> SET hive.security.authorization.enabled=true;

hive> CREATE DATABASE edsstuff;
```

```
hive> USE edsstuff;

hive> CREATE TABLE a (id INT);
Authorization failed:No privilege 'Create' found for outputs
{ database:edsstuff}. Use show grant to get more details.

hive> GRANT CREATE ON DATABASE edsstuff TO USER edward;

hive> CREATE TABLE a (id INT);

hive> CREATE EXTERNAL TABLE ab (id INT);
```

Similarly, we can grant ALTER privileges:

```
hive> ALTER TABLE a REPLACE COLUMNS (a int , b int);
Authorization failed:No privilege 'Alter' found for inputs
{ database:edsstuff, table:a}. Use show grant to get more details.

hive> GRANT ALTER ON TABLE a TO USER edward;

hive> ALTER TABLE a REPLACE COLUMNS (a int , b int);
```

Note that altering a table to add a partition does not require ALTER privileges:

```
hive> ALTER TABLE a_part_table ADD PARTITION (b=5);
```

UPDATE privileges are required to load data into a table:

```
hive> LOAD DATA INPATH '${env:HIVE_HOME}/NOTICE'
    > INTO TABLE a_part_table PARTITION (b=5);
Authorization failed:No privilege 'Update' found for outputs
{ database:edsstuff, table:a_part_table}. Use show grant to get more details.

hive> GRANT UPDATE ON TABLE a_part_table TO USER edward;

hive> LOAD DATA INPATH '${env:HIVE_HOME}/NOTICE'
    > INTO TABLE a_part_table PARTITION (b=5);
Loading data to table edsstuff.a_part_table partition (b=5)
```

Dropping a table or partition requires DROP privileges:

```
hive> ALTER TABLE a_part_table DROP PARTITION (b=5);
Authorization failed:No privilege 'Drop' found for inputs
{ database:edsstuff, table:a_part_table}. Use show grant to get more details.
```

Querying from a table or partition requires SELECT privileges:

```
hive> SELECT id FROM a_part_table;
Authorization failed:No privilege 'Select' found for inputs
{ database:edsstuff, table:a_part_table, columnName:id}. Use show
grant to get more details.

hive> GRANT SELECT ON TABLE a_part_table TO USER edward;

hive> SELECT id FROM a_part_table;
```

The syntax `GRANT SELECT(COLUMN)` is currently accepted but does nothing.

You can also grant all privileges:

```
hive> GRANT ALL ON TABLE a_part_table TO USER edward;
```

Partition-Level Privileges

It is very common for Hive tables to be partitioned. By default, privileges are granted on the table level. However, privileges can be granted on a per-partition basis. To do this, set the table property `PARTITION_LEVEL_PRIVILEGE` to `TRUE`:

```
hive> CREATE TABLE authorize_part (key INT, value STRING)
    > PARTITIONED BY (ds STRING);

hive> ALTER TABLE authorization_part
    > SET TBLPROPERTIES ("PARTITION_LEVEL_PRIVILEGE"="TRUE");
Authorization failed:No privilege 'Alter' found for inputs
{database:default, table:authorization_part}.
Use show grant to get more details.

hive> GRANT ALTER ON table authorization_part to user edward;

hive> ALTER TABLE authorization_part
    > SET TBLPROPERTIES ("PARTITION_LEVEL_PRIVILEGE"="TRUE");

hive> GRANT SELECT ON TABLE authorization_part TO USER edward;

hive> ALTER TABLE authorization_part ADD PARTITION (ds='3');

hive> ALTER TABLE authorization_part ADD PARTITION (ds='4');

hive> SELECT * FROM authorization_part WHERE ds='3';

hive> REVOKE SELECT ON TABLE authorization_part partition (ds='3') FROM USER edward;

hive> SELECT * FROM authorization_part WHERE ds='3';
Authorization failed:No privilege 'Select' found for inputs
{ database:default, table:authorization_part, partitionName:ds=3, columnName:key}.
Use show grant to get more details.

hive> SELECT * FROM authorization_part WHERE ds='4';
OK
Time taken: 0.146 seconds
```

Automatic Grants

Regular users will want to create tables and not bother with granting privileges to themselves to perform subsequent queries, etc. Earlier, we showed that you might want to grant `ALL` privileges, by default, but you can narrow the allowed privileges instead.

The property `hive.security.authorization.createtable.owner.grants` determines the automatically granted privileges for a table given to the user who created it. In the following example, rather than granting `ALL` privileges, the users are automatically granted `SELECT` and `DROP` privileges for their own tables:

```
<property>
  <name>hive.security.authorization.createtable.owner.grants</name>
  <value>select,drop</value>
</property>
```

Similarly, specific users can be granted automatic privileges on tables as they are created. The variable `hive.security.authorization.createtable.user.grants` controls this behavior. The following example shows how a Hive administrator `admin1` and user `edward` are granted privileges to read every table, while `user1` can only create tables:

```
<property>
  <name>hive.security.authorization.createtable.user.grants</name>
  <value>admin1,edward:select;user1:create</value>
</property>
```

Similar properties exist to automatically grant privileges to groups and roles. The names of the properties are `hive.security.authorization.createtable.group.grants` for groups and `hive.security.authorization.createtable.role.grants` for roles. The values of the properties follow the same format just shown.

CHAPTER 19

Locking

While HiveQL is an SQL dialect, Hive lacks the traditional support for locking on a column, row, or query, as typically used with update or insert queries. Files in Hadoop are traditionally write-once (although Hadoop does support limited append semantics). Because of the write-once nature and the streaming style of MapReduce, access to fine-grained locking is unnecessary.

However, since Hadoop and Hive are multi-user systems, locking and coordination are valuable in some situations. For example, if one user wishes to lock a table, because an `INSERT OVERWRITE` query is changing its content, and a second user attempts to issue a query against the table at the same time, the query could fail or yield invalid results.

Hive can be thought of as a fat client, in the sense that each Hive CLI, Thrift server, or web interface instance is completely independent of the other instances. Because of this independence, locking must be coordinated by a separate system.

Locking Support in Hive with Zookeeper

Hive includes a locking feature that uses *Apache Zookeeper (http://zookeeper.apache .org/)* for locking. Zookeeper implements highly reliable distributed coordination. Other than some additional setup and configuration steps, Zookeeper is invisible to Hive users.

To set up Zookeeper, designate one or more servers to run its server processes. Three Zookeeper nodes is a typical minimum size, to provide a quorum and to provide sufficient redundancy.

For our next example, we will use three nodes: `zk1.site.pvt`, `zk2.site.pvt`, and `zk3.site.pvt`.

Download and extract a Zookeeper release. In the following commands, we will install Zookeeper in the */opt* directory, requiring `sudo` access (a later version of Zookeeper, if any, will probably work fine, too):

```
$ cd /opt
$ sudo curl -o http://www.ecoficial.com/am/zookeeper/stable/zookeeper-3.3.3.tar.gz
$ sudo tar -xf zookeeper-3.3.3.tar.gz
$ sudo ln -s zookeeper-3.3.3 zookeeper
```

Make a directory for Zookeeper to store its data:

```
$ sudo mkdir /var/zookeeper
```

Create the Zookeeper configuration file */opt/zookeeper/conf/zoo.cfg* with the following contents, edited as appropriate for your installation:

```
tickTime=2000
dataDir=/var/zookeeper
clientPort=2181
initLimit=5
syncLimit=2
server.1=zk1.site.pvt:2888:3888
server.2=zk2.site.pvt:2888:3888
server.3=zk3.site.pvt:2888:3888
```

On each server, create a *myid* file and ensure the contents of the file matches the ID from the configuration. For example, for the file on the `zk1.site.pvt` node, you could use the following command to create the file:

```
$ sudo echo 1 > /var/zookeeper/myid
```

Finally, start Zookeeper:

```
$ sudo /opt/zookeeper/bin/zkServer.sh start
```

 We are starting the process as root, which is generally not recommended for most processes. You could use any standard techniques to run this file as a different user.

Once the Zookeeper nodes are in communication with each other, it will be possible to create data on one Zookeeper node and read it from the other. For example, run this session on one node:

```
$ /opt/zookeeper/bin/zkCli.sh -server zk1.site.pvt:2181
[zk: zk1.site.pvt:2181(CONNECTED) 3] ls /
[zookeeper]
[zk: zk1.site.pvt:2181(CONNECTED) 4] create /zk_test my_data
Created /zk_test
```

Then, run this session on a different node or a different terminal window on the first node:

```
$ /opt/zookeeper/bin/zkCli.sh -server zk1.site.pvt:2181
[zk: zk1.site.pvt:2181(CONNECTED) 0] ls /
[zookeeper, zk_test]
[zk: zk1.site.pvt:2181(CONNECTED) 1]
```

Whew! Okay, the hard part is over. Now we need to configure Hive so it can use these Zookeeper nodes to enable the concurrency support.

In the *$HIVE_HOME/hive-site.xml* file, set the following properties:

```
<property>
  <name>hive.zookeeper.quorum</name>
  <value>zk1.site.pvt,zk1.site.pvt,zk1.site.pvt</value>
  <description>The list of zookeeper servers to talk to.
  This is only needed for read/write locks.</description>
</property>

<property>
  <name>hive.support.concurrency</name>
  <value>true</value>
  <description>Whether Hive supports concurrency or not.
  A Zookeeper instance must be up and running for the default
  Hive lock manager to support read-write locks.</description>
</property>
```

With these settings configured, Hive automatically starts acquiring locks for certain queries. You can see all current locks with the SHOW LOCKS command:

```
hive> SHOW LOCKS;
default@people_20111230 SHARED
default@places  SHARED
default@places@hit_date=20111230          SHARED
...
```

The following more focused queries are also supported, where the ellipsis would be replaced with an appropriate partition specification, assuming that places is partitioned:

```
hive> SHOW LOCKS places EXTENDED;
default@places  SHARED
...
hive> SHOW LOCKS places PARTITION (...);
default@places  SHARED
...
hive> SHOW LOCKS places PARTITION (...) EXTENDED;
default@places  SHARED
...
```

There are two types of locks provided by Hive, and they are enabled automatically when the concurrency feature is enabled. A *shared* lock is acquired when a table is read. Multiple, concurrent shared locks are allowed.

An *exclusive* lock is required for all other operations that modify the table in some way. They not only freeze out other table-mutating operations, they also prevent queries by other processes.

When the table is partitioned, acquiring an exclusive lock on a partition causes a shared lock to be acquired on the table itself to prevent incompatible concurrent changes from occurring, such as attempting to drop the table while a partition is being modified. Of course, an exclusive lock on the table globally affects all partitions.

Explicit, Exclusive Locks

You can also manage locks explicitly. For example, suppose one Hive session creates an exclusive lock on table people:

```
hive> LOCK TABLE people EXCLUSIVE;
```

Here is another Hive session attempt to query the locked table:

```
hive> SELECT COUNT(*) FROM people;
conflicting lock present for default@people mode SHARED
FAILED: Error in acquiring locks: locks on the underlying objects
cannot be acquired. retry after some time
```

The table can be unlocked using the UNLOCK TABLE statement, after which queries from other sessions will work again:

```
hive> UNLOCK TABLE people;
```

CHAPTER 20

Hive Integration with Oozie

Apache Oozie is a workload scheduler for Hadoop: *http://incubator.apache.org/oozie/*.

You may have noticed Hive has its own internal workflow system. Hive converts a query into one or more stages, such as a *map reduce stage* or a *move task stage*. If a stage fails, Hive cleans up the process and reports the errors. If a stage succeeds, Hive executes subsequent stages until the entire job is done. Also, multiple Hive statements can be placed inside an HQL file and Hive will execute each query in sequence until the file is completely processed.

Hive's system of workflow management is excellent for single jobs or jobs that run one after the next. Some workflows need more than this. For example, a user may want to have a process in which step one is a custom MapReduce job, step two uses the output of step one and processes it using Hive, and finally step three uses `distcp` to copy the output from step 2 to a remote cluster. These kinds of workflows are candidates for management as Oozie Workflows (*http://incubator.apache.org/oozie/*).

Oozie Workflow jobs are Directed Acyclical Graphs (DAGs) of actions. Oozie Coordinator jobs are recurrent Oozie Workflow jobs triggered by time (frequency) and data availability. An important feature of Oozie is that the state of the workflow is detached from the client who launches the job. This detached (fire and forget) job launching is useful; normally a Hive job is attached to the console that submitted it. If that console dies, the job is half complete.

Oozie Actions

Oozie has several prebuilt actions. Some are listed below with their description:

MapReduce
> The user supplies the MapperClass, the ReducerClass, and sets `conf` variables

Shell
> A shell command with arguments is run as an action

Java action
> A Java class with a main method is launched with optional arguments

Pig
> A *Pig* script is run

Hive
> A Hive HQL query is run

DistCp
> Run a `distcp` command to copy data to or from another HDFS cluster

Hive Thrift Service Action

The built-in Hive action works well but it has some drawbacks. It uses Hive as a fat client. Most of the Hive distributions, including JARs and configuration files, need to be copied into the workflow directory. When Oozie launches an action, it will launch from a random *TaskTracker* node. There may be a problem reaching the metastore if you have your metastore setup to only allow access from specific hosts. Since Hive can leave artifacts like the *hive-history* file or some */tmp* entries if a job fails, make sure to clean up across your pool of *TaskTrackers*.

The fat-client challenges of Hive have been solved (mostly) by using Hive Thrift Service (see Chapter 16). The `HiveServiceBAction` (Hive Service "plan B" Action) leverages the Hive Thrift Service to launch jobs. This has the benefits of funneling all the Hive operations to a predefined set of nodes running Hive service:

```
$ cd ~
$ git clone git://github.com/edwardcapriolo/hive_test.git
$ cd hive_test
$ mvn wagon:download-single
$ mvn exec:exec
$ mvn install

$ cd ~
$ git clone git://github.com/edwardcapriolo/m6d_oozie.git
$ mvn install
```

A Two-Query Workflow

A workflow is created by setting up a specific directory hierarchy with required JAR files, a *job.properties* file and a *workflow.xml* file. This hierarchy has to be stored in HDFS, but it is best to assemble the folder locally and then copy it to HDFS:

```
$ mkdir myapp
$ mkdir myapp/lib
$ cp $HIVE_HOME/lib/*.jar myapp/lib/
$ cp m6d_oozie-1.0.0.jar myapp/lib/
$ cp hive_test-4.0.0.jar myapp/lib/
```

The *job.properties* sets the name of the filesystem and the *JobTracker*. Also, additional properties can be set here to be used as Hadoop Job Configuration properties:

The *job.properties* file:

```
nameNode=hdfs://rs01.hadoop.pvt:34310
jobTracker=rjt.hadoop.pvt:34311
queueName=default
oozie.libpath=/user/root/oozie/test/lib
oozie.wf.application.path=${nameNode}/user/root/oozie/test/main
```

The *workflow.xml* is the file where actions are defined:

```
<workflow-app xmlns="uri:oozie:workflow:0.2" name="java-main-wf">
    <start to="create-node"/>
    <!--The create-node actual defines a table if it does not
    already exist-->
    <action name="create-node">
        <java>
            <job-tracker>${jobTracker}</job-tracker>
            <name-node>${nameNode}</name-node>
            <configuration>
                <property>
                    <name>mapred.job.queue.name</name>
                    <value>${queueName}</value>
                </property>
            </configuration>
            <main-class>com.m6d.oozie.HiveServiceBAction</main-class>
            <arg>rhiveservice.hadoop.pvt</arg>
            <arg>10000</arg>
            <arg>CREATE TABLE IF NOT EXISTS zz_zz_abc (a int, b int)</arg>
        </java>
        <!-- on success proceded to query_node action -->
        <ok to="query_node"/>
        <!-- on fail end the job unsuccessfully-->
        <error to="fail"/>
    </action>

    <!-- populate the contents of the table with an
    insert overwrite query -->
    <action name="query_node">
        <java>
            <job-tracker>${jobTracker}</job-tracker>
            <name-node>${nameNode}</name-node>
            <configuration>
                <property>
                    <name>mapred.job.queue.name</name>
                    <value>${queueName}</value>
                </property>
            </configuration>
            <main-class>com.m6d.oozie.HiveServiceBAction</main-class>
            <arg>rhiveservice.hadoop.pvt</arg>
            <arg>10000</arg>
            <arg>INSERT OVERWRITE TABLE zz_zz_abc SELECT dma_code,site_id
    FROM BCO WHERE dt=20120426 AND offer=4159 LIMIT 10</arg>
        </java>
```

```
        <ok to="end"/>
        <error to="fail"/>
    </action>

    <kill name="fail">
        <message>Java failed, error message
        [${wf:errorMessage(wf:lastErrorNode())}]</message>
    </kill>
    <end name="end"/>
</workflow-app>
```

Oozie Web Console

The Oozie web console is helpful for troubleshooting jobs. Oozie launches each action inside a map task and captures all the input and output. Oozie does a good job presenting this information as well as providing links to job status pages found on the Hadoop *JobTracker* web console.

Here is a screenshot of the Oozie web console.

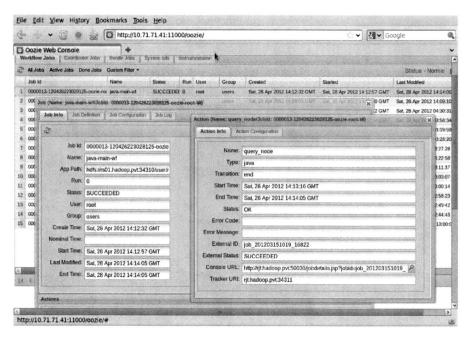

Variables in Workflows

A workflow based on completely static queries is useful but not overly practical. Most of the use cases for Oozie run a series of processes against files for today or this week.

In the previous workflow, you may have noticed the KILL tag and the interpolated variable inside of it:

```
<kill name="fail">
  <message>Java failed, error message
    [${wf:errorMessage(wf:lastErrorNode())}]</message>
</kill>
```

Oozie provides an ETL to access variables. Key-value pairs defined in *job.properties* can be referenced this way.

Capturing Output

Oozie also has a tag `<captureOutput/>` that can be placed inside an action. Output captured can be emailed with an error or sent to another process. Oozie sets a Java property in each action that can be used as a filename to write output to. The code below shows how this property is accessed:

```
private static final String
OOZIE_ACTION_OUTPUT_PROPERTIES = "oozie.action.output.properties";

public static void main(String args[]) throws Exception {
  String oozieProp = System.getProperty(OOZIE_ACTION_OUTPUT_PROPERTIES);
}
```

Your application can output data to that location.

Capturing Output to Variables

We have discussed both capturing output and Oozie variables; using them together provides what you need for daily workflows.

Looking at our previous example, we see that we are selecting data from a hardcoded day FROM BCO WHERE dt=20120426. We would like to run this workflow every day so we need to substitute the hardcoded dt=20120426 with a date:

```
<action name="create_table">
    <java>
        <job-tracker>${jobTracker}</job-tracker>
        <name-node>${nameNode}</name-node>
        <configuration>
            <property>
                <name>mapred.job.queue.name</name>
                <value>${queueName}</value>
            </property>
        </configuration>
        <main-class>test.RunShellProp</main-class>
        <arg>/bin/date</arg>
        <arg>+x=%Y%m%d</arg>
        <capture-output />
    </java>
    <ok to="run_query"/>
```

```
        <error to="fail"/>
    </action>
```

This will produce output like:

```
$ date +x=%Y%m%d
x=20120522
```

You can then access this output later in the process:

```
<arg>You said ${wf:actionData('create_table')['x']}</arg>
```

There are many more things you can do with Oozie, including integrating Hive jobs with jobs implemented with other tools, such as Pig, Java MapReduce, etc. See the Oozie website for more details.

CHAPTER 21

Hive and Amazon Web Services (AWS)

—Mark Grover

One of the services that Amazon provides as a part of Amazon Web Services (AWS) is Elastic MapReduce (EMR). With EMR comes the ability to spin up a cluster of nodes on demand. These clusters come with Hadoop and Hive installed and configured. (You can also configure the clusters with *Pig* and other tools.) You can then run your Hive queries and terminate the cluster when you are done, only paying for the time you used the cluster. This section describes how to use Elastic MapReduce, some best practices, and wraps up with pros and cons of using EMR versus other options.

You may wish to refer to the online AWS documentation available at *http://aws.amazon .com/elasticmapreduce/* while reading this chapter. This chapter won't cover all the details of using Amazon EMR with Hive. It is designed to provide an overview and discuss some practical details.

Why Elastic MapReduce?

Small teams and start-ups often don't have the resources to set up their own cluster. An in-house cluster is a fixed cost of initial investment. It requires effort to set up and servers and switches as well as maintaining a Hadoop and Hive installation.

On the other hand, Elastic MapReduce comes with a variable cost, plus the installation and maintenance is Amazon's responsibility. This is a huge benefit for teams that can't or don't want to invest in their own clusters, and even for larger teams that need a test bed to try out new tools and ideas without affecting their production clusters.

Instances

An Amazon cluster is comprised of one or more instances. Instances come in various sizes, with different RAM, compute power, disk drive, platform, and I/O performance. It can be hard to determine what size would work the best for your use case. With EMR, it's easy to start with small instance sizes, monitor performance with tools like Ganglia, and then experiment with different instance sizes to find the best balance of cost versus performance.

Before You Start

Before using Amazon EMR, you need to set up an Amazon Web Services (AWS) account. The *Amazon EMR Getting Started Guide* (*http://docs.amazonwebservices.com/ElasticMapReduce/latest/GettingStartedGuide/Welcome.html*) provides instructions on how to sign up for an AWS account.

You will also need to create an Amazon *S3 bucket* for storing your input data and retrieving the output results of your Hive processing.

When you set up your AWS account, make sure that all your Amazon EC2 instances, key pairs, security groups, and EMR jobflows are located in the same *region* to avoid cross-region transfer costs. Try to locate your Amazon S3 buckets and EMR jobflows in the same *availability zone* for better performance.

Although Amazon EMR supports several versions of Hadoop and Hive, only some combinations of versions of Hadoop and Hive are supported. See the Amazon EMR documentation to find out the supported version combinations of Hadoop and Hive.

Managing Your EMR Hive Cluster

Amazon provides multiple ways to bring up, terminate, and modify a Hive cluster. Currently, there are three ways you can manage your EMR Hive cluster:

EMR AWS Management Console (web-based frontend)
> This is the easiest way to bring up a cluster and requires no setup. However, as you start to scale, it is best to move to one of the other methods.

EMR Command-Line Interface
> This allows users to manage a cluster using a simple Ruby-based CLI, named `elastic-mapreduce`. The Amazon EMR online documentation describes how to install and use this CLI.

EMR API
> This allows users to manage an EMR cluster by using a language-specific SDK to call EMR APIs. Details on downloading and using the SDK are available in the Amazon EMR documentation. SDKs are available for Android, iOS, Java, PHP, Python, Ruby, Windows, and .NET. A drawback of an SDK is that sometimes particular SDK wrapper implementations lag behind the latest version of the AWS API.

It is common to use more than one way to manage Hive clusters.

Here is an example that uses the Ruby `elastic-mapreduce` CLI to start up a single-node Amazon EMR cluster with Hive configured. It also sets up the cluster for interactive use, rather than for running a job and exiting. This cluster would be ideal for learning Hive:

```
elastic-mapreduce --create --alive --name "Test Hive" --hive-interactive
```

If you also want *Pig* available, add the `--pig-interface` option.

Next you would log in to this cluster as described in the Amazon EMR documentation.

Thrift Server on EMR Hive

Typically, the Hive Thrift server (see Chapter 16) listens for connections on port 10000. However, in the Amazon Hive installation, this port number depends on the version of Hive being used. This change was implemented in order to allow users to install and support concurrent versions of Hive. Consequently, Hive v0.5.X operates on port 10000, Hive v0.7.X on 10001, and Hive v0.7.1 on 10002. These port numbers are expected to change as newer versions of Hive get ported to Amazon EMR.

Instance Groups on EMR

Each Amazon cluster has one or more nodes. Each of these nodes can fit into one of the following three instance groups:

Master Instance Group

This instance group contains exactly one node, which is called the master node. The master node performs the same duties as the conventional Hadoop master node. It runs the `namenode` and `jobtracker` daemons, but it also has Hive installed on it. In addition, it has a MySQL server installed, which is configured to serve as the *metastore* for the EMR Hive installation. (The embedded *Derby* metastore that is used as the default metastore in Apache Hive installations is not used.) There is also an *instance controller* that runs on the master node. It is responsible for launching and managing other instances from the other two instance groups. Note that this instance controller also uses the MySQL server on the master node. If the MySQL server becomes unavailable, the instance controller will be unable to launch and manage instances.

Core Instance Group

The nodes in the core instance group have the same function as Hadoop slave nodes that run both the `datanode` and `tasktracker` daemons. These nodes are used for MapReduce jobs and for the *ephemeral storage* on these nodes that is used for HDFS. Once a cluster has been started, the number of nodes in this instance group can only be increased but not decreased. It is important to note that *ephemeral storage* will be lost if the cluster is terminated.

Task Instance Group

This is an optional instance group. The nodes in this group also function as Hadoop slave nodes. However, they only run the `tasktracker` processes. Hence, these nodes are used for MapReduce tasks, but not for storing HDFS *blocks*. Once the cluster has been started, the number of nodes in the task instance group can be increased or decreased.

The task instance group is convenient when you want to increase cluster capacity during hours of peak demand and bring it back to normal afterwards. It is also useful when using *spot instances* (discussed below) for lower costs without risking the loss of data when a node gets removed from the cluster.

If you are running a cluster with just a single node, the node would be a master node and a core node at the same time.

Configuring Your EMR Cluster

You will often want to deploy your own configuration files when launching an EMR cluster. The most common files to customize are *hive-site.xml*, *.hiverc*, *hadoop-env.sh*. Amazon provides a way to override these configuration files.

Deploying hive-site.xml

For overriding *hive-site.xml*, upload your custom *hive-site.xml* to S3. Let's assume it has been uploaded to *s3n://example.hive.oreilly.com/tables/hive_site.xml*.

It is recommended to use the newer `s3n` "scheme" for accessing S3, which has better performance than the original `s3` scheme.

If you are starting you cluster via the `elastic-mapreduce` Ruby client, use a command like the following to spin up your cluster with your custom *hive-site.xml*:

```
elastic-mapreduce --create --alive --name "Test Hive" --hive-interactive \
--hive-site=s3n://example.hive.oreilly.com/conf/hive_site.xml
```

If you are using the SDK to spin up a cluster, use the appropriate method to override the *hive-site.xml* file. After the bootstrap actions, you would need two config steps, one for installing Hive and another for deploying *hive-site.xml*. The first step of installing Hive is to call `--install-hive` along with `--hive-versions` flag followed by a comma-separated list of Hive versions you would like to install on your EMR cluster.

The second step of installing Hive site configuration calls `--install-hive-site` with an additional parameter like `--hive-site=s3n://example.hive.oreilly.com/tables/hive_site.xml` pointing to the location of the *hive-site.xml* file to use.

Deploying a .hiverc Script

For *.hiverc*, you must first upload to S3 the file you want to install. Then you can either use a config step or a bootstrap action to deploy the file to your cluster. Note that *.hiverc* can be placed in the user's home directory or in the *bin* directory of the Hive installation.

Deploying .hiverc using a config step

At the time of this writing, the functionality to override the *.hiverc* file is not available in the Amazon-provided Ruby script, named `hive-script`, which is available at *s3n:// us-east-1.elasticmapreduce/libs/hive/hive-script*.

Consequently, *.hiverc* cannot be installed as easily as *hive-site.xml*. However, it is fairly straightforward to extend the Amazon-provided `hive-script` to enable installation of *.hiverc*, if you are comfortable modifying Ruby code. After implementing this change to `hive-script`, upload it to S3 and use that version instead of the original Amazon version. Have your modified script install *.hiverc* to the user's home directory or to the *bin* directory of the Hive installation.

Deploying a .hiverc using a bootstrap action

Alternatively, you can create a custom bootstrap script that transfers *.hiverc* from S3 to the user's home directory or Hive's *bin* directory of the master node. In this script, you should first configure `s3cmd` on the cluster with your S3 access key so you can use it to download the *.hiverc* file from S3. Then, simply use a command such as the following to download the file from S3 and deploy it in the home directory:

```
s3cmd get s3n://example.hive.oreilly.com/conf/.hiverc ~/.hiverc
```

Then use a bootstrap action to call this script during the cluster creation process, just like you would any other bootstrap action.

Setting Up a Memory-Intensive Configuration

If you are running a memory-intensive job, Amazon provides some predefined bootstrap actions that can be used to fine tune the Hadoop configuration parameters. For example, to use the memory-intensive bootstrap action when spinning up your cluster, use the following flag in your `elastic-mapreduce --create` command (wrapped for space):

```
--bootstrap-action
    s3n://elasticmapreduce/bootstrap-actions/configurations/latest/memory-intensive
```

Persistence and the Metastore on EMR

An EMR cluster comes with a MySQL server installed on the master node of the cluster. By default, EMR Hive uses this MySQL server as its metastore. However, all data stored on the cluster nodes are deleted once you terminate your cluster. This includes the data stored on the master node metastore, as well! This is usually unacceptable because you would like to retain your table schemas, etc., in a persistent metastore.

You can use one of the following methods to work around this limitation:

Use a persistent metastore external to your EMR cluster
> The details on how to configure your Hive installation to use an external metastore are in "Metastore Using JDBC" on page 28. You can use the Amazon RDS (Relational Data Service), which is based on MySQL, or another, in-house database server as a metastore. This is the best choice if you want to use the same metastore for multiple EMR clusters or the same EMR cluster running more than one version of Hive.

Leverage a start-up script
> If you don't intend to use an external database server for your metastore, you can still use the master node metastore in conjunction with your start-up script. You can place your create table statements in `startup.q`, as follows:

```
CREATE EXTERNAL TABLE IF NOT EXISTS emr_table(id INT, value STRING)
PARTITIONED BY (dt STRING)
LOCATION 's3n://example.hive.oreilly.com/tables/emr_table';
```

> It is important to include the `IF NOT EXISTS` clause in your create statement to ensure that the script doesn't try to re-create the table on the master node metastore if it was previously created by a prior invocation of *startup.q*.

> At this point, we have our table definitions in the master node metastore but we haven't yet imported the partitioning metadata. To do so, include a line like the following in your *startup.q* file after the create table statement:

```
ALTER TABLE emr_table RECOVER PARTITIONS;
```

> This will populate all the partitioning related metadata in the metastore. Instead of your custom start-up script, you could use *.hiverc*, which will be sourced automatically when Hive CLI starts up. (We'll discuss this feature again in "EMR Versus EC2 and Apache Hive" on page 254).

> The benefit of using *.hiverc* is that it provides automatic invocation. The disadvantage is that it gets executed on *every* invocation of the Hive CLI, which leads to unnecessary overhead on subsequent invocations.

The advantage of using your custom start-up script is that you can more strictly control when it gets executed in the lifecycle of your workflow. However, you will have to manage this invocation yourself. In any case, a side benefit of using a file to store Hive queries for initialization is that you can track the changes to your DDL via version control.

 As your meta information gets larger with more tables and more partitions, the start-up time using this system will take longer and longer. This solution is not suggested if you have more than a few tables or partitions.

MySQL dump on S3

Another, albeit cumbersome, alternative is to back up your metastore before you terminate the cluster and restore it at the beginning of the next workflow. S3 is a good place to persist the backup while the cluster is not in use.

Note that this metastore is not shared amongst different versions of Hive running on your EMR cluster. Suppose you spin up a cluster with both Hive v0.5 and v0.7.1 installed. When you create a table using Hive v0.5, you won't be able to access this table using Hive v0.7.1. If you would like to share the metadata between different Hive versions, you will have to use an external persistent metastore.

HDFS and S3 on EMR Cluster

HDFS and S3 have their own distinct roles in an EMR cluster. All the data stored on the cluster nodes is deleted once the cluster is terminated. Since HDFS is formed by *ephemeral storage* of the nodes in the core instance group, the data stored on HDFS is lost after cluster termination.

S3, on the other hand, provides a persistent storage for data associated with the EMR cluster. Therefore, the input data to the cluster should be stored on S3 and the final results obtained from Hive processing should be persisted to S3, as well.

However, S3 is an expensive storage alternative to HDFS. Therefore, intermediate results of processing should be stored in HDFS, with only the final results saved to S3 that need to persist.

Please note that as a side effect of using S3 as a source for input data, you lose the Hadoop data locality optimization, which may be significant. If this optimization is crucial for your analysis, you should consider importing "hot" data from S3 onto HDFS before processing it. This initial overhead will allow you to make use of Hadoop's data locality optimization in your subsequent processing.

Putting Resources, Configs, and Bootstrap Scripts on S3

You should upload all your bootstrap scripts, configuration scripts (e.g., *hive-site.xml* and *.hiverc*), resources (e.g., files that need to go in the distributed cache, UDF or streaming JARs), etc., onto S3. Since EMR Hive and Hadoop installations natively understand S3 paths, it is straightforward to work with these files in subsequent Hadoop jobs.

For example, you can add the following lines in *.hiverc* without any errors:

```
ADD FILE s3n://example.hive.oreilly.com/files/my_file.txt;
ADD JAR s3n://example.hive.oreilly.com/jars/udfs.jar;
CREATE TEMPORARY FUNCTION my_count AS 'com.oreilly.hive.example.MyCount';
```

Logs on S3

Amazon EMR saves the log files to the S3 location pointed to by the `log-uri` field. These include logs from bootstrap actions of the cluster and the logs from running daemon processes on the various cluster nodes. The `log-uri` field can be set in the *credentials.json* file found in the installation directory of the `elastic-mapreduce` Ruby client. It can also be specified or overridden explicitly when spinning up the cluster using `elastic-mapreduce` by using the `--log-uri` flag. However, if this field is not set, those logs will not be available on S3.

If your workflow is configured to terminate if your job encounters an error, any logs on the cluster will be lost after the cluster termination. If your `log-uri` field is set, these logs will be available at the specified location on S3 even after the cluster has been terminated. They can be an essential aid in debugging the issues that caused the failure.

However, if you store logs on S3, remember to purge unwanted logs on a frequent basis to save yourself from unnecessary storage costs!

Spot Instances

Spot instances allows users to bid on unused Amazon capacity to get instances at cheaper rates compared to on-demand prices. Amazon's online documentation describes them in more detail.

Depending on your use case, you might want instances in all three instance groups to be spot instances. In this case, your entire cluster could terminate at any stage during the workflow, resulting in a loss of intermediate data. If it's "cheap" to repeat the calculation, this might not be a serious issue. An alternative is to persist intermediate data periodically to S3, as long as your jobs can start again from those snapshots.

Another option is to only include the nodes in the task instance group as spot nodes. If these spot nodes get taken out of the cluster because of unavailability or because the spot prices increased, the workflow will continue with the master and core nodes, but with no data loss. When spot nodes get added to the cluster again, MapReduce tasks can be delegated to them, speeding up the workflow.

Using the `elastic-mapreduce` Ruby client, spot instances can be ordered by using the `--bid-price` option along with a bid price. The following example shows a command to create a cluster with one master node, two core nodes and two spot nodes (in the task instance group) with a bid price of 10 cents:

```
elastic-mapreduce --create --alive --hive-interactive \
--name "Test Spot Instances" \
--instance-group master --instance-type m1.large \
--instance-count 1 --instance-group core \
--instance-type m1.small --instance-count 2 --instance-group task \
--instance-type m1.small --instance-count 2 --bid-price 0.10
```

If you are spinning up a similar cluster using the Java SDK, use the following `Instance GroupConfig` variables for master, core, and task instance groups:

```
InstanceGroupConfig masterConfig = new InstanceGroupConfig()
.withInstanceCount(1)
.withInstanceRole("MASTER")
.withInstanceType("m1.large");
InstanceGroupConfig coreConfig = new InstanceGroupConfig()
.withInstanceCount(2)
.withInstanceRole("CORE")
.withInstanceType("m1.small");
InstanceGroupConfig taskConfig = new InstanceGroupConfig()
.withInstanceCount(2)
.withInstanceRole("TASK")
.withInstanceType("m1.small")
.withMarket("SPOT")
.withBidPrice("0.05");
```

 If a map or reduce task fails, Hadoop will have to start them from the beginning. If the same task fails four times (configurable by setting the MapReduce properties `mapred.map.max.attempts` for map tasks and `mapred.reduce.max.attempts` for reduce tasks), the entire job will fail. If you rely on too many spot instances, your job times may be unpredictable or fail entirely by *TaskTrackers* getting removed from the cluster.

Security Groups

The Hadoop *JobTracker* and *NameNode* User Interfaces are accessible on port 9100 and 9101 respectively in the EMRmaster node. You can use *ssh* tunneling or a dynamic SOCKS proxy to view them.

In order to be able to view these from a browser on your client machine (outside of the Amazon network), you need to modify the Elastic MapReduce master security group via your AWS Web Console. Add a new custom TCP rule to allow inbound connections from your client machine's IP address on ports 9100 and 9101.

EMR Versus EC2 and Apache Hive

An elastic alternative to EMR is to bring up several Amazon EC2 nodes and install Hadoop and Hive on a custom Amazon Machine Image (AMI). This approach gives you more control over the version and configuration of Hive and Hadoop. For example, you can experiment with new releases of tools before they are made available through EMR.

The drawback of this approach is that customizations available through EMR may not be available in the Apache Hive release. As an example, the S3 filesystem is not fully supported on Apache Hive [see JIRA HIVE-2318 (*https://issues.apache.org/jira/browse/HIVE-2318*)]. There is also an optimization for reducing start-up time for Amazon S3 queries, which is only available in EMR Hive. This optimization is enabled by adding the following snippet in your *hive-site.xml*:

```
<property>
  <name>hive.optimize.s3.query</name>
  <value>true</value>
  <description> Improves Hive query performance for Amazon S3 queries
  by reducing their start up time </description>
</property>
```

Alternatively, you can run the following command on your Hive CLI:

```
set hive.optimize.s3.query=true;
```

Another example is a command that allows the user to recover partitions if they exist in the correct directory structure on HDFS or S3. This is convenient when an external process is populating the contents of the Hive table in appropriate partitions. In order to track these partitions in the metastore, one could run the following command, where emr_table is the name of the table:

```
ALTER TABLE emr_table RECOVER PARTITIONS;
```

Here is the statement that creates the table, for your reference:

```
CREATE EXTERNAL TABLE emr_table(id INT, value STRING)
PARTITIONED BY (dt STRING)
LOCATION 's3n://example.hive.oreilly.com/tables/emr_table';
```

Wrapping Up

Amazon EMR provides an elastic, scalable, easy-to-set-up way to bring up a cluster with Hadoop and Hive ready to run queries as soon as it boots. It works well with data stored on S3. While much of the configuration is done for you, it is flexible enough to allow users to have their own custom configurations.

CHAPTER 22

HCatalog

—*Alan Gates*

Introduction

Using Hive for data processing on Hadoop has several nice features beyond the ability to use an SQL-like language. It's ability to store metadata means that users do not need to remember the schema of the data. It also means they do not need to know where the data is stored, or what format it is stored in. This decouples data producers, data consumers, and data administrators. Data producers can add a new column to the data without breaking their consumers' data-reading applications. Administrators can relocate data to change the format it is stored in without requiring changes on the part of the producers or consumers.

The majority of heavy Hadoop users do not use a single tool for data production and consumption. Often, users will begin with a single tool: Hive, Pig, MapReduce, or another tool. As their use of Hadoop deepens they will discover that the tool they chose is not optimal for the new tasks they are taking on. Users who start with analytics queries with Hive discover they would like to use Pig for ETL processing or constructing their data models. Users who start with Pig discover they would like to use Hive for analytics type queries.

While tools such as Pig and MapReduce do not require metadata, they can benefit from it when it is present. Sharing a metadata store also enables users across tools to share data more easily. A workflow where data is loaded and normalized using MapReduce or Pig and then analyzed via Hive is very common. When all these tools share one metastore, users of each tool have immediate access to data created with another tool. No loading or transfer steps are required.

HCatalog exists to fulfill these requirements. It makes the Hive metastore available to users of other tools on Hadoop. It provides connectors for MapReduce and Pig so that users of those tools can read data from and write data to Hive's warehouse. It has a command-line tool for users who do not use Hive to operate on the metastore with Hive DDL statements. It also provides a notification service so that workflow tools, such as Oozie, can be notified when new data becomes available in the warehouse.

HCatalog is a separate Apache project from Hive, and is part of the Apache Incubator. The Incubator is where most Apache projects start. It helps those involved with the project build a community around the project and learn the way Apache software is developed. As of this writing, the most recent version is HCatalog 0.4.0-incubating. This version works with Hive 0.9, Hadoop 1.0, and Pig 0.9.2.

MapReduce

Reading Data

MapReduce uses a Java class `InputFormat` to read input data. Most frequently, these classes read data directly from HDFS. `InputFormat` implementations also exist to read data from HBase, Cassandra, and other data sources. The task of the `InputFormat` is twofold. First, it determines how data is split into sections so that it can be processed in parallel by MapReduce's map tasks. Second, it provides a `RecordReader`, a class that MapReduce uses to read records from its input source and convert them to keys and values for the map task to operate on.

HCatalog provides `HCatInputFormat` to enable MapReduce users to read data stored in Hive's data warehouse. It allows users to read only the partitions of tables and columns that they need. And it provides the records in a convenient list format so that users do not need to parse them.

 `HCatInputFormat` implements the Hadoop 0.20 API, `org.apache.hadoop` `.mapreduce`, not the Hadoop 0.18 `org.apache.hadoop.mapred` API. This is because it requires some features added in the MapReduce (0.20) API. This means that a MapReduce user will need to use this interface to interact with HCatalog. However, Hive requires that the underlying `InputFormat` used to read data from disk be a `mapred` implementation. So if you have data formats you are currently using with a MapReduce `InputFormat`, you can use it with HCatalog. `InputFormat` is a class in the mapreduce API and an interface in the `mapred` API, hence it was referred to as a class above.

When initializing `HCatInputFormat`, the first thing to do is specify the table to be read. This is done by creating an `InputJobInfo` class and specifying the database, table, and partition filter to use.

InputJobInfo.java

```java
/**
 * Initializes a new InputJobInfo
 * for reading data from a table.
 * @param databaseName the db name
 * @param tableName the table name
 * @param filter the partition filter
 */
public static InputJobInfo create(String databaseName,
    String tableName,
    String filter) {
    ...
}
```

databaseName name indicates the Hive database (or schema) the table is in. If this is null then the default database will be used. The tableName is the table that will be read. This must be non-null and refer to a valid table in Hive. filter indicates which partitions the user wishes to read. If it is left null then the entire table will be read. Care should be used here, as reading all the partitions of a large table can result in scanning a large volume of data.

Filters are specified as an SQL-like where clause. They should reference only partition columns of the data. For example, if the table to be read is partitioned on a column called datestamp, the filter might look like datestamp = "2012-05-26". Filters can contain =, >, >=, <, <=, and, and or as operators.

There is a bug in the ORM mapping layer used by Hive v0.9.0 and earlier that causes filter clauses with >, >=, <, or <= to fail.

> To resolve this bug, you can apply the patch *HIVE-2084.D2397.1.patch* from *https://issues.apache.org/jira/browse/HIVE-2084* and rebuild your version of Hive. This does carry some risks, depending on how you deploy Hive. See the discussion on the JIRA entry.

This InputJobInfo instance is then passed to HCatInputFormat via the method setIn put along with the instance of Job being used to configure the MapReduce job:

```java
Job job = new Job(conf, "Example");
InputJobInfo inputInfo = InputJobInfo.create(dbName, inputTableName, filter));
HCatInputFormat.setInput(job, inputInfo);
```

The map task will need to specify HCatRecord as a value type. The key type is not important, as HCatalog does not provide keys to the map task. For example, a map task that reads data via HCatalog might look like:

```java
public static class Map extends
    Mapper<WritableComparable, HCatRecord, Text, Text> {

    @Override
    protected void map(
```

```
        WritableComparable key,
        HCatRecord value,
        org.apache.hadoop.mapreduce.Mapper<WritableComparable,
            HCatRecord, Text, HCatRecord>.Context context) {
      ...
    }
}
```

HCatRecord is the class that HCatalog provides for interacting with records. It presents
a simple get and set interface. Records can be requested by position or by name. When
requesting columns by name, the schema must be provided, as each individual HCatRe
cord does not keep a reference to the schema. The schema can be obtained by calling
HCatInputFormat.getOutputSchema(). Since Java does not support overloading of functions by return type, different instances of get and set are provided for each data type.
These methods use the object versions of types rather than scalar versions (that is
java.lang.Integer rather than int). This allows them to express null as a value. There
are also implementations of get and set that work with Java Objects:

```
// get the first column, as an Object and cast it to a Long
Long cnt = record.get(0);

// get the column named "cnt" as a Long
Long cnt = record.get("cnt", schema);

// set the column named "user" to the string "fred"
record.setString("user", schema, "fred");
```

Often a program will not want to read all of the columns in an input. In this case it
makes sense to trim out the extra columns as quickly as possible. This is particularly
true in columnar formats like RCFile, where trimming columns early means reading
less data from disk. This can be achieved by passing a schema that describes the desired
columns. This must be done during job configuration time. The following example will
configure the user's job to read only two columns named user and url:

```
HCatSchema baseSchema = HCatBaseInputFormat.getOutputSchema(context);
List<HCatFieldSchema> fields = new List<HCatFieldSchema>(2);
fields.add(baseSchema.get("user"));
fields.add(baseSchema.get("url"));
HCatBaseInputFormat.setOutputSchema(job, new HCatSchema(fields));
```

Writing Data

Similar to reading data, when writing data, the database and table to be written to need
to be specified. If the data is being written to a partitioned table and only one partition
is being written, then the partition to be written needs to be specified as well:

```
/**
 * Initializes a new OutputJobInfo instance for writing data from a table.
 * @param databaseName the db name
 * @param tableName the table name
 * @param partitionValues The partition values to publish to, can be null or empty Map
 */
```

```
public static OutputJobInfo create(String databaseName,
                                   String tableName,
                                   Map<String, String> partitionValues) {
    ...
}
```

The databaseName name indicates the Hive database (or schema) the table is in. If this is null then the default database will be used. The tableName is the table that will be written to. This must be non-null and refer to a valid table in Hive. partitionValues indicates which partition the user wishes to create. If only one partition is to be written, the map must uniquely identify a partition. For example, if the table is partitioned by two columns, entries for both columns must be in the map. When working with tables that are not partitioned, this field can be left null. When the partition is explicitly specified in this manner, the partition column need not be present in the data. If it is, it will be removed by HCatalog before writing the data to the Hive warehouse, as Hive does not store partition columns with the data.

It is possible to write to more than one partition at a time. This is referred to as dynamic partitioning, because the records are partitioned dynamically at runtime. For dynamic partitioning to be used, the values of the partition column(s) must be present in the data. For example, if a table is partitioned by a column "datestamp," that column must appear in the data collected in the reducer. This is because HCatalog will read the partition column(s) to determine which partition to write the data to. As part of writing the data, the partition column(s) will be removed.

Once an OutputJobInfo has been created, it is then passed to HCatOutputFormat via the static method setOutput:

```
OutputJobInfo outputInfo = OutputJobInfo.create(dbName, outputTableName, null));
HCatOutputFormat.setOutput(job, outputInfo);
```

When writing with HCatOutputFormat, the output key type is not important. The value must be HCatRecord. Records can be written from the reducer, or in map only jobs from the map task.

Putting all this together in an example, the following code will read a partition with a datestamp of *20120531* from the table rawevents, count the number of events for each user, and write the result to a table cntd:

```
public class MRExample extends Configured implements Tool {

  public static class Map extends
    Mapper<WritableComparable, HCatRecord, Text, LongWritable> {

    protected void map(WritableComparable key,
                       HCatRecord value,
                       Mapper<WritableComparable, HCatRecord,
                         Text, LongWritable>.Context context)
                       throws IOException, InterruptedException {
      // Get our schema from the Job object.
      HCatSchema schema = HCatBaseInputFormat.getOutputSchema(context);
```

```
    // Read the user field
    String user = value.get("user", schema);
    context.write(new Text(user), new LongWritable(1));
  }
}

public static class Reduce extends Reducer<Text, LongWritable,
    WritableComparable, HCatRecord> {

  protected void reduce(Text key, Iterable<LongWritable> values,
      Reducer<Text, LongWritable,
      WritableComparable, HCatRecord>.Context context)
      throws IOException ,InterruptedException {

    List<HCatFieldSchema> columns = new ArrayList<HCatFieldSchema>(2);
    columns.add(new HCatFieldSchema("user", HCatFieldSchema.Type.STRING, ""));
    columns.add(new HCatFieldSchema("cnt", HCatFieldSchema.Type.BIGINT, ""));
    HCatSchema schema = new HCatSchema(columns);

    long sum = 0;
    Iterator<IntWritable> iter = values.iterator();
    while (iter.hasNext()) sum += iter.next().getLong();
    HCatRecord output = new DefaultHCatRecord(2);
    record.set("user", schema, key.toString());
    record.setLong("cnt", schema, sum);
    context.write(null, record);
  }
}

public int run(String[] args) throws Exception {
  Job job = new Job(conf, "Example");
  // Read the "rawevents" table, partition "20120531", in the default
  // database
  HCatInputFormat.setInput(job, InputJobInfo.create(null, "rawevents",
      "datestamp='20120531'"));
  job.setInputFormatClass(HCatInputFormat.class);
  job.setJarByClass(MRExample.class);
  job.setMapperClass(Map.class);
  job.setReducerClass(Reduce.class);
  job.setMapOutputKeyClass(Text.class);
  job.setMapOutputValueClass(LongWritable.class);
  job.setOutputKeyClass(WritableComparable.class);
  job.setOutputValueClass(DefaultHCatRecord.class);
  // Write into "cntd" table, partition "20120531", in the default database
  HCatOutputFormat.setOutput(job
      OutputJobInfo.create(null, "cntd", "ds=20120531"));
  job.setOutputFormatClass(HCatOutputFormat.class);
  return (job.waitForCompletion(true) ? 0 : 1);
}

public static void main(String[] args) throws Exception {
  int exitCode = ToolRunner.run(new MRExample(), args);
  System.exit(exitCode);
}
}
```

Command Line

Since HCatalog utilizes Hive's metastore, Hive users do not need an additional tool to interact with it. They can use the Hive command-line tool as before. However, for HCatalog users that are not also Hive users, a command-line tool hcat is provided. This tool is very similar to Hive's command line. The biggest difference is that it only accepts commands that do not result in a MapReduce job being spawned. This means that the vast majority of DDL (Data Definition Language, or operations that define the data, such as creating tables) are supported:

```
$ /usr/bin/hcat -e "create table rawevents (user string, url string);"
```

The command line supports the following options:

Option	Explanation	Example
-e	Execute DDL provided on the command line	hcat -e "show tables;"
-f	Execute DDL provided in a script file	hcat -f setup.sql
-g	See the security section below	
-p	See the security section below	
-D	Port for the Cassandra server	hcat -Dlog.level=INFO
-h	Port for the Cassandra server	hcat -h

The SQL operations that HCatalog's command line does *not* support are:

- SELECT
- CREATE TABLE AS SELECT
- INSERT
- LOAD
- ALTER INDEX REBUILD
- ALTER TABLE CONCATENATE
- ALTER TABLE ARCHIVE
- ANALYZE TABLE
- EXPORT TABLE
- IMPORT TABLE

Security Model

HCatalog does not make use of Hive's authorization model. However, user authentication in HCatalog is identical to Hive. Hive attempts to replicate traditional database authorization models. However, this has some limitations in the Hadoop ecosystem.

Since it is possible to go directly to the filesystem and access the underlying data, authorization in Hive is limited. This can be resolved by having all files and directories that contain Hive's data be owned by the user running Hive jobs. This way other users can be prevented from reading or writing data, except through Hive. However, this has the side effect that all UDFs in Hive will then run as a super user, since they will be running in the Hive process. Consequently, they will have read and write access to all files in the warehouse.

The only way around this in the short term is to declare UDFs to be a privileged operation and only allow those with proper access to create UDFs, though there is no mechanism to enforce this currently. This may be acceptable in the Hive context, but in Pig and MapReduce where user-generated code is the rule rather than the exception, this is clearly not acceptable.

To resolve these issues, HCatalog instead delegates authorization to the storage layer. In the case of data stored in HDFS, this means that HCatalog looks at the directories and files containing data to see if a user has access to the data. If so, he will be given identical access to the metadata. For example, if a user has permission to write to a directory that contains a table's partitions, she will also have permission to write to that table.

This has the advantage that it is truly secure. It is not possible to subvert the system by changing abstraction levels. The disadvantage is that the security model supported by HDFS is much poorer than is traditional for databases. In particular, features such as column-level permissions are not possible. Also, users can only be given permission to a table by being added to a filesystem group that owns that file.

Architecture

As explained above, HCatalog presents itself to MapReduce and Pig using their standard input and output mechanisms. HCatLoader and HCatStorer are fairly simple since they sit atop HCatInputFormat and HCatOutputFormat, respectively. These two MapReduce classes do a fair amount of work to integrate MapReduce with Hive's metastore.

Figure 22-1 shows the HCatalog architecture.

HCatInputFormat communicates with Hive's metastore to obtain information about the table and partition(s) to be read. This includes finding the table schema as well as schema for each partition. For each partition it must also determine the actual Input Format and SerDe to use to read the partition. When HCatInputFormat.getSplits is called, it instantiates an instance of the InputFormat for each partition and calls getSplits on that InputFormat. These are then collected together and the splits from all the partitions returned as the list of InputSplits.

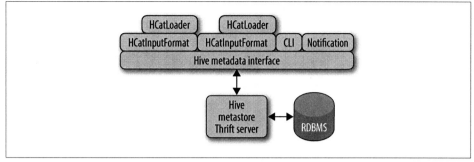

Figure 22-1. HCatalog architecture diagram

Similarly, the RecordReaders from each underlying InputFormat are used to decode the partitions. The HCatRecordReader then converts the values from the underlying Record Reader to HCatRecords via the SerDe associated with the partition. This includes padding each partition with any missing columns. That is, when the table schema contains columns that the partition schema does not, columns with null values must be added to the HCatRecord. Also, if the user has indicated that only certain columns are needed, then the extra columns are trimmed out at this point.

HCatOutputFormat also communicates with the Hive metastore to determine the proper file format and schema for writing. Since HCatalog only supports writing data in the format currently specified for the table, there is no need to open different OutputFor mats per partition. The underlying OutputFormat is wrapped by HCatOutputFormat. A RecordWriter is then created per partition that wraps the underlying RecordWriter, while the indicated SerDe is used to write data into these new records. When all of the partitions have been written, HCatalog uses an OutputCommitter to commit the data to the metastore.

CHAPTER 23

Case Studies

Hive is in use at a multitude of companies and organizations around the world. This case studies chapter details interesting and unique use cases, the problems that were present, and how those issues were solved using Hive as a unique data warehousing tool for petabytes of data.

m6d.com (Media6Degrees)

Data Science at M6D Using Hive and R

by Ori Stitelman

In this case study we examine one of many approaches our data science team, here at m6d, takes toward synthesizing the immense amount of data that we are able to extract using Hive. m6d is a display advertising prospecting company. Our role is to create machine learning algorithms that are specifically tailored toward finding the best new prospects for an advertising campaign. These algorithms are layered on top of a delivery engine that is tied directly into a myriad of real time bidding exchanges that provide a means to purchase locations on websites to display banner advertisements on behalf of our clients. The m6d display advertising engine is involved in billions of auctions a day and tens of millions of advertisements daily. Naturally, such a system produces an immense amount of data. A large portion of the records that are generated by our company's display advertising delivery system are housed in m6d's Hadoop cluster and, as a result, Hive is the primary tool our data science team uses to interact with the these logs.

Hive gives our data science team a way to extract and manipulate large amounts of data. In fact, it allows us to extract samples and summarize data that prior to using Hive could not be analyzed as efficiently, or at all, because of the immense size. Despite the fact that Hive allows us access to huge amounts of data at rates many times faster than before, it does not change the fact that most of the tools that we were previously familiar with as data scientists are not always able to analyze data samples of the size we can now produce. In summary, Hive provides us a great tool to extract huge amounts of data; however, the toolbox of data science, or statistical learning, methods that we as data scientists are used to using cannot easily accommodate the new larger data sets without substantial changes.

Many different software packages have been developed or are under development for both supervised and unsupervised learning on large data sets. Some of these software packages are stand alone software implementations, such as Vowpal Wabbit and BBR, while others are implementations within a larger infrastructure such as Mahout for Hadoop or the multitude of "large data" packages for R. A portion of these algorithms take advantage of parallel programing approaches while others rely on different methods to achieve scalability.

The primary tool for statistical learning for several of the data scientists in our team is R. It provides a large array of packages that are able to perform many statistical learning methods. More importantly, we have a lot of experience with it, know how its packages perform, understand their features, and are very familiar with its documentation. However, one major drawback of R is that by default it loads the entire data set into memory. This is a major limitation considering that the majority of the data sets that we extract from Hive and are able to analyze today are much larger than what can fit in memory. Moreover, once the data in R is larger than what is able to fit in memory, the system will start swapping, which leads to the system thrashing and massive decreases in processing speed.[1]

In no way are we advocating ignoring the new tools that are available. Obviously, it is important to take advantage of the best of these scalable technologies, but only so much time can be spent investigating and testing new technology. So now we are left with a choice of either using the new tools that are available for large data sets or downsampling our data to fit into the tools that we are more familiar with. If we decide to use the new tools, we can gain signal by letting our data learn off of more data, and as a result the variance in our estimates will decrease. This is particularly appealing in situations where the outcome is very rare. However, learning these new tools takes time and there is an opportunity cost of using that time to learn new tools rather than answering other questions that have particular value to the company.

Alternatively, we can downsample the data to obtain something that can fit in the old tools we have at our disposal, but must deal with a loss of signal and increased variance in our estimates. However, this allows us to deal with tools with which we are familiar and the features that they provide. Thus, we are able to retain the functionality of our current toolbox at the price of losing some signal. However, these are not the only two possible approaches. In this case study, we highlight a way that we can both retain the functionality of the current toolbox as well as gain signal, or decrease variance, by using a larger sample, or all, of the data available to us.

1. *http://www.r-bloggers.com/taking-r-to-the-limit-large-datasets-predictive-modeling-with-pmml-and-adapa/*

Figure 23-1 shows the probability of converting versus the score from an algorithm designed to rank prospects for an advertising campaign. Higher scores should indicate a higher probability of conversion. This plot clearly shows that the top individuals are converting at a lower rate than some of the lower scoring browsers. That is, browsers with scores greater than 1 convert at a lower rate than individuals with scores between 0.5 and 1.0. Considering that some campaigns only target a very small percentage of the overall population, it is important the best prospects are among the top scorers.

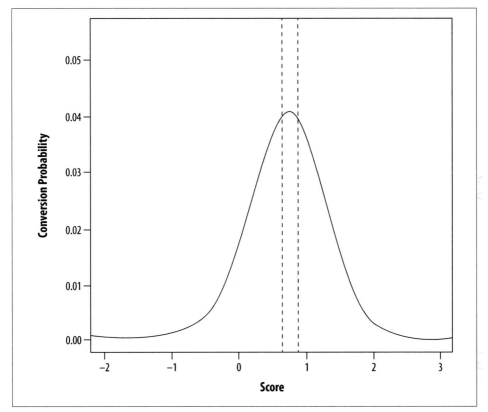

Figure 23-1. Probability of conversion versus score

The line that expresses the relationship between the score and the conversion probability seen in Figure 23-1 is generated using a generalized additive model (GAM) in the statistical programming package R.[2] The details about GAMs will not be presented here. For the purpose of this case study it can be thought of as a black box that produces for each score a prediction of the conversion rate. The browsers can then be re-ranked

2. For more details on the use of generalized additive models (GAM), see Hastie et al. 2001. The R package used to implement the GAM for the purpose of the analysis presented here is the mgcv package available at *http://cran.r-project.org/*.

based on the predicted conversion rate; thus, the predicted conversion rate becomes the new score.

The new ranking can be generated in the following way. First, extract the scores for each individual browser and then follow them for some designated period of time, say five days, and record if they took the desired action, and thus converted. Consider a Hive table called scoretable that has the following information and is partitioned on date and subpartitioned by offer.

Name	Type	Description
score	double	The score is the score generated by the initial algorithm that does not necessarily rank order appropriately.
convert	int	The variable convert is a binary variable that is equal to one if the individual browser takes the desired action in the following five days and equal to zero if not.
date	int	The day that the browser was given the particular score.
offer	int	An ID of an offer.

The following query can then be used to extract a set of data from scoretable for use in R to estimate the GAM line that predicts conversion for different levels of score like in the preceding table:

```
SELECT score,convert
FROM scoretable
WHERE date >= (…)  AND date <= (…)
AND offer = (…);
1.2347 0
3.2322 1
0.0013 0
0.3441 0
```

This data is then loaded into R and the following code is used to create the predicted conversion probability versus score, as in the preceding table:

```
library(mgcv)
g1=gam(convert~s(score),family=binomial,data=[data frame name])
```

The issue with this approach is that it only can be used for a limited number of days of data because the data set gets too large and R begins thrashing for any more than three days of data. Moreover, it takes approximately 10 minutes of time for each campaign to do this for about three days of data. So, running this analysis for about 300 campaigns for a single scoring method took about 50 hours for three days of data.

By simply extracting the data from Hive in a slightly different way and making use of the feature of the gam function in mgcv that allows for frequency weights, the same analysis may be done using more data, and thus gaining more signal, at a much faster rate. This is done by selecting the data from Hive by rounding the score to the nearest hundredth and getting frequency weights for each rounded score, convert combination by using a GROUP BY query. This is a very common approach for dealing with large data sets and in the case of these scores there should be no loss of signal due to rounding because there is no reason to believe that individuals with scores that differ by less than 0.001 are any different from each other. The following query would select such a data set:

```
SELECT round(score,2) as score,convert,count(1) AS freq
       FROM scoretable
       WHERE date >= [start.date] and date <= [end.date] and offer = [chosen.offer]
       GROUP BY round(score,2),convert;
1.23 0 500
3.23 1 22
0.00 0 127
0.34 0 36
```

The resulting data set is significantly smaller than the original approach presented that does not use frequency weights. In fact, the initial data set for each offer consisted of millions of records, and this new data set consists of approximately 6,500 rows per offer. The new data is then loaded into R and the following code may be used to generate the new GAM results:

```
library(mgcv)
g2=gam(convert~s(score),family=binomial,weights=freq,
 data=[frequency weight data frame name])
```

(We wrapped the line.)

The previously presented approach took 10 minutes per offer to create the GAM for only three days of data, compared to the frequency-weighted approach which was able to create the GAM based on seven days of data in approximately 10 seconds. Thus, by using frequency weights, the analysis for the 300 campaigns was able to be done in 50 minutes compared to 50 hours using the originally presented approach. This increase in speed was also realized while using more than twice the amount of data resulting in more precise estimates of the predicted conversion probabilities. In summary, the frequency weights allowed for a more precise estimate of the GAM in significantly less time.

In the presented case study, we showed how by rounding the continuous variables and grouping like variables with frequency weights, we were both able to get more precise estimates by using more data and fewer computational resources, resulting in quicker estimates. The example shown was for a model with a single feature, score. In general, this is an approach that will work well for a low number of features or a larger number of sparse features. The above approach may be extended to higher dimensional problems as well using some other small tricks. One way this can be done for a larger number of variables is by bucketing the variables, or features, into binary variables and then using GROUP BY queries and frequency weights for those features. However, as the number of features increases, and those features are not sparse, there is little value gained by such an approach and other alternative methods must be explored, or software designed for larger data sets must be embraced.

M6D UDF Pseudorank

by David Ha and Rumit Patel

Sorting data and identifying the top N elements is straightforward. You order the whole data set by some criteria and limit the result set to N. But there are times when you need to group like elements together and find the top N elements within that group only. For example, identifying the top 10 requested songs for each recording artist or the top 100 best-selling items per product category and country. Several database platforms define a rank() function that can support these scenarios, but until Hive provides an implementation, we can create a user-defined function to produce the results we want. We will call this function p_rank() for psuedorank, leaving the name rank() for the Hive implementation.

Say we have the following product sales data and we want to see the top three items per category and country:

Category	Country	Product	Sales
movies	us	chewblanca	100
movies	us	war stars iv	150
movies	us	war stars iii	200
movies	us	star wreck	300
movies	gb	titanus	100
movies	gb	spiderella	150
movies	gb	war stars iii	200
movies	gb	war stars iv	300
office	us	red pens	30
office	us	blue pens	50
office	us	black pens	60
office	us	pencils	70
office	gb	rulers	30
office	gb	blue pens	40
office	gb	black pens	50
office	gb	binder clips	60

In most SQL systems:

```
SELECT
  category,country,product,sales,rank
FROM (
 SELECT
   category,country,product, sales,
   rank() over (PARTITION BY category, country ORDER BY sales DESC) rank
 FROM p_rank_demo) t
WHERE rank <= 3
```

To achieve the same result using HiveQL, the first step is partitioning the data into groups, which we can achieve using the DISTRIBUTE BY clause. We must ensure that all rows with the same category and country are sent to the same reducer:

```
DISTRIBUTE BY
  category,
  country
```

The next step is ordering the data in each group by descending sales using the SORT BY clause. While ORDER BY effects a total ordering across all data, SORT BY affects the ordering of data on a specific reducer. You must repeat the partition columns named in the DISTRIBUTE BY clause:

```
SORT BY
  category,
  country,
  sales DESC
```

Putting everything together, we have:

```
ADD JAR p-rank-demo.jar;
CREATE TEMPORARY FUNCTION p_rank AS 'demo.PsuedoRank';

SELECT
  category,country,product,sales,rank
FROM (
 SELECT
   category,country,product,sales,
   p_rank(category, country) rank
 FROM (
   SELECT
     category,country,product,
     sales
   FROM p_rank_demo
   DISTRIBUTE BY
     category,country
   SORT BY
     category,country,sales desc) t1) t2
WHERE rank <= 3
```

The subquery t1 organizes the data so that all data belonging to the same category and country are sorted by descending sales count. The next query t2 then uses p_rank() to assign a rank to each row within the group. The outermost query filters the rank to be in the top three:

Category	Country	Product	Sales	Rank
movies	gb	war stars iv	300	1
movies	gb	war stars iii	200	2
movies	gb	spiderella	150	3
movies	us	star wreck	300	1
movies	us	war stars iii	200	2
movies	us	war stars iv	150	3
office	gb	binder clips	60	1
office	gb	black pens	50	2
office	gb	blue pens	40	3
office	us	pencils	70	1
office	us	black pens	60	2
office	us	blue pens	50	3

p_rank() is implemented as a generic UDF whose parameters are all the identifying attributes of the group, which, in this case, are category and country. The function remembers the previous arguments, and so long as the successive arguments match, it increments and returns the rank. Whenever the arguments do not match, the function resets the rank back to 1 and starts over.

This is just one simple example of how p_rank() can be used. You can also find the 10th to 15th bestsellers by category and country. Or, if you precalculate the counts of products in each category and country, you can use p_rank() to calculate percentiles using a join. For example, if there were 1,000 products in the "movies" and "us" group, the 50th, 70th, and 95th quantiles would have rank 500, 700, and 950, respectively. Please know that p_rank() is not a direct substitute for rank() because there will be differences in some circumstances. rank() returns the same value when there are ties, but p_rank() will keep incrementing, so plan accordingly and test with your data.

Lastly, here is the implementation. It is public domain so feel free to use, improve, and modify it to suit your needs:

```
package demo;

import org.apache.hadoop.hive.ql.exec.UDFArgumentException;
import org.apache.hadoop.hive.ql.metadata.HiveException;
import org.apache.hadoop.hive.ql.udf.generic.GenericUDF;
import org.apache.hadoop.hive.serde2.objectinspector.ObjectInspector;
import org.apache.hadoop.hive.serde2.objectinspector.primitive.
  PrimitiveObjectInspectorFactory;

public class PsuedoRank extends GenericUDF {
  /**
   * The rank within the group. Resets whenever the group changes.
   */
```

```java
private long rank;

/**
 * Key of the group that we are ranking. Use the string form
 * of the objects since deferred object and equals do not work
 * as expected even for equivalent values.
 */
private String[] groupKey;

@Override
public ObjectInspector initialize(ObjectInspector[] oi)
    throws UDFArgumentException {
  return PrimitiveObjectInspectorFactory.javaLongObjectInspector;
}

@Override
public Object evaluate(DeferredObject[] currentKey) throws HiveException {
  if (!sameAsPreviousKey(currentKey)) {
    rank = 1;
  }
  return new Long(rank++);
}

/**
 * Returns true if the current key and the previous keys are the same.
 * If the keys are not the same, then sets {@link #groupKey} to the
 * current key.
 */
private boolean sameAsPreviousKey(DeferredObject[] currentKey)
    throws HiveException {
  if (null == currentKey && null == groupKey) {
    return true;
  }
  String[] previousKey = groupKey;
  copy(currentKey);
  if (null == groupKey && null != previousKey) {
    return false;
  }
  if (null != groupKey && null == previousKey) {
    return false;
  }
  if (groupKey.length != previousKey.length) {
    return false;
  }
  for (int index = 0; index < previousKey.length; index++) {
    if (!groupKey[index].equals(previousKey[index])) {
      return false;
    }
  }
  return true;
}

/**
 * Copies the given key to {@link #groupKey} for future
 * comparisons.
```

```
*/
private void copy(DeferredObject[] currentKey)
    throws HiveException {
  if (null == currentKey) {
    groupKey = null;
  } else {
    groupKey = new String[currentKey.length];
    for (int index = 0; index < currentKey.length; index++) {
      groupKey[index] = String.valueOf(currentKey[index].get());
    }
  }
}

@Override
public String getDisplayString(String[] children) {
  StringBuilder sb = new StringBuilder();
  sb.append("PsuedoRank (");
  for (int i = 0; i < children.length; i++) {
    if (i > 0) {
      sb.append(", ");
    }
    sb.append(children[i]);
  }
  sb.append(")");
  return sb.toString();
}
}
```

M6D Managing Hive Data Across Multiple MapReduce Clusters

Although Hadoop clusters are designed to scale from 10 to 10,000 nodes, sometimes deployment-specific requirements involve running more than one filesystem or Job-Tracker. At M6D, we have such requirements, for example we have hourly and daily process reports using Hadoop and Hive that are business critical and must complete in a timely manner. However our systems also support data science and sales engineers that periodically run ad hoc reporting. While using the fair share scheduler and capacity scheduler meets many of our requirements, we need more isolation than schedulers can provide. Also, because HDFS has no snapshot or incremental backup type features, we require a solution that will prevent an accidental delete or drop table operations from destroying data.

Our solution is to run two distinct Hadoop deployments. Data can have a replication factor of two or three on the primary deployment and additionally be replicated to a second deployment. This decision allows us to have guaranteed resources dedicated to our time-sensitive production process as well as our ad hoc users. Additionally, we protected against any accidental drop tables or data deletes. This design does incur some overhead in having to administer two deployments and setup and administer the replication processes, but this overhead is justified in our case.

Our two deployments are known as *production* and *research*. They each have their own dedicated Data Nodes and Task Trackers. Each *NameNode* and *JobTracker* is a failover setup using DRBD and Linux-HA. Both deployments are on the same switching network (Tables 23-1 and 23-2).

Table 23-1. Production

NameNode	hdfs.hadoop.pvt:54310
JobTracker	jt.hadoop.pvt:54311

Table 23-2. Research

NameNode	rs01.hadoop.pvt:34310
JobTracker	rjt.hadoop.pvt:34311

Cross deployment queries with Hive

A given table `zz_mid_set` exists on Production and we wish to be able to query it from Research without having to transfer the data between clusters using `distcp`. Generally, we try to avoid this because it breaks our isolation design but it is nice to know that this can be done.

Use the `describe extended` command to determine the columns of a table as well as its location:

```
hive> set fs.default.name;
fs.default.name=hdfs://hdfs.hadoop.pvt:54310
hive> set mapred.job.tracker;
mapred.job.tracker=jt.hadoop.pvt:54311
hive> describe extended zz_mid_set;
OK
adv_spend_id    int
transaction_id  bigint
time      string
client_id       bigint
visit_info      string
event_type      tinyint
level   int

location:hdfs://hdfs.hadoop.pvt:54310/user/hive/warehouse/zz_mid_set
Time taken: 0.063 seconds
hive> select count(1) from zz_mid_set;
1795928
```

On the second cluster, craft a second `CREATE TABLE` statement with the same columns. Create the second table as `EXTERNAL`, in this way if the table is dropped on the second cluster the files are not deleted on the first cluster. Notice that for the location we specified a full URI. In fact, when you specify a location as a relative URI, Hive stores it as a full URI:

```
hive> set fs.default.name;
fs.default.name=hdfs://rs01.hadoop.pvt:34310
hive> set mapred.job.tracker;
mapred.job.tracker=rjt.hadoop.pvt:34311
hive> CREATE TABLE EXTERNAL table_in_another_cluster
( adv_spend_id int, transaction_id bigint, time string, client_id bigint,
visit_info string, event_type tinyint, level int)
LOCATION 'hdfs://hdfs.hadoop.pvt:54310/user/hive/warehouse/zz_mid_set';
hive> select count(*) FROM table_in_another_cluster;
1795928
```

It is important to note that this cross-deployment access works because both clusters have network access to each other. The TaskTrackers of the deployment we submit the job to will have to be able to access the NameNode and DataNodes of the other deployment. Hadoop was designed to move processing closer to data. This is done by scheduling tasks to run on nodes where the data is located. In this scenario TaskTrackers connect to another cluster's DataNodes. Which means a general performance decrease and network usage increase.

Replicating Hive data between deployments

Replicating Hadoop and Hive data is easier than replicating a traditional database. Unlike a database running multiple transactions that change the underlying data frequently, Hadoop and Hive data is typically "write once." Adding new partitions does not change the existing ones, and typically new partitions are added on time-based intervals.

Early iterations of replication systems were standalone systems that used `distcp` and generated Hive statements to add partitions on an interval. When we wanted to replicate a new table, we could copy an existing program and make changes for different tables and partitions. Over time we worked out a system that could do this in a more automated manner without having to design a new process for each table to replicate.

The process that creates the partition also creates an empty HDFS file named:

```
/replication/default.fracture_act/hit_date=20110304,mid=3000
```

The replication daemon constantly scans the replication hierarchy. If it finds a file, it looks up the table and partition in Hive's metadata. It then uses the results to replicate the partition. On a successful replication the file is then deleted.

Below is the main loop of the program. First, we do some checking to make sure the table is defined in the source and destination metastores:

```
public void run(){
    while (goOn){
        Path base = new Path(pathToConsume);
        FileStatus [] children = srcFs.listStatus(base);
        for (FileStatus child: children){
            try {
                openHiveService();
                String db = child.getPath().getName().split("\\.")[0];
```

```
String hiveTable = child.getPath().getName().split("\\.")[1];
Table table = srcHive.client.get_table(db, hiveTable);
if (table == null){
  throw new RuntimeException(db+" "+hiveTable+
    " not found in source metastore");
}
Table tableR = destHive.client.get_table(db,hiveTable);
if (tableR == null){
  throw new RuntimeException(db+" "+hiveTable+
    " not found in dest metastore");
}
```

Using the database and table name we can look up the location information inside the metastore. We then do a sanity check to ensure the information does not already exist:

```
URI localTable = new URI(tableR.getSd().getLocation());
FileStatus [] partitions = srcFs.listStatus(child.getPath());
for (FileStatus partition : partitions){
  try {
    String replaced = partition.getPath().getName()
    .replace(",", "/").replace("'","");
    Partition p = srcHive.client.get_partition_by_name(
    db, hiveTable, replaced);
URI partUri = new URI(p.getSd().getLocation());
String path = partUri.getPath();
    DistCp distCp = new DistCp(destConf.conf);
    String thdfile = "/tmp/replicator_distcp";
    Path tmpPath = new Path(thdfile);
destFs.delete(tmpPath,true);
    if (destFs.exists( new Path(localTable.getScheme()+
      "://"+localTable.getHost()+":"+localTable.getPort()+path) ) ){
      throw new RuntimeException("Target path already exists "
      +localTable.getScheme()+"://"+localTable.getHost()+
      ":"+localTable.getPort()+path );
    }
```

Hadoop DistCP is not necessarily made to be run programmatically. However, we can pass a string array identical to command-line arguments to its main function. After, we check to confirm the returned result was a 0:

```
String [] dargs = new String [4];
dargs[0]="-log";
dargs[1]=localTable.getScheme()+"://"+localTable.getHost()+":"+
  localTable.getPort()+thdfile;
dargs[2]=p.getSd().getLocation();
dargs[3]=localTable.getScheme()+"://"+localTable.getHost()+":"+
  localTable.getPort()+path;
int result =ToolRunner.run(distCp,dargs);
if (result != 0){
  throw new RuntimeException("DistCP failed "+ dargs[2] +" "+dargs[3]);
}
```

Finally, we re-create the ALTER TABLE statement that adds the partition:

```
String HQL = "ALTER TABLE "+hiveTable+
    " ADD PARTITION ("+partition.getPath().getName()
```

```
            +") LOCATION '"+path+"'";
          destHive.client.execute("SET hive.support.concurrency=false");
          destHive.client.execute("USE "+db);
          destHive.client.execute(HQL);
          String [] results=destHive.client.fetchAll();
          srcFs.delete(partition.getPath(),true);
        } catch (Exception ex){
          ex.printStackTrace();
        }
      } // for each partition
    } catch (Exception ex) {
      //error(ex);
      ex.printStackTrace();
    }
  } // for each table
  closeHiveService();
  Thread.sleep(60L*1000L);
  } // end run loop
} // end run
```

Outbrain

by David Funk

Outbrain is the leading content-discovery platform.

In-Site Referrer Identification

Sometimes, when you're trying to aggregate your traffic, it can be tricky to tell where it's actually coming from, especially for traffic coming from elsewhere in your site. If you have a site with a lot of URLs with different structures, you can't simply check that the referrer URLs match the landing page.

Cleaning up the URLs

What we want is to correctly group each referrer as either In-site, Direct, or Other. If it's Other, we'll just keep the actual URL. That way you can tell your internal traffic apart from Google searches to your site, and so on and so forth. If the referrer is blank or null, we'll label it as Direct.

From here on out, we'll assume that all our URLs are already parsed down to the host or domain, whatever level of granularity you're aiming for. Personally, I like using the domain because it's a little simpler. That said, Hive only has a host function, but not domain.

If you just have the raw URLs, there are a couple of options. The host, as given below, gives the full host, like *news.google.com* or *www.google.com*, whereas the domain would truncate it down to the lowest logical level, like *google.com* or *google.co.uk*.

```
Host = PARSE_URL(my_url, 'HOST'')
```

Or you could just use a UDF for it. Whatever, I don't care. The important thing is that we're going to be using these to look for matches, so just make your choice based on your own criteria.

Determining referrer type

So, back to the example. We have, let's say, three sites: *mysite1.com*, *mysite2.com*, and *mysite3.com*. Now, we can convert each pageview's URL to the appropriate class. Let's imagine a table called `referrer_identification`:

```
ri_page_url STRING
ri_referrer_url STRING
```

Now, we can easily add in the referrer type with a query:

```
SELECT ri_page_url, ri_referrer_url,
  CASE
    WHEN ri_referrer_url is NULL or ri_referrer_url = '' THEN 'DIRECT'
    WHEN ri_referrer_url is in ('mysite1.com','mysite2.com','mysite3.com') THEN 'INSITE'
    ELSE ri_referrer_url
  END as ri_referrer_url_classed
FROM
  referrer_identification;
```

Multiple URLs

This is all pretty simple. But what if we're an ad network? What if we have hundreds of sites? What if each of the sites could have any number of URL structures?

If that's the case, we probably also have a table that has each URL, as well as what site it belongs to. Let's call it `site_url`, with a schema like:

```
su_site_id INT
su_url STRING
```

Let's also add one more field to our earlier table, `referrer_identification`:

```
ri_site_id INT
```

Now we're in business. What we want to do is go through each referrer URL and see if it matches with anything of the same site ID. If anything matches, it's an In-site referrer. Otherwise, it's something else. So, let's query for that:

```
SELECT
  c.c_page_url as ri_page_url,
  c.c_site_id as ri_site_id,
  CASE
    WHEN c.c_referrer_url is NULL or c.c_referrer_url = '' THEN 'DIRECT'
    WHEN c.c_insite_referrer_flags > 0 THEN 'INSITE'
    ELSE c.c_referrer_url
  END as ri_referrer_url_classed
FROM
(SELECT
  a.a_page_url as c_page_url,
  a.a_referrer_url as c_referrer_url,
```

```
    a.a_site_id as c_site_id,
    SUM(IF(b.b_url <> '', 1, 0)) as c_insite_referrer_flags
FROM
(SELECT
  ri_page_url as a_page_url,
  ri_referrer_url as a_referrer_url,
  ri_site_id as a_site_id
FROM
  referrer_identification
) a
LEFT OUTER JOIN
(SELECT
  su_site_id as b_site_id,
  su_url as b_url
FROM
  site_url
) b
ON
  a.a_site_id = b.b_site_id and
  a.a_referrer_url = b.b_url
) c
```

A few small notes about this. We use the outer join in this case, because we expect there to be some external referrers that won't match, and this will let them through. Then, we just catch any cases that did match, and if there were any, we know they came from somewhere in the site.

Counting Uniques

Let's say you want to calculate the number of unique visitors you have to your site/network/whatever. We'll use a ridiculously simple schema for our hypothetical table, daily_users:

```
du_user_id STRING
du_date STRING
```

However, if you have too many users and not enough machines in your cluster, it might begin to have trouble counting users over a month:

```
SELECT
 COUNT(DISTINCT du_user_id)
FROM
 daily_users
WHERE
  du_date >= '2012-03-01' and
  du_date <= '2012-03-31'
```

In all likelihood, your cluster is probably able to make it through the map phase without too much problems, but starts having issues around the reduce phase. The problem is that it's able to access all the records but it can't count them all at once. Of course, you can't count them day by day, either, because there might be some redundancies.

Why this is a problem

Counting uniques is O(n), where n is the number of records, but it has a high constant factor. We could maybe come up with some clever way to cut that down a little bit, but it's much easier to cut down your n. While it's never good to have a high O(n), most of the real problems happen further along. If you have something that takes $n^{1.1}$ time to run, who cares if you only have n=2 versus n=1. It's slower, sure, but nowhere near the difference between n=1 and n=100.

So, if each day has m entries, and an average of x redundancies, our first query would have n= 31*m. We can reduce this to n=31*(m–x) by building a temp table to save deduped versions for each day.

Load a temp table

First, create the temp table:

```
CREATE TABLE daily_users_deduped (dud_user_id STRING)
PARTITIONED BY (dud_date STRING)
ROW FORMAT DELIMITED
FIELDS TERMINATED BY '\t';
```

Then we write a template version of a query to run over each day, and update it to our temp table. I like to refer to these as "metajobs," so let's call this mj_01.sql:

```
INSERT OVERWRITE TABLE daily_users_deduped
PARTITION (dud_date = ':date:')

SELECT DISTINCT
  du_user_id
FROM
  daily_users
WHERE
  du_date = ':date:'
```

Next, we write a script that marks this file up, runs it, and repeats it for every date in a range. For this, we have three functions, modify_temp_file, which replaces a variable name with fire_query, which basically runs hive -f on a file, and then a function to delete the file:

```
start_date = '2012-03-01'
end_date = '2012-03-31'

for date in date_range(start_date, end_date):
  femp_file = modify_temp_file('mj_01.sql',{':date:':my_date})
  fire_query(temp_file)
  delete(temp_file)
```

Querying the temp table

Run the script, and you've got a table with a n=31*(m-x). Now, you can query the deduped table without as big a reduce step to get through.

```
SELECT
  COUNT(DISTINCT (dud_uuid)
FROM
  daily_users_deduped
```

If that's not enough, you can then dedupe sets of dates, maybe two at a time, whatever the interval that works for you. If you still have trouble, you could hash your user IDs into different classes, maybe based on the first character, to shrink n even further.

The basic idea remains, if you limit the size of your n, a high O(n) isn't as big of a deal.

Sessionization

For analyzing web traffic, we often want to be able to measure engagement based on various criteria. One way is to break up user behavior into sessions, chunks of activity that represent a single "use." A user might come to your site several times a day, a few days a month, but each visit is certainly not the same.

So, what is a session? One definition is a string of activity, not separated by more than 30 minutes. That is, if you go to your first page, wait five minutes, go to the second page, it's the same session. Wait 30 minutes exactly until the third page, still the same session. Wait 31 minutes until that fourth page, and the session will be broken; rather than the fourth pageview, it would be the first page of the second session.

Once we've got these broken out, we can look at properties of the session to see what happened. The ubiquitous case is to compare referrers to your page by session length. So, we might want to find out if Google or Facebook give better engagement on your site, which we might measure by session length.

At first glance, this seems perfect for an iterative process. For each pageview, keep counting backwards until you find the page that was first. But Hive isn't iterative.

You can, however, figure it out. I like to break this into four phases.

1. Identify which pageviews are the session starters, or "origin" pages.
2. For every pageview, bucket it in with the correct origin page.
3. Aggregate all the pageviews for each origin page.
4. Label each origin page, then calculate engagement for each session.

This leaves a table where each row represents a full session, which you can then query for whatever you want to find out.

Setting it up

Let's define our table, session_test:

```
st_user_id STRING
st_pageview_id STRING
st_page_url STRING
```

```
st_referrer_url STRING
st_timestamp DOUBLE
```

Most of this is pretty straightforward, though I will mention that `st_pageview_id` is basically a unique ID to represent each transaction, in this case a pageview. Otherwise, it could be confusing if you happened to have multiple views of the same page. For the purposes of this example, the timestamp will be in terms of seconds.

Finding origin pageviews

All right, let's start with step one (shocking!). How do we find which pageviews are the session starters? Well, if we assume any break of more than 30 minutes implies a new session, than any session starter can't have any activity that precedes it by 30 minutes or less. This is a great case for conditional sums. What we want to do is count up how many times, for each pageview. Then, anything with a count of zero must be an origin case.

In order to do this, we need to compare every pageview that could precede it. This is a pretty expensive move, as it requires performing a cross-product. To prevent this from blowing up to unmanageable size, we should group everything on criteria that limits it as much as possible. In this case, it's just the user ID, but if you have a large network of independent sites, you might also want to group based on each source, as well:

```
CREATE TABLE sessionization_step_one_origins AS

SELECT
  c.c_user_id as ssoo_user_id,
  c.c_pageview_id as ssoo_pageview_id,
  c.c_timestamp as ssoo_timestamp
FROM
      (SELECT
    a.a_user_id as c_user_id,
    a.a_pageview_id as c_pageview_id,
    a.a_timestamp as c.c_timestamp,
    SUM(IF(a.a_timestamp + 1800 >= b.b_timestamp AND
        a.a_timestamp < b.b_timestamp,1,0)) AS c_nonorigin_flags
  FROM
    (SELECT
      st_user_id as a_user_id,
      st_pageview_id as a_pageview_id,
      st_timestamp as a_timestamp
    FROM
      session_test
    ) a
    JOIN
    (SELECT
      st_user_id as b_user_id,
      st_timestamp as b_timestamp
    FROM
      session_test
    ) b
    ON
```

```
      a.a_user_id = b.b_user_id
  GROUP BY
    a.a_user_id,
    a.a_pageview_id,
    a.a_timestamp
  ) c
WHERE
  c.c_nonorigin_flags
```

That's a bit much, isn't it? The important part is to count the flags that are not of a session origin, which is where we define `c_nonorigin_flags`. Basically, counting up how many reasons why it isn't the session starter. Aka, this line:

```
SUM(IF(a.a_timestamp + 1800 >= b.b_timestamp AND
    a.a_timestamp < b.b_timestamp,1,0)) as c_nonorigin_flags
```

Let's break this up, part by part. First, everything is in terms of subquery a. We only use b to qualify those candidates. So, the first part, the `a.a_timestamp + 1800 >= b.b_timestamp`, is just asking if the candidate timestamp is no more than 30 minutes prior to the qualifying timestamp. The second part, `a.a_timestamp < b.b_timestamp` adds a check to make sure that it is earlier, otherwise every timestamp that occurred later than it's qualifier would trigger a false positive. Plus, since this is a cross-product, it prevents a false positive by using the candidate as its own qualifier.

Now, we're left with a table, `sessionization_step_one_origins`, with a schema of:

```
ssoo_user_id STRING
ssoo_pageview_id STRING
ssoo_timestamp DOUBLE
```

Bucketing PVs to origins

Which is probably a good reason to start on step two, finding which pageview belongs to which origin. It's pretty simple to do this, every pageview's origin must be the one immediately prior to it. For this, we take another big join to check for the minimum difference between a pageview's timestamp and all the potential origin pageviews:

```
CREATE TABLE sessionization_step_two_origin_identification AS

SELECT
  c.c_user_id as sstoi_user_id,
  c.c_pageview_id as sstoi_pageview_id,
  d.d_pageview_id as sstoi_origin_pageview_id
FROM
(SELECT
  a.a_user_id as c_user_id,
  a.a_pageview_id as c_pageview_id,
  MAX(IF(a.a_timestamp >= b.b_timestamp, b.b_timestamp, NULL)) as c_origin_timestamp
FROM
(SELECT
  st_user_id as a_user_id,
  st_pageview_id as a_pageview_id,
  st_timestamp as a_timestamp
FROM
```

```
  session_test
) a
JOIN
(SELECT
  ssoo_user_id as b_user_id,
  ssoo_timestamp as b_timestamp
FROM
  sessionization_step_one_origins
) b
ON
  a.a_user_id = b.b_user_id
GROUP BY
  a.a_user_id,
  a.a_pageview_id
) c
JOIN
(SELECT
  ssoo_usr_id as d_user_id,
  ssoo_pageview_id as d_pageview_id,
  ssoo_timestamp as d_timestamp
FROM
  sessionization_step_one_origins
) d
ON
  c.c_user_id = d.d_user_id and
  c.c_origin_timestamp = d.d_timestamp
```

There's a lot to mention here. First, let's look at this line:

```
MAX(IF(a.a_timestamp >= b.b_timestamp, b.b_timestamp, NULL)) as c_origin_timestamp
```

Again, we use the idea of qualifiers and candidates, in this case b are the candidates for every qualifier a. An origin candidate can't come later than the pageview, so for every case like that, we want to find the absolute latest origin that meets that criteria. The null is irrelevant, because we are guaranteed to have a minimum, because there is always at least one possible origin (even if it's itself). This doesn't give us the origin, but it gives us the timestamp, which we can use as a fingerprint for what the origin should be.

From here, it's just a matter of matching up this timestamp with all the other potential origins, and we know which origin each pageview belongs to. We're left with the table `sessionization_step_two_origin_identification`, with the following schema:

```
sstoi_user_id STRING
sstoi_pageview_id STRING
sstoi_origin_pageview_id STRING
```

It's worth mentioning that this isn't the only way to identify the origin pageviews. You could do it based on the referrer, labeling any external referrer, homepage URL, or blank referrer (indicating direct traffic) as a session origin. You could base it on an action, only measuring activity after a click. There are plenty of options, but the important thing is simply to identify what the session origins are.

Aggregating on origins

At this point, it's all pretty easy. Step three, where we aggregate on origins, is really, really simple. For each origin, count up how many pageviews match to it:

```
CREATE TABLE sessionization_step_three_origin_aggregation AS

SELECT
  a.a_user_id as sstoa_user_id,
  a.a_origin_pageview_id as sstoa_origin_pageview_id,
  COUNT(1) as sstoa_pageview_count
FROM
  (SELECT
    ssoo_user_id  as a_user_id
    ssoo_pageview_id as a_origin_pageview_id
  FROM
    sessionization_step_one_origins
  ) a
  JOIN
  (SELECT
    sstoi_user_id as b_user_id,
    sstoi_origin_pageview_id as b_origin_pageview_id
  FROM
    sessionization_step_two_origin_identification
  ) b
ON
  a.a_user_id = b.b_user_id and
  a.a_origin_pageview_id = b.b_origin_pageview_id
GROUP BY
  a.a_user_id,
  a.a_origin_pageview_id
```

Aggregating on origin type

Now, this last step we could have avoided by keeping all the qualitative info about a pageview, particularly the origins, in one of the earlier steps. However, if you have a lot of details you want to pay attention to, it can sometimes be easier to add it in at the end. Which is step four:

```
CREATE TABLE sessionization_step_four_qualitative_labeling

SELECT
  a.a_user_id as ssfql_user_id,
  a.a_origin_pageview_id as ssfql_origin_pageview_id,
  b.b_timestamp as ssfql_timestamp,
  b.b_page_url as ssfql_page_url,
  b.b_referrer_url as ssfql_referrer_url,
  a.a_pageview_count as ssqfl_pageview_count
(SELECT
  sstoa_user_id as a_user_id,
  sstoa_origin_pageview_id as a_origin_pageview_id,
  sstoa_pageview_count as a_pageview_count
FROM
  sessionization_step_three_origin_aggregation
) a
```

```
JOIN
(SELECT
    st_user_id as b_user_id,
    st_pageview_id as b_pageview_id,
    st_page_url as b_page_url,
    st_referrer_url as b_referrer_url,
    st_timestamp as b_timestamp
FROM
    session_test
) b
ON
    a.a_user_id = b.b_user_id and
    a.a_origin_pageview_id = b.b_pageview_id
```

Measure engagement

Now, with our final table, we can do whatever we want. Let's say we want to check the number of sessions, average pageviews per session, weighted average pageviews per session, and the max or min. We could pick whatever criteria we want, or none at all, but in this case, let's do it by referrer URL so we can find out the answer to which traffic source gives the best engagement. And, just for kicks, let's also check who gives us the most unique users:

```
SELECT
    PARSE_URL(ssfql_referrer_url, 'HOST') as referrer_host,
    COUNT(1) as session_count,
    AVG(ssfql_pageview_count) as avg_pvs_per_session,
    SUM(ssfq_pageview_count)/COUNT(1) as weighted_avg_pvs_per_session,
    MAX(ssfql_pageview_count) as max_pvs_per_session,
    MIN(ssfql_pageview_count) as min_pvs_per_session,
    COUNT(DISTINCT ssfql_usr_id) as unique_users
FROM
    sessionization_step_three_origin_aggregation
GROUP BY
    PARSE_URL(ssfql_referrer_url, 'HOST') as referrer_host
```

And there we have it. We could check which page URL gives the best engagement, figure out who the power users are, whatever. Once we've got it all in a temp table, especially with a more complete set of qualitative attributes, we can answer all sorts of questions about user engagement.

NASA's Jet Propulsion Laboratory

The Regional Climate Model Evaluation System

by Chris A. Mattmann, Paul Zimdars, Cameron Goodale, Andrew F. Hart, Jinwon Kim, Duane Waliser, Peter Lean

Since 2009, our team at NASA's Jet Propulsion Laboratory (JPL) has actively led the development of a Regional Climate Model Evaluation System (RCMES). The system, originally funded under the American Recovery and Reinvestment Act (ARRA) has the following goals:

- Facilitate the evaluation and analysis of regional climate model simulation outputs via the availability of the reference data sets of quality-controlled observations and assimilations especially from spaceborne sensors, an efficient database structure, a collection of computational tools for calculating the metrics for model evaluation metrics and diagnostics, and relocatable and friendly user interfaces.

- Easily bring together a number of complex, and heterogeneous software tools and capability for data access, representation, regridding, reformatting, and visualization so that the end product such as a bias plot can be easily delivered to the end user.

- Support regional assessments of climate variability, and impacts, needed to inform decision makers (e.g., local governments, agriculture, state government, hydrologists) so that they can make critical decisions with large financial and societal impact.

- Overcome data format and metadata heterogeneity (e.g., NetCDF3/4, CF metadata conventions, HDF4/5, HDF-EOS metadata conventions).

- Deal with spatial and temporal differences, (e.g., line up the data alongside a 180/80 lat-lon grid—such as converting from, for example, a 360/360 lat-lon grid —and making sure data, that may be originally daily, is properly comparable with monthly data.

- Elastically scaling up, performing a regional study that requires specific remote sensing data, and climate model output data, performing a series of analyses, and then destroying that particular instance of the system. In other words, supporting transient analyses, and rapid construction/deconstruction of RCMES instances.

Figure 23-2 shows the architecture and data flow of the Regional Climate Model Evaluation System

In support of these goals, we have constructed a multifaceted system shown in Figure 23-2. Reading the diagram from left to right, available reference data sets from observations and assimilations, especially from satellite-based remote sensing, enters the system according to the desired climate parameters useful for climate model evaluation. Those parameters are stored in various mission data sets, and those data sets are housed in several external repositories, eventually fed into the database component (RCMED: Regional Climate Model Evaluation Database) of RCMES.

As an example, AIRS is NASA's Atmospheric Infrared Sounder and provides parameters including surface air temperature, temperature, and geopotential; MODIS is NASA's Moderate Imaging Spectroradiometer and provides parameters including cloud fraction; and TRMM is NASA's Tropical Rainfall Measurement Mission and provides parameters including monthly precipitation. This information is summarized

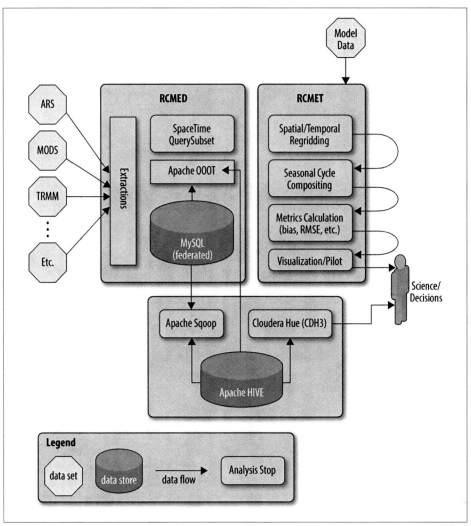

Figure 23-2. JPL Architecture Diagram.

in our RCMES system website parameter table, *http://rcmes.jpl.nasa.gov/rcmed/param eters/*, and shown in Figure 23-3.

Data sets are loaded into the RCMED using the Apache OODT extractor framework and the desired parameters, their values, spatial and temporal constraints (and optionally height) are loaded and potentially transformed (e.g., normalized, put on same coordinate system, converted from unit values) into a MySQL database. The data loaded into that MySQL database, RCMED, is exposed to external clients via a Space/ Time query and subsetting web service; the description of which is a topic of a separate

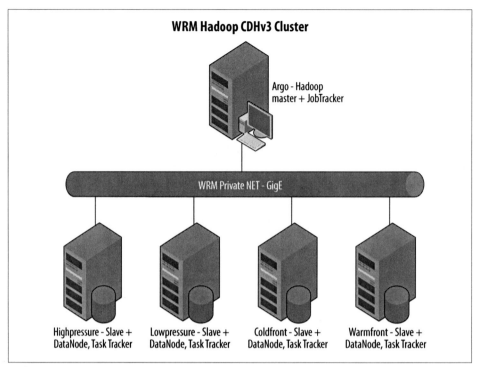

WRM Hadoop CDHv3 Cluster

Argo - Hadoop
master + JobTracker

WRM Private NET - GigE

Highpressure - Slave +
DataNode, Task Tracker

Lowpressure - Slave +
DataNode, Task Tracker

Coldfront - Slave +
DataNode, Task Tracker

Warmfront - Slave +
DataNode, Task Tracker

Figure 23-3. JPL Physical Architecture Diagram

study. For all intents and purposes, it provides the same capabilities that the OPeNDAP technology does.

The right side of the diagram shows the Regional Climate Model Evaluation Toolkit (RCMET). It provides users with the ability to take in the reference data from RCMED and climate model output data produced elsewhere and to re-grid these datasets in order to match them spatially and temporally in preparation for the comparison of the reference and model data for the evaluation of model output against the user-selected reference data. At that point, the system allows for seasonal cycle compositing (e.g., all Januaries, or all summer months for N years), and for preparing the data for eventual metrics calculation, that is, comparison of the values of the model output against the remote sensing data observation parameters and their values. The system supports several metrics, such as bias computation, Root Mean Squared Error (RMSE), and the generation of relevant visualizations, including traditional plots and Taylor diagrams for science use/decision making.

Our Experience: Why Hive?

So, where does Hive come in to play? After loading 6 billion rows of (latitude, longitude, time, data point value, height) tuples into MySQL, the system fell down and experienced data loss. This is probably due in part to our naïve strategy of storing all of the data points in a single table. Over time, we evolved this strategy to break tables down by dataset and by parameter, which helped but added needless overhead that we didn't want to spend cycles engineering around.

Instead, we decided to experiment with the Apache Hive technology. We installed Hive 0.5+20 using CDHv3 and Apache Hadoop (0.20.2+320). CDHv3 came with a number of other relevant tools including Sqoop, and Hue, which we leveraged in our architecture, shown in the bottom portion of Figure 23-3.

We used Apache Sqoop to dump out the data into Hive, and then wrote an Apache OODT wrapper that queried Hive for the data by Space/Time and provided it back to the RCMET and other users (shown in the middle portion of Figure 23-2). The full architecture for the RCMES cluster is shown in Figure 23-3. We had five machines, including a master/slave configuration as shown in the diagram, connected by a private network running GigE.

Some Challenges and How We Overcame Them

During the migration of data from MySQL to Hive, we experienced slow response times while doing simple tasks such as a count DB query (e.g., hive> select count(data point_id) from dataPoint;). We initially loaded up around 2.5 billion data points in a single table and noticed that on our machine configuration, Hive took approximately 5–6 minutes to do a count of these 2.5 billion records (15–17 minutes for the full 6.8 billion records). The reduce portion was fast (we were experiencing a single reduce phase since we were using a count * benchmark) but the map stage took the remainder of the time (~95%). Our system at the time consisted of six (4 x quad-core) systems with approximately 24 GB of RAM each (all of the machines shown in Figure 23-3, plus another "borrowed machine" of similar class from another cluster).

We attempted to add more nodes, increase map tasktrackers (many different #s), change DFS block size (32 M, 64 M, 128 MB, 256 M), leverage LZO compression, and alter many other configuration variables (io.sort.factor, io.sort.mb) without much success in lowering the time to complete the count. We did notice a high I/O wait on the nodes no matter how many task trackers we ran. The size of the database was approximately ~200GB and with MySQL it took a few seconds to do both the 2.5 billion and 6.7 billion count.

Members of the Hive community jumped in and provided us with insight, ranging from mentioning that HDFS read speed is about 60 MB/sec comparing to about 1 GB/sec on local disk, depending of course on network speed, and namenode workload. The numbers suggested by the community member suggested that we needed roughly 16 mappers in the Hadoop job to match with the I/O performance of a local non-Hadoop task. In addition, Hive community members suggested that we increase the number of mappers (increase parallelism) by reducing the split size (input size) for each mapper, noting we should examine the following parameters: mapred.min.split.size, `mapred.max.split.size`, `mapred.min.split.size.per.rack`, and `mapred.min.split.size` `.per.node`, and suggesting that the parameters should be set to a value of 64 MB. Finally, the community suggested that we look at a benchmark that only counts rows by using `count(1)` instead of `count (datapoint_id)`, as the latter is faster since no column reference means no decompression and deserialization, e.g., if you store your table in `RCFile` format.

Based on the above feedback, we were able to tune our Hive cluster for RCMES to respond to a count query benchmark, and to a space/time query from RCMET for billions of rows in under 15 seconds, using the above-mentioned resources, making Hive a viable and great choice for our system architecture.

Conclusion

We have described our use of Apache Hive in the JPL Regional Climate Model Evaluation System. We leveraged Hive during a case study wherein we wanted to explore cloud-based technology alternatives to MySQL, and configuration requirements needed to make it scale to the level of tens of billions of rows, and to elastically destroy and re-create the data stored within.

Hive did a great job of meeting our system needs and we are actively looking for more ways to closely integrate it into the RCMES system.

Photobucket

Photobucket is the largest dedicated photo-hosting service on the Internet. Started in 2003 by Alex Welch and Darren Crystal, Photobucket quickly became one of the most popular sites on the Internet and attracted over one hundred million users and billions of stored and shared media. User and system data is spread across hundreds of MySQL instances, thousands of web servers, and petabytes of filesystem.

Big Data at Photobucket

Prior to 2008, Photobucket didn't have a dedicated analytics system in-house. Questions from the business users were run across hundreds of MySQL instances and the results aggregated manually in Excel.

In 2008, Photobucket embarked on implementing its first data warehouse dedicated to answering the increasingly complex data questions being asked by a fast-growing company.

The first iteration of the data warehouse was built using an open source system with a Java SQL optimizer and a set of underlying PostGreSQL databases. The previous system worked well into 2009, but the shortcomings in the architecture became quickly evident. Working data sets quickly became larger than the available memory; coupled with the difficulty in repartitioning the data across the PostGreSQL nodes forced us to scale up when we really wanted to scale out.

In 2009, we started to investigate systems that would allow us to scale out, as the amount of data continued to grow and still meet our SLA with the business users. Hadoop quickly became the favorite for consuming and analyzing the terabytes of data generated daily by the system, but the difficulty of writing MapReduce programs for simple ad hoc questions became a negative factor for full implementation. Thankfully, Facebook open sourced Hive a few weeks later and the barriers to efficiently answering ad hoc business questions were quickly smashed.

Hive demonstrates many advantages over the previous warehouse implementation. Here are a few examples of why we chose Hadoop and Hive:

1. Ability to handle structured and unstructured data
2. Real-time streaming of data into HDFS from Flume, Scribe, or MountableHDFS
3. Extend functionality through UDFs
4. A well-documented, SQL-like interface specifically built for OLAP versus OLTP

What Hardware Do We Use for Hive?

Dell R410, 4 × 2 TB drives with 24 GB RAM for the data nodes, and Dell R610, 2 × 146 GB (RAID 10) drives with 24 GB RAM for the management hardware.

What's in Hive?

The primary goal of Hive at Photobucket is to provide answers about business functions, system performance, and user activity. To meet these needs, we store nightly dumps of MySQL data sets from across hundreds of servers, terabytes of logfiles from web servers and custom log formats ingested through Flume. This data helps support many groups throughout the company, such as executive management, advertising, customer support, product development, and operations just to name a few. For historical data, we keep the partition of all data created on the first day of the month for MySQL data and 30+ days of log files. Photobucket uses a custom ETL framework for migrating MySQL data into Hive. Log file data is streamed into HDFS using Flume and picked up by scheduled Hive processes.

Who Does It Support?

Executive management relies on Hadoop to provide reports surrounding the general health of the business. Hive allows us to parse structured database data and unstructured click stream data and distill the data into a format requested by the business stakeholder.

Advertising operations uses Hive to sift through historical data for forecast and define quotas for ad targeting.

Product development is far and away the group generating the largest number of ad hoc queries. As with any user base, segments change and evolve over time. Hive is important because it allows us to run A/B tests across current and historical data to gauge relevancy of new products in a quickly changing user environment.

Providing our users with a best-in-class system is the most important goal at Photo-bucket. From an operations perspective, Hive is used to generate rollup data partitioned across multiple dimensions. Knowing the most popular media, users, and referring domains is important for many levels across the company. Controlling expenses is important to any organization. A single user can quickly consume large amounts of system resources, significantly increasing monthly expenditures. Hive is used to identify and analyze rogue users; to determine which ones are within our Terms of Service and which are not. Operations also uses Hive to run A/B tests defining new hardware requirements and generating ROI calculations. Hive's ability to abstract users from underlying MapReduce code means questions can be answered in hours or days instead of weeks.

SimpleReach

by Eric Lubow

At SimpleReach, we use Cassandra to store our raw data from all of our social network polling. The format of the row key is an account ID (which is a MongoDB ObjectId) and a content item ID (with a MD5 hash of the URL of the content item being tracked) separated by an underscore which we split on to provide that data in the result set. The columns in the row are composite columns that look like the ones below:

```
4e87f81ca782f3404200000a_8c825814de0ac34bb9103e2193a5b824
=> (column=meta:published-at, value=1330979750000, timestamp=1338919372934628)
=> (column=hour:1338876000000_digg-diggs, value=84, timestamp=1338879756209142)
=> (column=hour:1338865200000_googleplus-total, value=12, timestamp=1338869007737888)
```

In order for us to be able to query on composite columns, we need to know the hex value of the column name. In our case, we want to know the hex value of the column name (*meta:*'published-at').

The hex equivalent is below: `00046D65746100000C7075626C69736865642D617400` = `meta:published-at`

Once the column name is converted to hexadecimal format, Hive queries are run against it. The first part of the query is the `LEFT SEMI JOIN`, which is used to mimic a SQL subselect. All the references to `SUBSTR` and `INSTR` are to handle the case of composite columns. Since it is known in advance that characters 10–23 of the "hour:*" columns (i.e., `SUBSTR(r.column_name,10,13)`) is a timestamp and therefore we can crop it out and use it in the returned data or for matching. The `INSTR` is used to match column names and ensure the result set always has the same columns in the same place in the output. The SUBSTR is used for matching as part of the Ruby function. The SUBSTR returns a timestamp (long) in milliseconds since epoch and the start_date and end_date are also a timestamp in milliseconds since epoch. This means that the passed in values can be matched to a part of the column name.

The goal of this query is to export our data from Cassandra into a CSV file to give aggregated data dumps to our publishers. It is done via a Resque (offline) job that is kicked off through our Rails stack. Having a full CSV file means that all columns in the header must be accounted for in the Hive query (meaning that zeros need to be put to fill places where there is no data). We do that by pivoting our wide rows into fixed column tables using the CASE statement.

Here is the HiveQL for the CSV file:

```
SELECT CAST(SUBSTR(r.column_name, 10, 13) AS BIGINT) AS epoch,
SPLIT(r.row_key, '_')[0] AS account_id,
SPLIT(r.row_key, '_')[1] AS id,
SUM(CAST(CASE WHEN INSTR(r.column_name, 'pageviews-total') > 0
THEN r.value ELSE '0' END AS INT)) AS pageviews,
SUM(CAST(CASE WHEN INSTR(r.column_name, 'digg-digg') > 0
THEN r.value ELSE '0' END AS INT)) AS digg,
SUM(CAST(CASE WHEN INSTR(r.column_name, 'digg-referrer') > 0
THEN r.value ELSE '0' END AS INT)) AS digg_ref,
SUM(CAST(CASE WHEN INSTR(r.column_name, 'delicious-total') > 0
THEN r.value ELSE '0' END AS INT)) AS delicious,
SUM(CAST(CASE WHEN INSTR(r.column_name, 'delicious-referrer') > 0
THEN r.value ELSE '0' END AS INT)) AS delicious_ref,
SUM(CAST(CASE WHEN INSTR(r.column_name, 'googleplus-total') > 0
THEN r.value ELSE '0' END AS INT)) AS google_plus,
SUM(CAST(CASE WHEN INSTR(r.column_name, 'googleplus-referrer') > 0
THEN r.value ELSE '0' END AS INT)) AS google_plus_ref,
SUM(CAST(CASE WHEN INSTR(r.column_name, 'facebook-total') > 0
THEN r.value ELSE '0' END AS INT)) AS fb_total,
SUM(CAST(CASE WHEN INSTR(r.column_name, 'facebook-referrer') > 0
THEN r.value ELSE '0' END AS INT)) AS fb_ref,
SUM(CAST(CASE WHEN INSTR(r.column_name, 'twitter-tweet') > 0
THEN r.value ELSE '0' END AS INT)) AS tweets,
SUM(CAST(CASE WHEN INSTR(r.column_name, 'twitter-referrer') > 0
THEN r.value ELSE '0' END AS INT)) AS twitter_ref,
SUM(CAST(CASE WHEN INSTR(r.column_name, 'linkedin-share') > 0
THEN r.value ELSE '0' END AS INT)) AS linkedin,
SUM(CAST(CASE WHEN INSTR(r.column_name, 'linkedin-referrer') > 0
THEN r.value ELSE '0' END AS INT)) AS linkedin_ref,
SUM(CAST(CASE WHEN INSTR(r.column_name, 'stumbleupon-total') > 0
THEN r.value ELSE '0' END AS INT)) AS stumble_total,
SUM(CAST(CASE WHEN INSTR(r.column_name, 'stumbleupon-referrer') > 0
THEN r.value ELSE '0' END AS INT)) AS stumble_ref,
SUM(CAST(CASE WHEN INSTR(r.column_name, 'social-actions') > 0
THEN r.value ELSE '0' END AS INT)) AS social_actions,
SUM(CAST(CASE WHEN INSTR(r.column_name, 'referrer-social') > 0
THEN r.value ELSE '0' END AS INT)) AS social_ref,
MAX(CAST(CASE WHEN INSTR(r.column_name, 'score-realtime') > 0
```

```
THEN r.value ELSE '0.0' END AS DOUBLE)) AS score_rt
FROM content_social_delta r
LEFT SEMI JOIN (SELECT row_key
FROM content
WHERE HEX(column_name) = '00046D65746100000C7075626C69736865642D617400'
AND CAST(value AS BIGINT) >= #{start_date}
AND CAST(value AS BIGINT) <= #{end_date}
) c ON c.row_key = SPLIT(r.row_key, '_')[1]
WHERE INSTR(r.column_name, 'hour') > 0
AND CAST(SUBSTR(r.column_name, 10, 13) AS BIGINT) >= #{start_date}
AND CAST(SUBSTR(r.column_name, 10, 13) AS BIGINT) <= #{end_date}
GROUP BY CAST(SUBSTR(r.column_name, 10, 13) AS BIGINT),
SPLIT(r.row_key, '_')[0],
SPLIT(r.row_key, '_')[1]
```

The output of the query is a comma-separated value (CSV) file, an example of which
is below (wrapped for length with a blank line between each record for clarity):

```
epoch,account_id,id,pageviews,digg,digg_ref,delicious,delicious_ref,
google_plus,google_plus_ref,fb_total,fb_ref,tweets,twitter_ref,
linkedin,linkedin_ref,stumble_total,stumble_ref,social_actions,social_ref,score_rt

1337212800000,4eb331eea782f32acc000002,eaff81bd10a527f589f45c186662230e,
39,0,0,0,0,0,0,0,2,0,20,0,0,0,0,0,22,0

1337212800000,4f63ae61a782f327ce000007,940fd3e9d794b80012d3c7913b837dff,
101,0,0,0,0,0,0,44,63,11,16,0,0,0,0,0,55,79,69.64308064

1337212800000,4f6baedda782f325f4000010,e70f7d432ad252be439bc9cf1925ad7c,
260,0,0,0,0,0,0,8,25,15,34,0,0,0,0,0,23,59,57.23718477

1337216400000,4eb331eea782f32acc000002,eaff81bd10a527f589f45c186662230e,
280,0,0,0,0,0,0,37,162,23,15,0,0,0,2,56,179,72.45877173

1337216400000,4ebd76f7a782f30c9b000014,fb8935034e7d365e88dd5be1ed44b6dd,
11,0,0,0,0,0,0,0,1,1,4,0,0,0,0,0,5,29.74849901
```

Experiences and Needs from the Customer Trenches

A Karmasphere Perspective

By Nanda Vijaydev

Introduction

For over 18 months, Karmasphere has been engaged with a fast-growing number of
companies who adopted Hadoop and immediately gravitated towards Hive as the optimal way for teams of analysts and business users to use existing SQL skills with the
Hadoop environment. The first part of this chapter provides use case techniques that
we've seen used repeatedly in customer environments to advance Hive-based analytics.

The use case examples we cover are:

- Optimal data formatting for Hive
- Partitions and performance
- Text analytics with Hive functions including Regex, Explode and Ngram

As companies we've worked with plan for and move into production use of Hive, they look for incremental capabilities that make Hive-based access to Hadoop even easier to use, more productive, more powerful, and available to more people in their organization. When they wire Hadoop and Hive into their existing data architectures, they also want to enable results from Hive queries to be systematized, shared and integrated with other data stores, spreadsheets, BI tools, and reporting systems.

In particular, companies have asked for:

- Easier ways to ingest data, detect raw formats, and create metadata
- Work collaboratively in an integrated, multi-user environment
- Explore and analyze data iteratively
- Preserved and reusable paths to insight
- Finer-grain control over data, table, and column security, and compartmentalized access to different lines of business
- Business user access to analytics without requiring SQL skills
- Scheduling of queries for automated result generation and export to non-Hadoop data stores
- Integration with Microsoft Excel, Tableau, Spotfire, and other spreadsheet, reporting systems, dashboards, and BI tools
- Ability to manage Hive-based assets including queries, results, visualizations, and standard Hive components such as UDFs and SerDes

Use Case Examples from the Customer Trenches

Customer trenches #1: Optimal data formatting for Hive

One recurring question from many Hive users revolves around the format of their data and how to make that available in Hive.

Many data formats are supported out-of-the-box in Hive but some custom proprietary formats are not. And some formats that are supported raise questions for Hive users about how to extract individual components from within a row of data. Sometimes, writing a standard Hive SerDe that supports a custom data format is the optimal approach. In other cases, using existing Hive delimiters and exploiting Hive UDFs is the most convenient solution. One representative case we worked on was with a company using Hadoop and Hive to provide personalization services from the analysis of multiple input data streams. They were receiving logfiles from one of their data providers in a format that could not easily be split into columns. They were trying to figure out a way to parse the data and run queries without writing a custom SerDe.

The data had top header level information and multiple detailed information. The detailed section was a JSON nested within the top level object, similar to the data set below:

```
{ "top" : [
{"table":"user",
  "data":{
    "name":"John Doe","userid":"2036586","age":"74","code":"297994","status":1}},
{"table":"user",
  "data":{
    "name":"Mary Ann","userid":"14294734","age":"64","code":"142798","status":1}},
{"table":"user",
  "data":{
    "name":"Carl Smith","userid":"13998600","age":"36","code":"32866","status":1}},
{"table":"user",
  "data":{
    "name":"Anil Kumar":"2614012","age":"69","code":"208672","status":1}},
{"table":"user",
  "data":{
    "name":"Kim Lee","userid":"10471190","age":"53","code":"79365","status":1}}
]}
```

After talking with the customer, we realized they were interested in splitting individual columns of the detailed information that was tagged with "data" identifier in the above sample.

To help them proceed, we used existing Hive function get_json_object as shown below:

First step is to create a table using the sample data:

```
CREATE TABLE user (line string)
ROW FORMAT DELIMITED FIELDS TERMINATED BY '\n'
STORED AS TEXTFILE
LOCATION 'hdfs://hostname/user/uname/tablefolder/'
```

Then using Hive functions such as get_json_object, we could get to the nested JSON element and parse it using UDFs:

```
SELECT get_json_object(colo, '$.name') as name, get_json_object(colo, '$.userid') as uid,
get_json_object(colo, '$.age') as age, get_json_object(colo, '$.code') as code,
    get_json_object(colo, '$.status') as status
FROM
  (SELECT get_json_object(user.line, '$.data') as colo
   FROM user
   WHERE get_json_object(user.line, '$.data') is not null) temp;
```

Query details include:

- Extract the nested JSON object identified by data in the inner query as colo.
- Then the JSON object is split into appropriate columns using their names in the name value pair.

The results of the query are given below, with header information saved, as a CSV file:

```
"name","uid","age","code","status"
"John Doe","2036586","74","297994","1"
"Mary Ann","14294734","64","142798","1"
"Carl Smith","13998600","36","32866","1"
"Kim Lee","10471190","53","79365","1"
```

Customer trenches #2: Partitions and performance

Using partitions with data being streamed or regularly added to Hadoop is a use case we see repeatedly, and a powerful and valuable way of harnessing Hadoop and Hive to analyze various kinds of rapidly additive data sets. Web, application, product, and sensor logs are just some of the types of data that Hive users often want to perform *ad hoc*, repeated, and scheduled queries on.

Hive partitions, when set up correctly, allow users to query data only in specific partitions and hence improves performance significantly. To set up partitions for a table, files should be located in directories as given in this example:

```
hdfs://user/uname/folder/"yr"=2012/"mon"=01/"day"=01/file1, file2, file3
                        /"yr"=2012/"mon"=01/"day"=02/file4, file5
            …·······
                        /"yr"=2012/"mon"=05/"day"=30/file100, file101
```

With the above structure, tables can be set up with partition by year, month, and day. Queries can use *yr*, *mon*, and *day* as columns and restrict the data accessed to specific values during query time. If you notice the folder names, partitioned folders have identifiers such as *yr=* , *mon=*, and *day=*.

Working with one high tech company, we discovered that their folders did not have this explicit partition naming and they couldn't change their existing directory structure. But they still wanted to benefit from having partitions. Their sample directory structure is given below:

```
hdfs://user/uname/folder/2012/01/01/file1, file2, file3
                        /2012/01/02/file4, file5
            ······•
                        /2012/05/30/file100, file101
```

In this case, we can still add partitions by explicitly adding the location of the absolute path to the table using ALTER TABLE statements. A simple external script can read the directory and add the literal *yr=*, *mon=*, *day=* to an ALTER TABLE statement and provide the value of the folder (yr=2012, mon=01,…) to ALTER TABLE statements. The output of the script is a set of Hive SQL statements generated using the existing directory structure and captured into a simple text file.

```
ALTER TABLE tablename
ADD PARTITION (yr=2012, mon=01, day=01) location '/user/uname/folder/2012/01/01/';

ALTER TABLE tablename
ADD PARTITION (yr=2012, mon=01, day=02) location '/user/uname/folder/2012/01/02/';
```

```
...
ALTER TABLE tablename
ADD PARTITION (yr=2012, mon=05, day=30) location '/user/uname/folder/2012/05/30/';
```

When these statements are executed in Hive, the data in the specified directories automatically become available under defined logical partitions created using `ALTER TABLE` statements.

 You should make sure that your table is created with `PARTITIONED BY` columns for year, month, and day.

Customer trenches #3: Text analytics with Regex, Lateral View Explode, Ngram, and other UDFs

Many companies we work with have text analytics use cases which vary from simple to complex. Understanding and using Hive regex functions, n-gram functions and other string functions can address a number of those use cases.

One large manufacturing customer we worked with had lot of machine-generated compressed text data being ingested into Hadoop. The format of this data was:

1. Multiple rows of data in each file and a number of such files in time-partitioned buckets.
2. Within each row there were a number of segments separated by **/r/n** (carriage return and line feed).
3. Each segment was in the form of a "name: value" pair.

The use case requirement was to:

1. Read each row and separate individual segments as name-value pairs.
2. Zero in on specific segments and look for word counts and word patterns for analyzing keywords and specific messages.

The sample below illustrates this customer's data (text elided for space):

```
name:Mercury\r\ndescription:Mercury is the god of commerce, ...\r\ntype:Rocky planet
name:Venus\r\ndescription:Venus is the goddess of love...\r\ntype:Rocky planet
name:Earch\r\ndescription:Earth is the only planet ...\r\ntype:Rocky planet
name:Mars\r\ndescription: Mars is the god of War...\r\ntype:Rocky planet
name:Jupiter\r\ndescription:Jupiter is the King of the Gods...\r\ntype:Gas planet
name:Saturn\r\ndescription:Saturn is the god of agriculture...\r\ntype:Gas planet
name:Uranus\r\ndescription:Uranus is the God of the Heavens...\r\ntype:Gas planet
name:Neptune\r\ndescription:Neptune was the god of the Sea...\r\ntype:Gas planet
```

The data contains:

1. Planet names and their description with type.
2. Each row of data is separated by a delimiter.

3. Within each row there are three subsections, including "name," "description," and "type" separated by /r/n.

4. Description is a large text.

First step is to create the initial table with this sample data:

```
CREATE TABLE planets (col0 string)
ROW FORMAT DELIMITED FIELDS TERMINATED BY '\n'
STORED AS TEXTFILE
LOCATION 'hdfs://hostname/user/uname/planets/'
```

In the following, we run a series of queries, starting with a simple query and adding functions as we iterate. Note that the requirement can be met with queries written in several different ways. The purpose of the queries shown below is to demonstrate some of the key capabilities in Hive around text parsing.

First, we use a split function to separate each section of data into an array of individual elements:

```
SELECT split(col0, '(\\\\r\\\\n)') AS splits FROM planets;
```

Next, we explode the splits (array) into individual lines using the LATERAL VIEW EXPLODE function. Results of this query will have name-value pairs separated into individual rows. We select only those rows that start with description. The function LTRIM is also used to remove left spaces.

```
SELECT ltrim(splits) AS pairs FROM planets
LATERAL VIEW EXPLODE(split(col0, '(\\\\r\\\\n)')) col0 AS splits
WHERE ltrim(splits) LIKE 'desc%'
```

Now we separate the description line into name-value pair and select only the value data. This can be done in different ways. We use split by : and choose the value parameter:

```
SELECT (split(pairs, ':'))[1] AS txtval FROM (
SELECT ltrim(splits) AS pairs FROM planets
LATERAL VIEW EXPLODE(split(col0, '(\\\\r\\\\n)')) col0 AS splits
WHERE ltrim(splits) LIKE 'desc%')tmp1;
```

Notice the use of temporary identifiers tmp1 for the inner query. This is required when you use the output of a subquery as the input to outer query. At the end of step three, we have the value of the description segment within each row.

In the next step, we use ngrams to show the top 10 bigrams (2-gram) words from the description of planets. You could also use functions such as context_ngram, find_in_set, regex_replace, and others to perform various text-based analyses:

```
SELECT ngrams(sentences(lower(txtval)), 2, 10) AS bigrams FROM (
SELECT (split(pairs, ':'))[1] AS txtval FROM (
        SELECT ltrim(splits) AS pairs FROM planets
        LATERAL VIEW EXPLODE(split(col0, '(\\\\r\\\\n)')) col0 AS splits
        WHERE ltrim(splits) LIKE 'desc%') tmp1) tmp2;
```

Notice that we have used functions such as `lower` to convert to lowercase and sentences to tokenize each word in the text.

For additional information about the text analytics capabilities of Hive, see the functions listed in Chapter 3.

Apache Hive in production: Incremental needs and capabilities. Hive adoption continues to grow, as outlined by the use cases defined above. Companies across different industry segments and various sizes have benefited immensely by leveraging Hive in their Hadoop environments. A strong and active community of contributors and significant investments in Hive R&D efforts by leading Hadoop vendors ensures that Hive, already the SQL-based standard for Hadoop, will become the SQL-based standard within organizations that are leveraging Hadoop for Big Data analysis.

As companies invest significant resources and time in understanding and building Hive resources, in many cases we find they look for additional capabilities that enable them to build on their initial use of Hive and extend its reach faster and more broadly within their organizations. From working with these customers looking to take Hive to the next level, a common set of requirements have emerged.

These requirements include:

Collaborative multiuser environments

Hadoop enables new classes of analysis that were prohibitive computationally and economically with traditional RDBMS technologies. Hadoop empowers organizations to break down the data and people silos, performing analysis on every byte of data they can get their hands on, doing this all in a way that enables them to share their queries, results, and insights with other individuals, teams, and systems in the organization. This model implies that users with deep understanding of these different data sets need to collaborate in discovery, in the sharing of insights, and the availability of all Hive-based analytic assets across the organization.

Productivity enhancements

The current implementation of Hive offers a serial batch environment on Hadoop to run queries. This implies that once a user submits a query for job execution to the Hadoop cluster, they have to wait for the query to complete execution before they can execute another query against the cluster. This can limit user productivity.

One major reason for companies adopting Hive is that it enables their SQL-skilled data professionals to move faster and more easily to working with Hadoop. These users are usually familiar with graphical SQL editors in tools and BI products. They are looking for similar productivity enhancements like syntax highlighting and code completion.

Managing Hive assets

A recent McKinsey report predicted significant shortage of skilled workers to enable organizations to profit from their data. Technologies like Hive promise to help bridge that skills shortage by allowing people with an SQL skillset to perform analysis on Hadoop. However, organizations are realizing that just having Hive available to their users is not enough. They need to be able to manage Hive assets like queries (history and versions), UDFs, SerDes for later share and reuse. Organizations would like to build this living knowledge repository of Hive assets that is easily searchable by users.

Extending Hive for advanced analytics

Many companies are looking to re-create analysis they perform in the traditional RDBMS world in Hadoop. While not all capabilities in the SQL environment easily translate into Hive functions, due to inherent limitations of how data is stored, there are some advanced analytics functions like RANKING, etc., that are Hadoop-able. In addition, organizations have spent tremendous resources and time in building analytical models using traditional tools like SAS and SPSS and would like the ability to score these models on Hadoop via Hive queries.

Extending Hive beyond the SQL skill set

As Hadoop is gaining momentum in organizations and becoming a key fabric of data processing and analytics within IT infrastructure, it is gaining popularity amongst users with different skill sets and capabilities. While Hive is easily adopted by users with SQL skill sets, other less SQL savvy users are also looking for drag-and-drop capabilities like those available in traditional BI tools to perform analysis on Hadoop using Hive. The ability to support interactive forms on top of Hive, where a user is prompted to provide column values via simple web-based forms is an often-asked for capability.

Data exploration capabilities

Traditional database technologies provide data exploration capabilities; for example, a user can view min, max values for an integer column. In addition, users can also view visualizations of these columns to understand the data distribution before they perform analysis on the data. As Hadoop stores hundreds of terabytes of data, and often petabytes, similar capabilities are being requested by customers for specific use cases.

Schedule and operationalize Hive queries

As companies find insights using Hive on Hadoop, they are also looking to operationalize these insights and schedule them to run on a regular interval. While open source alternatives are currently available, these sometimes fall short when companies also want to manage the output of Hive queries; for example, moving result sets into a traditional RDBMS system or BI stack. To manage certain use cases, companies often have to manually string together various different open source tools or rely on poor performing JDBC connectors.

About Karmasphere. Karmasphere is a software company, based in Silicon Valley California, focused exclusively on bringing native Hadoop Big Data Analytics capabilities to teams of analysts and business users. Their flagship product, Karmasphere 2.0, is based on Apache Hive, extending it in a multi-user graphical workspace to enable:

- Reuse of standard Hive-based tables, SerDes and UDFs
- Social, project-based big data analytics for teams of analysts and business users
- Easy data ingestion to the cluster
- Heuristic-based recognition and table creation of many popular data formats
- Visual and iterative data exploration and analysis
- Graphical exploration of all Hive-based analytic assets
- Sharing and scheduling of queries, results and visualizations
- Easy integration with traditional spreadsheets, reporting, dashboard, and BI tools

Figure 23-4 shows a screenshot of Karmasphere 2.0's Hive-based Big Data Analytics Environment.

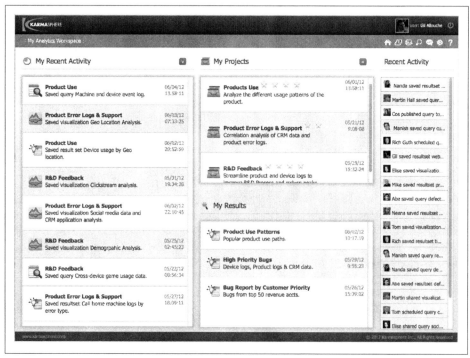

Figure 23-4. Screenshot of Karmasphere 2.0

Hive features survey

We'd like to get feedback on the importance of these needs and share them back with the growing Hive community. If you are interested in seeing what others think and would like to participate, please visit:

http://karmasphere.com/hive-features-survey.html

Glossary

Amazon Elastic MapReduce

Amazon's EMR is a hosted Hadoop service on top of Amazon EC2 (*Elastic Compute Cloud*).

Avro

Avro is a new serialization format developed to address some of the common problems associated with evolving other serialization formats. Some of the benefits are: rich data structures, fast binary format, support for remote procedure calls, and built-in schema evolution.

Bash

The "Bourne-Again Shell" that is the default interactive command shell for Linux and Mac OS X systems.

S3 Bucket

The term for the top-level container you own and manage when using S3. A user may have many buckets, analogous to the root of a physical hard drive.

Command-Line Interface

The *command-line interface* (CLI) can run "scripts" of Hive statements or all the user to enter statements interactively.

Data Warehouse

A repository of structured data suitable for analysis for reports, trends, etc. Warehouses are batch mode or offline, as opposed to providing real-time responsiveness for on-line activity, like ecommerce.

Derby

A lightweight *SQL* database that can be embedded in Java applications. It runs in the same process and saves its data to local files. It is used as the default *SQL* data store for Hive's *metastore*. See *http://db.apache.org/derby/* for more information.

Dynamic Partitions

A HiveQL extension to *SQL* that allows you to insert query results into table *partitions* where you leave one or more partition column values unspecified and they are determined dynamically from the query results themselves. This technique is convenient for partitioning a query result into a potentially large number of partitions in a new table, without having to write a separate query for each partition column value.

Ephemeral Storage

In the nodes for a virtual Amazon EC2 cluster, the on-node disk storage is called *ephemeral* because it will vanish when the cluster is shut down, in contrast to a physical cluster that is shut down. Hence, when using an EC2 cluster, such as an Amazon *Elastic MapReduce* cluster, it is important to back up important data to S3.

ExternalTable

A table using a storage location and contents that are outside of Hive's control. It is convenient for sharing data with other tools, but it is up to other processes to manage the life cycle of the data. That is, when an external table is created, Hive does not create the external directory (or directories for partitioned tables), nor are the directory and data files deleted when an external table is dropped.

Hadoop Distributed File System

(HDFS) A distributed, resilient file system for data storage that is optimized for scanning large contiguous blocks of data on hard disks. Distribution across a cluster provides horizontal scaling of data storage. Blocks of HDFS files are replicated across the cluster (by default, three times) to prevent data loss when hard drives or whole servers fail.

HBase

The *NoSQL* database that uses HDFS for durable storage of table data. HBase is a column-oriented, key-value store designed to provide traditional responsiveness for queries and row-level updates and insertions. *Column oriented* means that the data storage is organized on disk by groups of columns, called *column families*, rather than by row. This feature promotes fast queries for subsets of columns. *Key-value* means that rows are stored and fetched by a unique *key* and the *value* is the entire row. HBase does not provide an *SQL* dialect, but Hive can be used to query HBase tables.

Hive

A *data warehouse* tool that provides table abstractions on top of data resident in *HDFS*, *HBase* tables, and other stores. The *Hive Query Language* is a dialect of the *Structured Query Language*.

Hive Query Language

Hive's own dialect of the *Structured Query Language (SQL)*. Abbreviated HiveQL or HQL.

Input Format

The input format determines how input streams, usually from files, are split into records. A *SerDe* handles parsing the record into columns. A custom input format can be specified when creating a table using the `INPUTFORMAT` clause. The input format for the default `STORED AS TEXTFILE` specification is

implemented by the Java object named `org.apache.hadoop.mapreduce.lib.input. TextInputFormat`. See also *Output Format*.

JDBC

The Java Database Connection API provides access to *SQL* systems, including Hive, from Java code.

Job

In the *Hadoop* context, a *job* is a self-contained workflow submitted to *MapReduce*. It encompasses all the work required to perform a complete calculation, from reading input to generating output. The *MapReduce JobTracker* will decompose the *job* into one or more *tasks* for distribution and execution around the cluster.

JobTracker

The top-level controller of all jobs using *Hadoop's MapReduce*. The *JobTracker* accepts job submissions, determines what tasks to run and where to run them, monitors their execution, restarts failed tasks as needed, and provides a web console for monitoring job and task execution, viewing logs, etc.

Job Flow

A term used in *Amazon Elastic MapReduce (EMR)* for the sequence of *jobs* executed on a temporary EMR cluster to accomplish a particular goal.

JSON

JSON (JavaScript Object Notation) is a lightweight data serialization format used commonly in web-based applications.

Map

The mapping phase of a *MapReduce* process where an input set of key-value pairs are converted into a new set of key-value pairs. For each input key-value pair, there can be zero-to-many output key-value pairs. The input and output keys and the input and output values can be completely different.

MapR

A commercial distribution of Hadoop that replaces *HDFS* with the *MapR File System*

(MapR-FS), a high-performance, distributed file system.

MapReduce

A computation paradigm invented at Google and based loosely on the common data operations of mapping a collection of data elements from one form to another (the *map* phase) and reducing a collection to a single value or a smaller collection (the *reduce* phase). *MapReduce* is designed to scale computation horizontally by decomposing *map* and *reduce* steps into *tasks* and distributing those tasks across a cluster. The MapReduce runtime provided by Hadoop handles decomposition of a *job* into *tasks*, distribution around the cluster, movement of a particular task to the machine that holds the data for the task, movement of data to tasks (as needed), and automated re-execution of failed tasks and other error recovery and logging services.

Metastore

The service that maintains "metadata" information, such as table schemas. Hive requires this service to be running. By default, it uses a built-in *Derby SQL* server, which provides limited, single-process *SQL* support. Production systems must use a full-service relational database, such as MySQL.

NoSQL

An umbrella term for data stores that don't support the *relational model* for data management, dialects of the *structured query language*, and features like transactional updates. These data stores trade off these features in order to provide more cost-effective scalability, higher availability, etc.

ODBC

The Open Database Connection API provides access to *SQL* systems, including Hive, from other applications. Java applications typically use the *JDBC* API, instead.

Output Format

The output format determines how records are written to output streams, usually to files. A *SerDe* handles serialization of each record into an appropriate byte stream. A custom output format can be specified when creating a table using the `OUTPUTFORMAT` clause. The output format for the default `STORED AS TEXTFILE` specification is implemented by the Java object named `org .apache.hadoop.hive.ql.io.HiveIgnoreKey TextOutputFormat`. See also *Input Format*.

Partition

A subset of a table's data set where one column has the same value for all records in the subset. In Hive, as in most databases that support partitioning, each partition is stored in a physically separate location—in Hive's case, in a subdirectory of the root directory for the table. Partitions have several advantages. The column value corresponding to a partition doesn't have to be repeated in every record in the partition, saving space, and queries with `WHERE` clauses that restrict the result set to specific values for the partition columns can perform more quickly, because they avoid scanning the directories of nonmatching partition values. See also *dynamic partitions*.

Reduce

The reduction phase of a *MapReduce* process where the key-value pairs from the *map* phase are processed. A crucial feature of *MapReduce* is that all the key-value pairs from all the *map* tasks that have the same key will be sent together to the same reduce task, so that the collection of values can be "reduced" as appropriate. For example, a collection of integers might be added or averaged together, a collection of strings might have all duplicates removed, etc.

Relational Model

The most common model for database management systems, it is based on a logical model of data organization and manipulation. A declarative specification of the data structure and how it should be manipulated is supplied by the user, most typically using the *Structured Query Language*. The implementation translates these declarations into procedures for storing, retrieving, and manipulating the data.

S3

The distributed file system for Amazon Web Services. It can be used with or instead of *HDFS* when running *MapReduce* jobs.

SerDe

The Serializer/Deserializer or SerDe for short is used to parse the bytes of a record into columns or fields, the deserialization process. It is also used to create those record bytes (i.e., serialization). In contrast, the *Input Format* is used to split an input stream into records and the *Output Format* is used to write records to an output stream. A SerDe can be specified when a Hive table is created. The default SerDe supports the field and collection separators discussed in "Text File Encoding of Data Values" on page 45, as well as various optimizations such as a lazy parsing.

Structured Query Language

A language that implements the relational model for querying and manipulating data. Abbreviated *SQL*. While there is an ANSI standard for *SQL* that has undergone periodic revisions, all *SQL* dialects in widespread use add their own custom extensions and variations.

Task

In the *MapReduce* context, a *task* is the smallest unit of work performed on a single cluster node, as part of an overall *job*. By default each task involves a separate JVM process. Each *map* and *reduce* invocation will have its own task.

Thrift

An RPC system invented by Facebook and integrated into Hive. Remote processes can send Hive statements to Hive through Thrift.

User-Defined Aggregate Functions

User-defined functions that take multiple rows (or columns from multiple rows) and return a single "aggregation" of the data, such as a count of the rows, a sum or average

of number values, etc. The term is abbreviated UDAF. See also *user-defined functions* and *user-defined table generating functions*.

User-Defined Functions

Functions implemented by users of Hive to extend their behavior. Sometimes the term is used generically to include built-in functions and sometimes the term is used for the specific case of functions that work on a single row (or columns in a row) and return a single value, (i.e., which don't change the number of records). Abbreviated UDF. See also *user-defined aggregate functions* and *user-defined table generating functions*.

User-Defined Table Generating Functions

User-defined functions that take a column from a single record and expand it into multiple rows. Examples include the `explode` function that converts an array into rows of single fields and, for Hive v0.8.0 and later, converts a map into rows of key and value fields. Abbreviated UDTF. See also *user-defined functions* and *user-defined aggregate functions*.

References

Amazon Web Services, http://aws.amazon.com/.

Amazon DynamoDB, http://aws.amazon.com/dynamodb/.

Amazon Elastic MapReduce (Amazon EMR), http://aws.amazon.com/elasticmapreduce/.

Amazon Simple Storage Service (S3), http://aws.amazon.com/s3.

Cassandra Database, http://cassandra.apache.org/.

Apache HBase, http://hbase.apache.org/.

Apache Hive, http://hive.apache.org/.

Apache Hive Wiki: https://cwiki.apache.org/Hive/.

Apache Oozie, http://incubator.apache.org/oozie/.

Apache Pig, http://pig.apache.org/.

Apache Zookeeper, http://zookeeper.apache.org/.

Cascading, http://cascading.org.

Data processing on Hadoop without the hassle, https://github.com/nathanmarz/cascalog.

Easy, efficient MapReduce pipelines in Java and Scala, https://github.com/cloudera/crunch.

Datalog, http://en.wikipedia.org/wiki/Datalog.

C.J. Date, *The Relational Database Dictionary*, O'Reilly Media, 2006, ISBN 978-0-596-52798-3.

Jeffrey Dean and Sanjay Ghemawat, *MapReduce: simplified data processing on large clusters*, Proceeding OSDI '04 Proceedings of the 6th conference on Symposium on Operating Systems Design and Implementation - Volume 6, 2004.

Apache Derby, http://db.apache.org/derby/.

Jeffrey E.F. Friedl, *Mastering Regular Expressions, 3rd Edition*, O'Reilly Media, 2006, ISBN 978-0-596-52812-6.

Alan Gates, *Programming Pig*, O'Reilly Media, 2011, ISBN 978-1-449-30264-1.

Lars George, *HBase: The Definitive Guide*, O'Reilly Media, 2011, ISBN 978-1-449-39610-7.

Sanjay Ghemawat, Howard Gobioff, and Shun-Tak Leung, *The Google file system*, SOSP '03 Proceedings of the nineteenth ACM symposium on Operating systems principles, 2003.

Jan Goyvaerts and Steven Levithan, *Regular Expressions Cookbook, 2nd Edition*, O'Reilly Media, 2009, ISBN 978-1-449-31943-4.

Eben Hewitt, *Cassandra: The Definitive Guide*, O'Reilly Media, 2010, ISBN 978-1-449-39041-9.

Ashish Thusoo, et al, *Hive - a petabyte scale data warehouse using Hadoop*, 2010 IEEE 26th International Conference on Data Engineering (ICDE).

JDK 1.6 java.util.regex.Pattern Javadoc, http://docs.oracle.com/javase/6/docs/api/java/util/regex/Pattern.html.

The Java Tutorials, Lesson: Regular Expressions, http://docs.oracle.com/javase/tutorial/essential/regex/.

JSON, http://json.org/.

Apache Kafka: A high-throughput, distributed messaging system, http://incubator.apache.org/kafka/index.html.

Kerberos: The Network Authentication Protocol, http://web.mit.edu/kerberos.

MapR, the Next Generation Distribution for Apache Hadoop, http://mapr.com.

MarkLogic, http://www.marklogic.com/.

Wolfram Mathematica, http://www.wolfram.com/mathematica/.

Matlab: The Language of Technical Computing, http://www.mathworks.com/products/matlab/index.html.

GNU Octave, http://www.gnu.org/software/octave/.

Oracle XML DB, http://www.oracle.com/technetwork/database/features/xmldb/index.html.

The R Project for Statistical Computing, http://r-project.org/.

A Scala API for Cascading, https://github.com/twitter/scalding.

SciPy: Scientific Tools for Python, http://scipy.org.

Shark (Hive on Spark), http://shark.cs.berkeley.edu/.

Spark: Lightning-Fast Cluster Computing, http://www.spark-project.org/.

Storm: Distributed and fault-tolerant realtime computation: stream processing, continuous computation, distributed RPC, and more, https://github.com/nathanmarz/storm.

Tony Stubblebine, *Regular Expression Pocket Reference*, O'Reilly Media, 2003, ISBN 978-0-596-00415-6.

Dean Wampler, *Functional Programming for Java Developers*, O'Reilly Media, 2011, ISBN 978-1-449-31103-2.

Dean Wampler and Alex Payne, *Programming Scala*, O'Reilly Media, 2009, ISBN 978-0-596-15595-7.

Tom White, *Hadoop: The Definitive Guide, 3nd Edition*, O'Reilly Media, 2012, ISBN 978-1-449-31152-0.

XPath Specification, http://www.w3.org/TR/xpath/.

Index

Symbols

" (single quotes)
    regular expressions using, 55
*.domain.pvt, 27
.hiverc script, deploying, 249
; (semicolon)
    at end of lines in Hive queries, 36
    separating multiple queries, 34

A

^A ("Control" A) delimiters, 45, 47
AbstractGenericUDAFResolver, methods in, 174
ADD PARTITION clauses, ALTER TABLE ..., 63
aggregate functions, 85–87, 164–176
aggregate functions, UDF, 172–177
aggregates, calculating with streaming, 191–192
algorithms (case study), creating machine learning, 265–270
ALTER DATABASE command, 52
ALTER INDEX clauses, 118–119
ALTER TABLE ... ADD PARTITION clause, 63
ALTER TABLE ... ARCHIVE PARTITION clause, 70
ALTER TABLE ... TOUCH clause, in triggering execution hooks, 69
ALTER TABLE statements
    adding, modifying, and dropping partitions, 66
    altering storage properties, 68
    changing schemas with, 53, 66

columns
    adding, 68
    changing, 67
    deleting or replacing, 68
    renaming tables, 66
    table properties, altering, 68
Amazon Web Services (AWS)
    DynamoDB, 225
    Elastic MapReduce (EMR), 251
        about, 245–246, 305
        clusters, 246–248
        logs on S3, 252
        persistence and metastore on, 250–251
        security groups for, 253
        Thrift Server on, 247
        vs. EC2 and Hive, 254
    S3 system for
        about, 308
        accessing, 248
        deploying .hiverc script to, 249
        EMR logs on, 252
        moving data to, 62
        MySQL dump on, 251
        putting resources on, 252
        role on EMR cluster, 251
        support for, 62
    spot instances, 252–253
annotations, for use with functions, 184
ANSI SQL standard, 2, 49
Apache
    Cassandra, 2, 224–225
    DynamoDB, 2
    Hadoop (see Hadoop)
    HBase, 2, 8–9, 222–224
    Hive (see Hive)

We'd like to hear your suggestions for improving our indexes. Send email to *index@oreilly.com*.

Friedl, Jeffrey E.F., Mastering Regular
    Expressions, 3rd Edition, 97
FROM clause, 79
full-outer JOINs, 104
functions
    aggregate, 85–87, 164–176, 171, 172–177
    annotations, for use with, 184
    casting, 109
    deterministic, 184
    mathematical, 83–85
    other built-in, 88–90
    stateful, 184
    table generating, 87–88, 165–166
    User-Defined Functions (UDFs), 163
        (see also User-Defined Functions
        (UDFs))
    XPath (XML Path Language), 207–208

G

Gates, Alan, Programming Pig, 8
Generalized Additive Models (GAM), 267
GenericMR Tools, for streaming to Java, 194–
    196
GenericUDAs, 172–177
GenericUDFs vs. UDFs, 169–171
George, Lars, HBase: The Definitive Guide, 9
getClusterStatus method, 215
getQueryPlan() method, 216
getSchema() method, 215
Google Big Table, 8
Google File System, 3
Google Summer of Code project, JSON SerDe
    and, 208
Goyvaerts, Jan, Regular Expression Pocket
    Reference, 97
graphical interfaces, for interacting with Hive,
    6
Groovy, setting up to connect to HiveService,
    214
GROUP BY clause
    about, 97
    DISTRIBUTE BY clauses and, 108
    HAVING clause and, 97
groups, granting and revoking privileges for
    individual, 230–233
GZip compression, 148

H

Hadoop
    about, 1
    alternative higher-level libraries for, 9–10
    alternatives to Hive for, 8–9
    compression of data
        about, 145
        DefaultCodec, 147
        SnappyCodec, 147
    configuring, 24–29
    HAR file format, 152–154
    Hive in, 6–8
    InputFormat API, 145
    installing, 18–19
    installing Java for, 16–18
    JVM reuse as running parameter, 139–140
    launching components of MapReduce for,
        20–21
    operating systems for, 15
    runtime modes for, 19
    speculative execution in, 141–142
    testing installation of, 20
    using Hive for data processing, 255
hadoop dfs commands, defining alias for, 20
Hadoop Distributed File System (HDFS)
    about, 1, 4, 306
    HBase and, 9
    master node of, 51
    NameNode and, 7
    role on EMR cluster, 251
    Sort and Shuffle phase in, 5
Hadoop Java API, implementing algorithms
    using, 6
Hadoop JobTracker
    getting cluster status from, 215
Hadoop security, 227
Hadoop Streaming API, 187
Hadoop: The Definitive Guide (White), 12, 24
HADOOP_HOME, Hive using, 21
HAR (Hadoop ARchive), 152–154
HAVING clause, 97
HBase, 2, 8–9, 222–224, 306
HBase: The Definitive Guide (George), 9
hcat (command line tool), options supported
    by, 261
HCatalog
    about, 255–256
    architecture, 262–263
    command line tool, 261

X

Z

About the Authors

Edward Capriolo is currently System Administrator at Media6degrees, where he helps design and maintain distributed data storage systems for the Internet advertising industry.

Edward is a member of the Apache Software Foundation and a committer for the Hadoop-Hive project. He has experience as a developer, as well as a Linux and network administrator, and enjoys the rich world of open source software.

Dean Wampler is a Principal Consultant at Think Big Analytics, where he specializes in "Big Data" problems and tools like Hadoop and Machine Learning. Besides Big Data, he specializes in Scala, the JVM ecosystem, JavaScript, Ruby, functional and object-oriented programming, and Agile methods. Dean is a frequent speaker at industry and academic conferences on these topics. He has a Ph.D. in Physics from the University of Washington.

Jason Rutherglen is a software architect at Think Big Analytics and specializes in Big Data, Hadoop, search, and security.

Colophon

The animal on the cover of *Programming Hive* is a European hornet (*Vespa cabro*) and its hive. The European hornet is the only hornet in North America, introduced to the continent when European settlers migrated to the Americas. This hornet can be found throughout Europe and much of Asia, adapting its hive-building techniques to different climates when necessary.

The hornet is a social insect, related to bees and ants. The hornet's hive consists of one queen, a few male hornets (drones), and a large quantity of sterile female workers. The chief purpose of drones is to reproduce with the hornet queen, and they die soon after. It is the female workers who are responsible for building the hive, carrying food, and tending to the hornet queen's eggs.

The hornet's nest itself is the consistency of paper, since it is constructed out of wood pulp in several layers of hexagonal cells. The end result is a pear-shaped nest attached to its shelter by a short stem. In colder areas, hornets will abandon the nest in the winter and take refuge in hollow logs or trees, or even human houses, where the queen and her eggs will stay until the warmer weather returns. The eggs form the start of a new colony, and the hive can be constructed once again.

The cover image is from *Johnson's Natural History*. The cover font is Adobe ITC Garamond. The text font is Linotype Birka; the heading font is Adobe Myriad Condensed; and the code font is LucasFont's TheSansMonoCondensed.

Have it your way.

Get even more for your money.

Join the O'Reilly Community, and register the O'Reilly books you own. It's free, and you'll get:

- $4.99 ebook upgrade offer
- 40% upgrade offer on O'Reilly print books
- Membership discounts on books and events
- Free lifetime updates to ebooks and videos
- Multiple ebook formats, DRM FREE
- Participation in the O'Reilly community
- Newsletters
- Account management
- 100% Satisfaction Guarantee

Signing up is easy:

1. **Go to: oreilly.com/go/register**
2. **Create an O'Reilly login.**
3. **Provide your address.**
4. **Register your books.**

Note: English-language books only

To order books online:
oreilly.com/store

For questions about products or an order:
orders@oreilly.com

To sign up to get topic-specific email announcements and/or news about upcoming books, conferences, special offers, and new technologies:
elists@oreilly.com

For technical questions about book content:
booktech@oreilly.com

To submit new book proposals to our editors:
proposals@oreilly.com

O'Reilly books are available in multiple DRM-free ebook formats. For more information:
oreilly.com/ebooks

O'REILLY®

Spreading the knowledge of innovators · oreilly.com

CPSIA information can be obtained at www.ICGtesting.com
Printed in the USA
BVOW041740200912

300978BV00001B/1/P

9 781449 319335